S0-CAD-663

Scott, Foresman

Texas Edition

Discover SCIENCE

Authors

Dr. Michael R. Cohen
Professor of Science and Environmental Education
School of Education
Indiana University
Indianapolis, Indiana

Dr. Timothy M. Cooney
Chairperson K-12 Science Program
Malcolm Price Laboratory School
University of Northern Iowa
Cedar Falls, Iowa

Cheryl M. Hawthorne
Science Curriculum Specialist
Mathematics, Engineering, Science Achievement Program (MESA)
Stanford University
Stanford, California

Dr. Alan J. McCormack
Professor of Science Education
San Diego State University
San Diego, California

Dr. Jay M. Pasachoff
Director, Hopkins Observatory
Williams College
Williamstown, Massachusetts

Dr. Naomi Pasachoff
Research Associate
Williams College
Williamstown, Massachusetts

Karin L. Rhines
Science/Educational Consultant
Valhalla, New York

Dr. Irwin L. Slesnick
Professor of Biology
Western Washington University
Bellingham, Washington

Scott, Foresman and Company
Editorial Offices: Glenview, Illinois

Regional Offices: Sunnyvale, California • Tucker, Georgia •
Glenview, Illinois • Oakland, New Jersey • Dallas, Texas

Consultants

Special Content Consultant

Dr. Abraham S. Flexer
Science Education Consultant
Boulder, Colorado

Health Consultant

Dr. Julius B. Richmond
John D. MacArthur Professor of Health Policy
Director, Division of Health Policy Research and Education
Harvard University
Advisor on Child Health Policy
Children's Hospital of Boston
Boston, Massachusetts

Safety Consultant

Dr. Jack A. Gerlovich
Science Education Safety Consultant/Author
Des Moines, Iowa

Process Skills Consultant

Dr. Alfred DeVito
Professor Emeritus Science Education
Purdue University
West Lafayette, Indiana

Activity Consultants

Edward Al Pankow
Teacher
Petaluma City Schools
Petaluma, California

Valerie Pankow
Teacher and Writer
Petaluma City Schools
Petaluma, California

Science and Technology Consultant

Dr. David E. Newton
Adjunct Professor—Science and Social Issues
University of San Francisco
College of Professional Studies
San Francisco, California

Cooperative Learning Consultant

Dr. Robert E. Slavin
Director, Elementary School Program
Center for Research on Elementary and Middle Schools
Johns Hopkins University
Baltimore, Maryland

Gifted Education Consultants

Hilda P. Hobson
Teacher of the Gifted
W.B. Wicker School
Sanford, North Carolina

Christine Kuehn
Assistant Professor of Education
University of South Carolina
Columbia, South Carolina

Nancy Linkel York
Teacher of the Gifted
W.B. Wicker School
Sanford, North Carolina

Special Education Consultants

Susan E. Affleck
Classroom Teacher
Salt Creek Elementary School
Elk Grove Village, Illinois

Dr. Dale R. Jordan
Director
Jordan Diagnostic Center
Oklahoma City, Oklahoma

Dr. Shirley T. King
Learning Disabilities Teacher
Helfrich Park Middle School
Evansville, Indiana

Jeannie Rae McCoun
Learning Disabilities Teacher
Mary M. McClelland Elementary School
Indianapolis, Indiana

Thinking Skills Consultant

Dr. Joseph P. Riley II
Professor of Science Education
University of Georgia
Athens, Georgia

Reading Consultants

Patricia T. Hinske
Reading Specialist
Cardinal Stritch College
Milwaukee, Wisconsin

Dr. Robert A. Pavlik
Professor and Chairperson of Reading/Language Arts Department
Cardinal Stritch College

Dr. Alfredo Schifini
Reading Consultant
Downey, California

Cover painting commissioned by Scott, Foresman
Artist: Ben Verkaaik

ISBN: 0-673-42491-X

345678910RRW9897969594939291

Reviewers and Content Specialists

Dr. Ramona J. Anshutz
Science Specialist
Kansas State Department of Education
Topeka, Kansas

Teresa M. Auldridge
Science Education Consultant
Amelia, Virginia

Annette M. Barzal
Classroom Teacher
Willetts Middle School
Brunswick, Ohio

James Haggard Brannon
Classroom Teacher
Ames Community Schools
Ames, Iowa

Priscilla L. Callison
Science Teacher
Topeka Adventure Center
Topeka, Kansas

Rochelle F. Cohen
Education Coordinator
Indianapolis Head Start
Indianapolis, Indiana

Linda Lewis Cundiff
Classroom Teacher
R. F. Bayless Elementary School
Lubbock, Texas

Dr. Patricia Dahl
Classroom Teacher
Bloomington Oak Grove Intermediate School
Bloomington, Minnesota

Audrey J. Dick
Supervisor, Elementary Education
Cincinnati Public Schools
Cincinnati, Ohio

Nancy B. Drabik
Reading Specialist
George Washington School
Wyckoff, New Jersey

Bennie Y. Fleming
Science Supervisor
Providence School District
Providence, Rhode Island

Mike Graf
Classroom Teacher
Branch Elementary School
Arroyo Grande, California

Thelma Robinson Graham
Classroom Teacher
Pearl Spann Elementary School
Jackson, Mississippi

Robert G. Guy
Classroom Teacher
Big Lake Elementary School
Sedro-Woolley, Washington

Dr. Claude A. Hanson
Science Supervisor
Boise Public Schools
Boise, Idaho

Dr. Jean D. Harlan
Psychologist, Early Childhood Consultant
Lighthouse Counseling Associates
Racine, Wisconsin

Dr. Rebecca P. Harlin
Assistant Professor of Reading
State University of New York—Geneseo
Geneseo, New York

Richard L. Ingraham
Professor of Biology
San José State University
San José, California

Ron Jones
Science Coordinator
Salem Keizer Public Schools
Salem, Oregon

Sara A. Jones
Classroom Teacher
Burroughs-Molette Elementary School
Brunswick, Georgia

Dr. Judy LaCavera
Director of Curriculum and Instruction
Learning Alternatives
Vienna, Ohio

Jack Laubisch
K-12 Science, Health, and Outdoor Education Coordinator
West Clermont Local School District
Amelia, Ohio

Douglas M. McPhee
Classroom Teacher/Consultant
Del Mar Hills Elementary School
Del Mar, California

Larry Miller
Classroom Teacher
Caldwell Elementary School
Caldwell, Kansas

Dr. Robert J. Miller
Professor of Science Education
Eastern Kentucky University
Richmond, Kentucky

Sam Murr
Teacher—Elementary Gifted Science
Academic Center for Enrichment—Mid Del Schools
Midwest City—Del City, Oklahoma

Janet Nakai
Classroom Teacher
Community Consolidated School District #65
Evanston, Illinois

Patricia Osborne
Classroom Teacher
Valley Heights Elementary School
Waterville, Kansas

Elisa Pinzón-Umaña
Classroom Teacher
Coronado Academy
Albuquerque, New Mexico

Dr. Jeanne Phillips
Director of Curriculum and Instruction
Meridian Municipal School District
Meridian, Mississippi

Maria Guadalupe Ramos
Classroom Teacher
Metz Elementary School
Austin, Texas

Elissa Richards
Math/Science Teacher Leader
Granite School District
Salt Lake City, Utah

Mary Jane Roscoe
Teacher and Team Coordinator
Fairwood Alternative Elementary School of Individually Guided Education
Columbus, Ohio

Sister Mary Christelle Sawicki, C. S. S. F.
Science Curriculum Coordinator
Department of Catholic Education Diocese of Buffalo
Buffalo, New York

Ray E. Smalley
Classroom Teacher/Science Specialist
Cleveland School of Science
Cleveland, Ohio

Anita Snell
Elementary Coordinator for Early Childhood Education
Spring Branch Independent School District
Houston, Texas

Norman Sperling
Chabot Observatory
Oakland, California

Sheri L. Thomas
Classroom Teacher
McLouth Unified School District #342
McLouth, Kansas

Lisa D. Torres
Science Coordinator
Lebanon School District
Lebanon, New Hampshire

Alice C. Webb
Early Childhood Resource Teacher
Primary Education Office
Rockledge, Florida

Tina Ziegler
Classroom Teacher
Evanston, Illinois

Chapter 3 — Life on Earth Long Ago — 56

Unit 2 Physical Science 84

Chapter 6 Machines and Electricity 130

Unit 3 Earth Science 152

Chapter 7 Water and Air 154

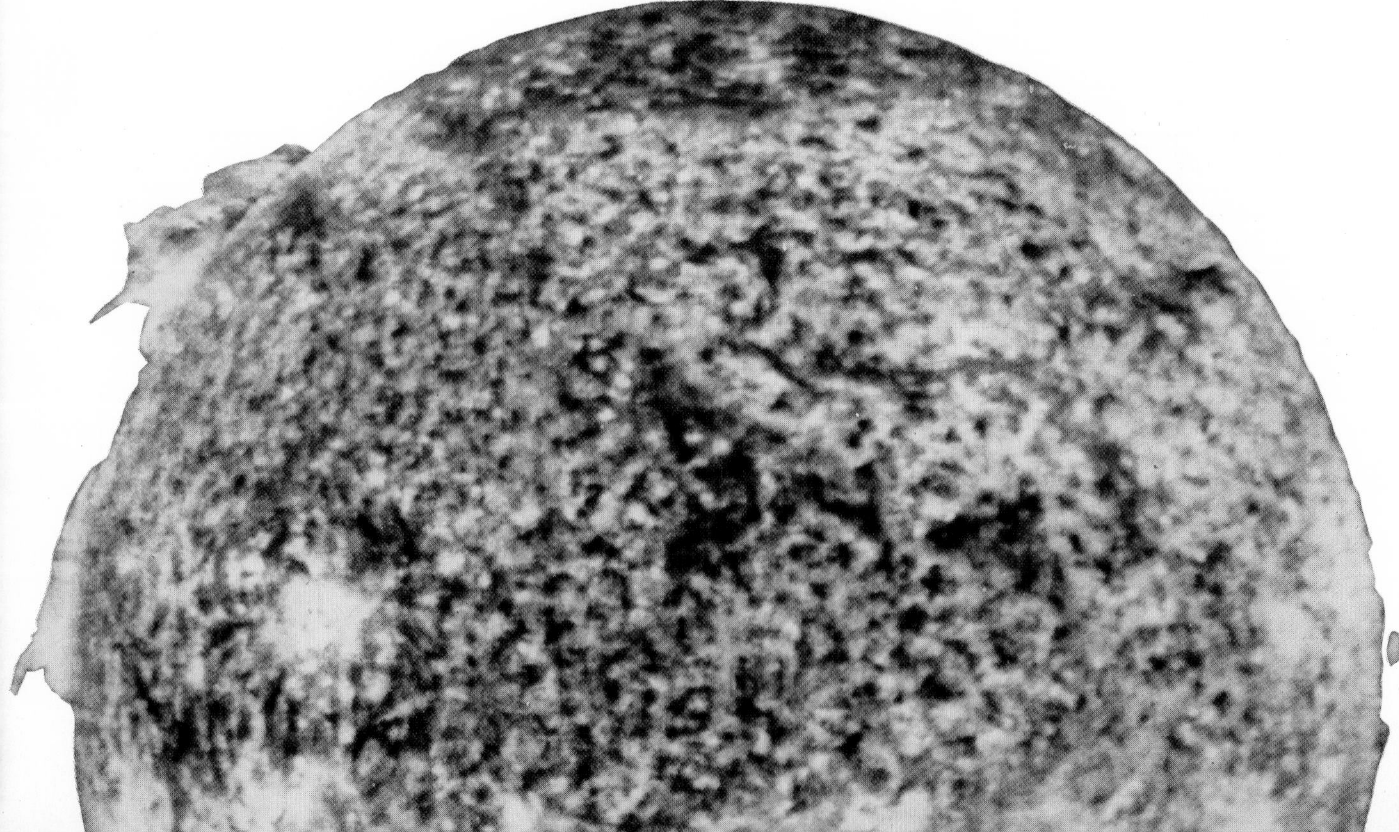

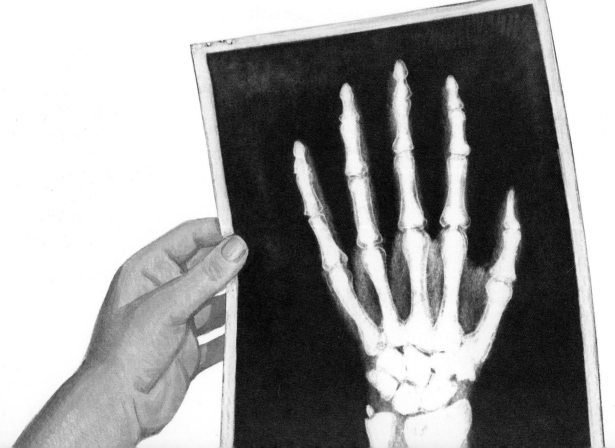

Chapter 11 Keeping Healthy 244

Discovering Science

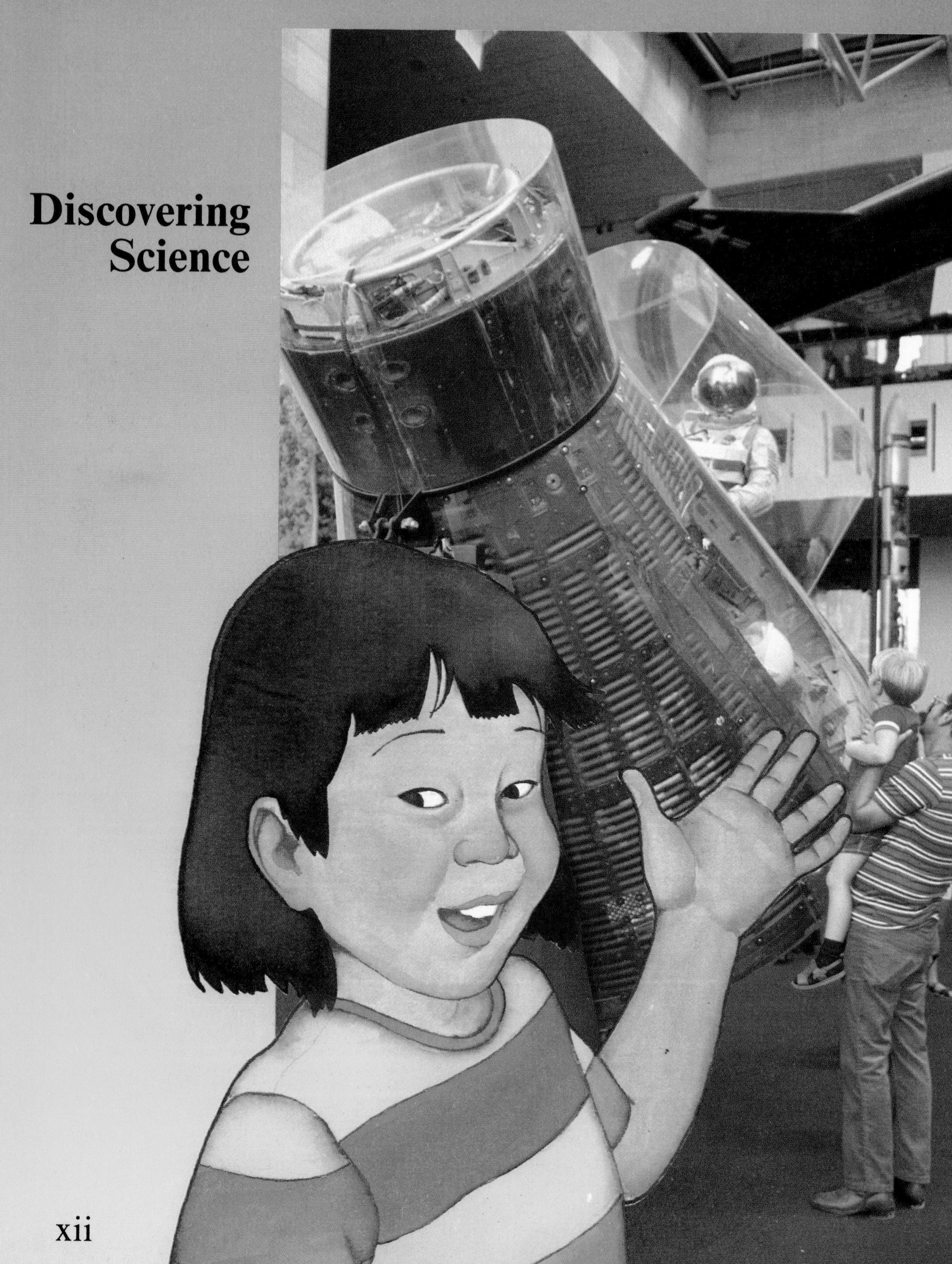

Scientific Methods

Jane has been reading about the sun and its planets at school. She knows that she lives on planet earth. The moon is the earth's closest neighbor in space. The sun and planets are farther away from earth than the moon. Jane wants to know more about the moon. So today she is visiting the Space Museum.

The museum has many exhibits with pictures, stories to read, videotapes, and other objects. Jane reads through the list of exhibits. Some exhibits help people learn about the sun, stars, and planets. Jane is glad to find an exhibit about the moon.

Jane hurries to the moon exhibit. Many pictures of the moon are hanging there. Jane cannot decide where to look first. She sees a picture that shows a person walking on the moon. The person is wearing a suit with a tank on the back. The tank has air to breathe. There is no air on the moon.

Jane wonders how people got to the moon. Then she sees pictures of the rockets that took them there. Jane hopes she can go to the moon some day.

Some of the tools and machines people use on the moon look strange to Jane. One machine looks like a car with no top. People used this machine to drive on the moon.

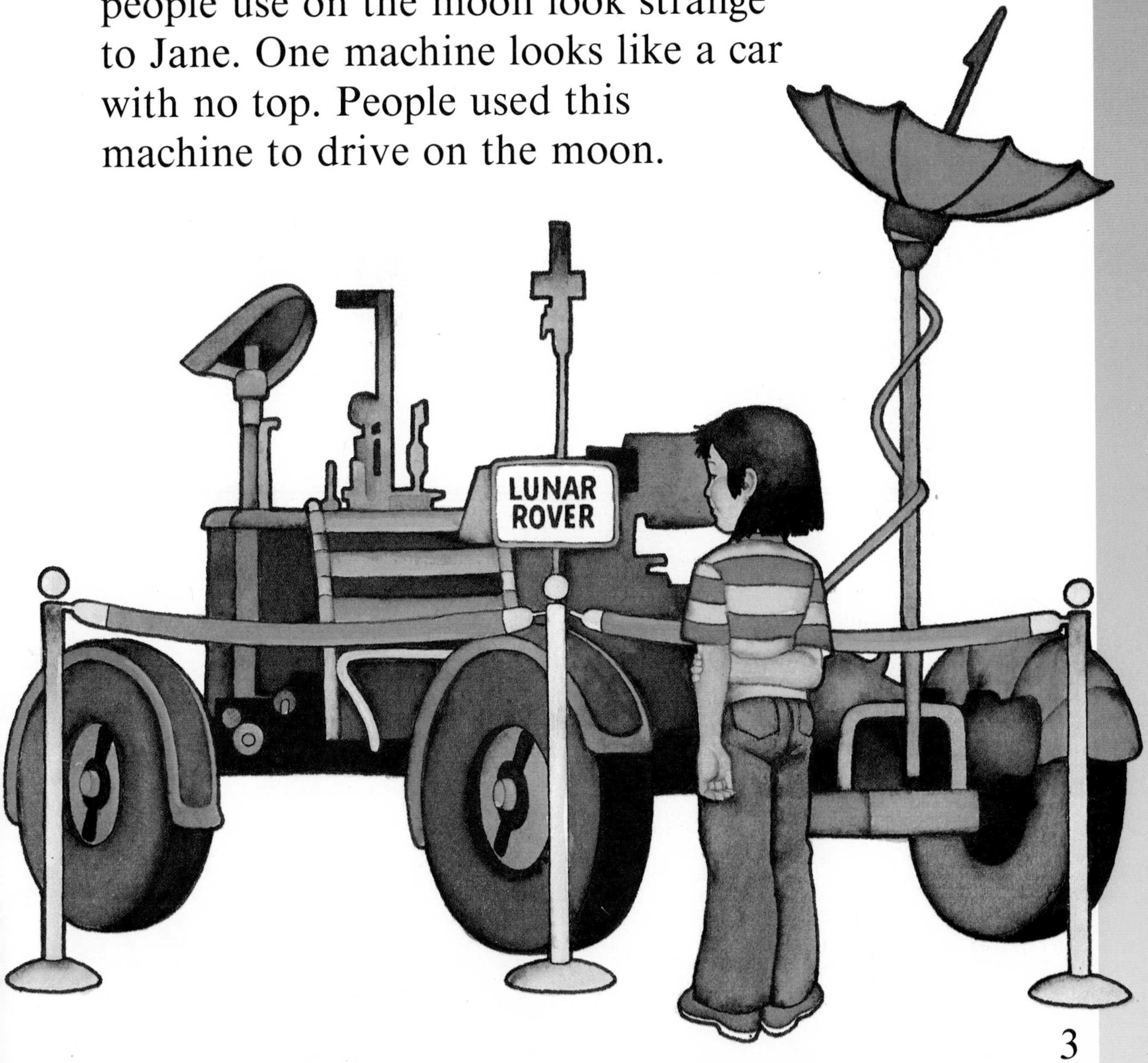

In all the pictures of the moon, Jane notices that the sky is black and filled with stars. She thinks the sky must always look black on the moon. Jane would miss seeing a blue sky if she went to the moon. She also notices no plants in the pictures. The ground is covered with rocks and dust.

In one part of the exhibit, Jane can see how the moon looks through a telescope. She looks for water on the moon. She does not see any oceans, lakes, or rivers. Now Jane knows why there are no plants growing on the moon. Plants need water to grow.

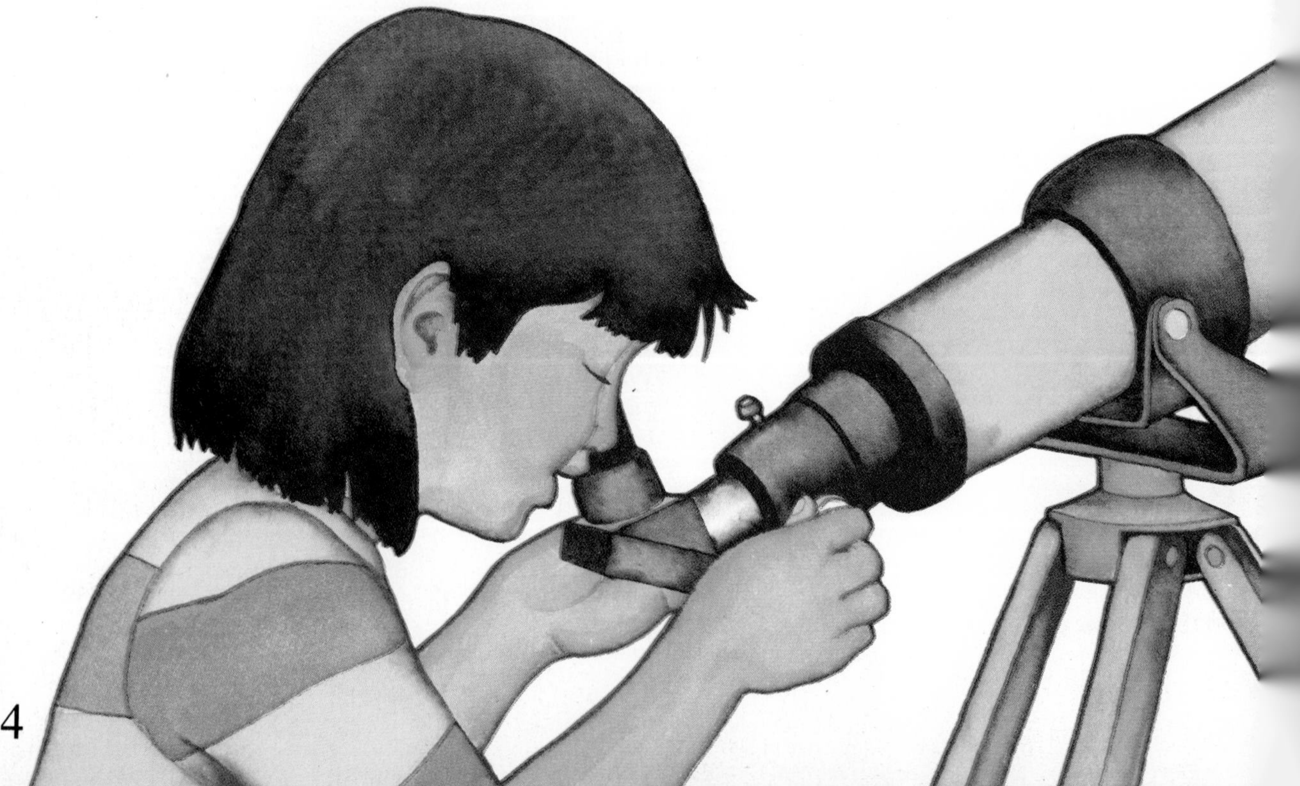

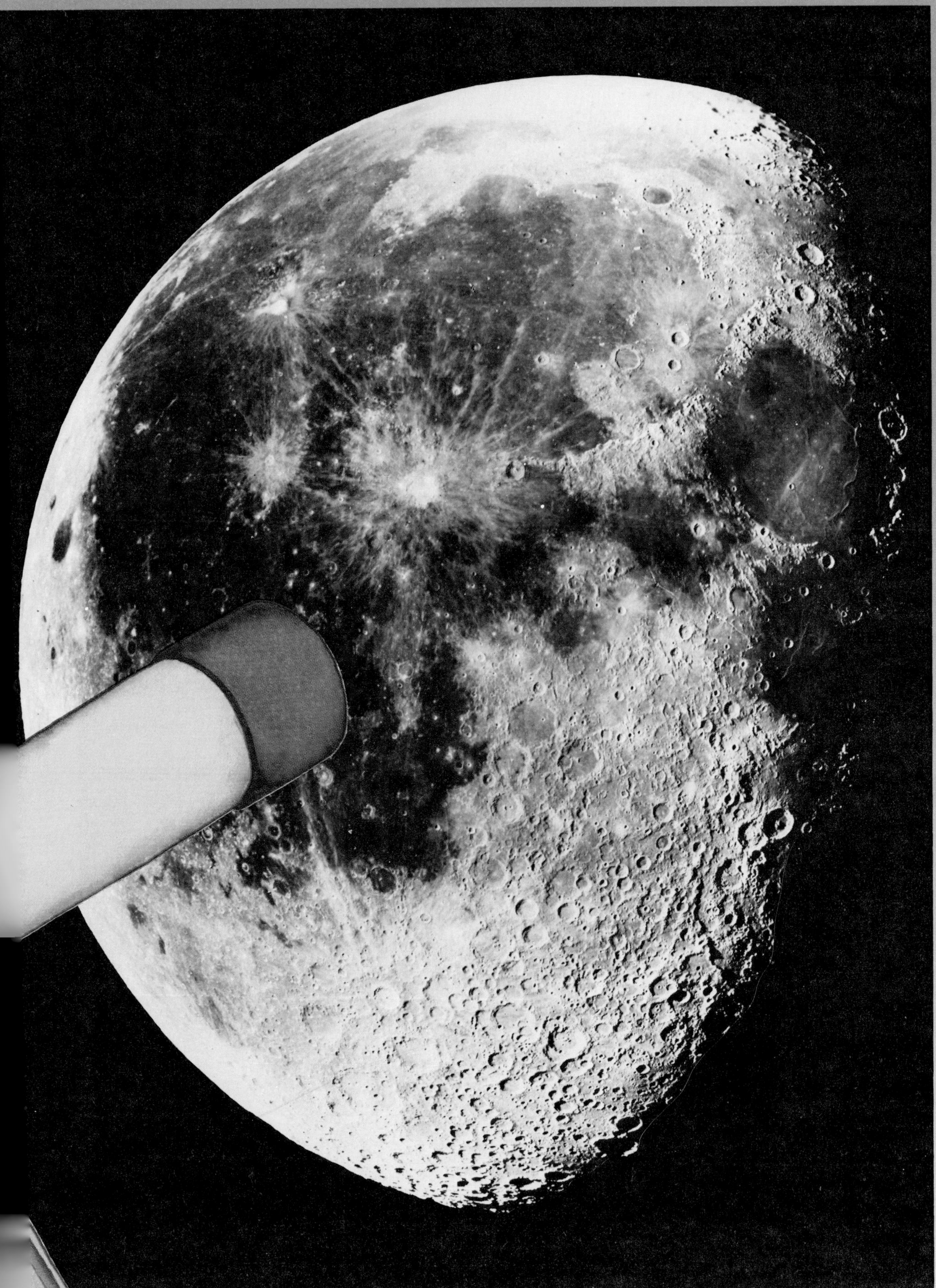

Jane is almost finished looking at the exhibit. But then she sees some pictures that show how the moon looks on different nights. The moon looks like a different shape in each picture. Jane knows the moon is always the same round shape. But on each night we see a different part of the moon that is lit up by the sun. So the moon looks like it changes shape. The lighted shapes we see are called the moon's phases.

Jane wonders how long it takes to really see all the phases of the moon. She can use a scientific method to find out.

Scientists use scientific methods to find answers to questions. These methods have certain steps. Scientists do not always use the steps in the same way. Often they use the steps in different order. Read on to see how Jane uses the steps. You can also use these steps to answer questions.

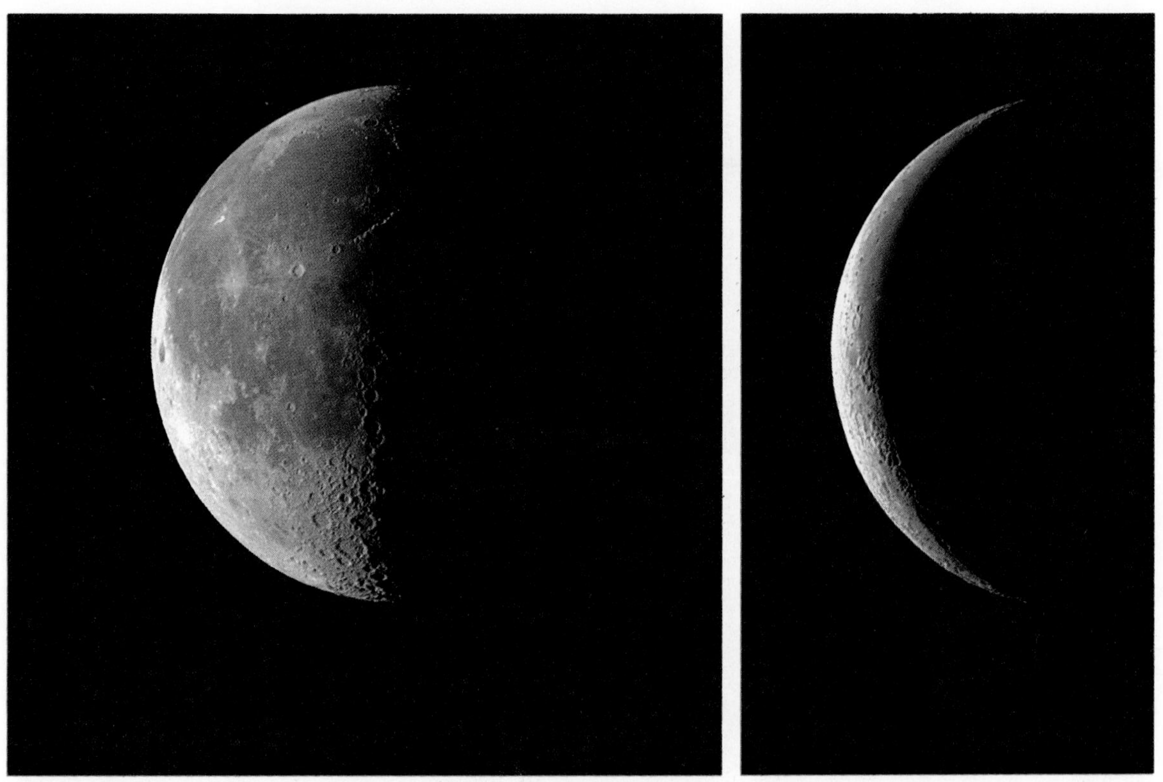

Explain the Problem

Jane has a question about the moon. How long does it take for the moon to go through all its phases?

Make Observations

Jane saw some pictures of the moon in the night sky. She noticed for a few nights how the moon changes shape.

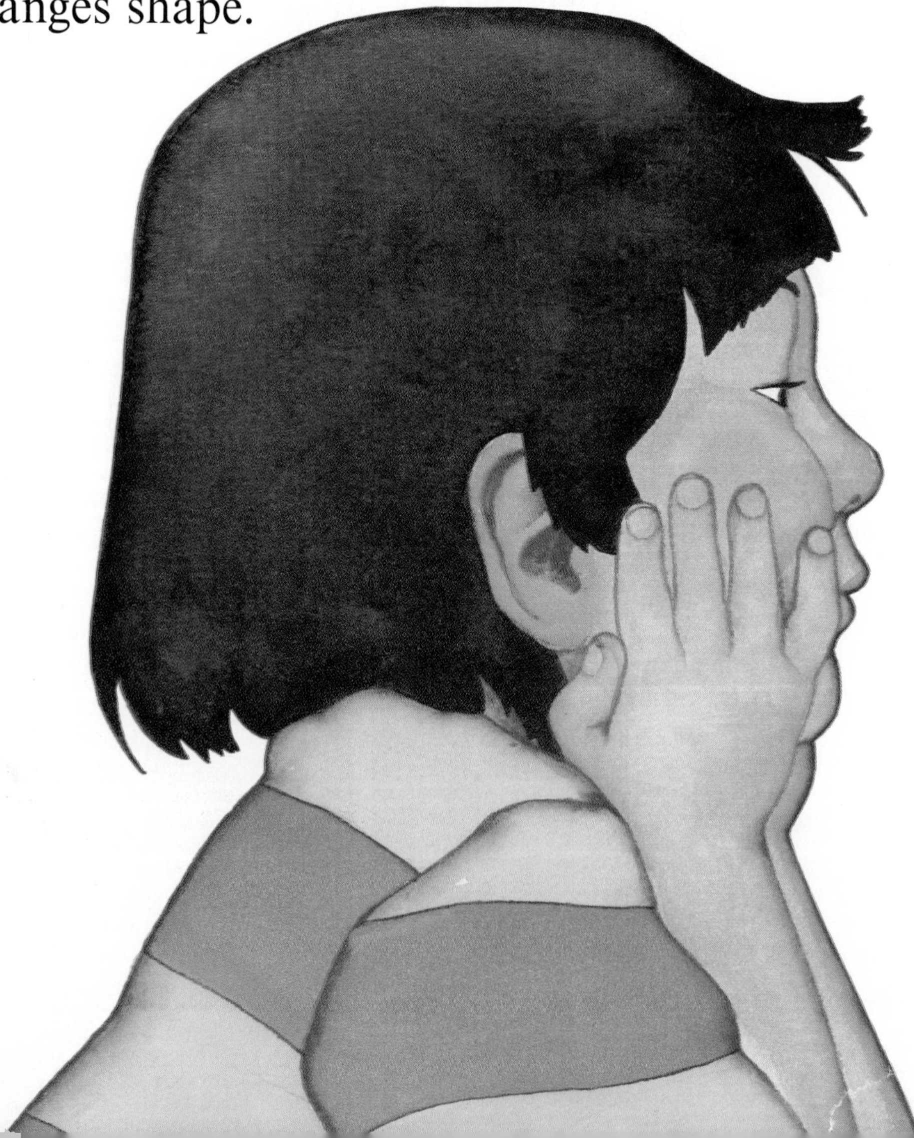

Give a Hypothesis

Jane thinks about her problem and observations. She gives this hypothesis. The moon takes about a month to go through all its phases.

Jane decides to do an experiment. Then she will know if her hypothesis is right. Jane looks for the moon each day and night. She carefully notices the shape of the part of the moon she can see.

Make a Chart

Jane decides to make a calendar with large boxes. Each day, she draws the moon shape in the right box. She continues to do this for one month.

Make Conclusions

Jane decides that her hypothesis is right. It takes about one month for the moon to go through all its phases. How is Jane's conclusion like her hypothesis?

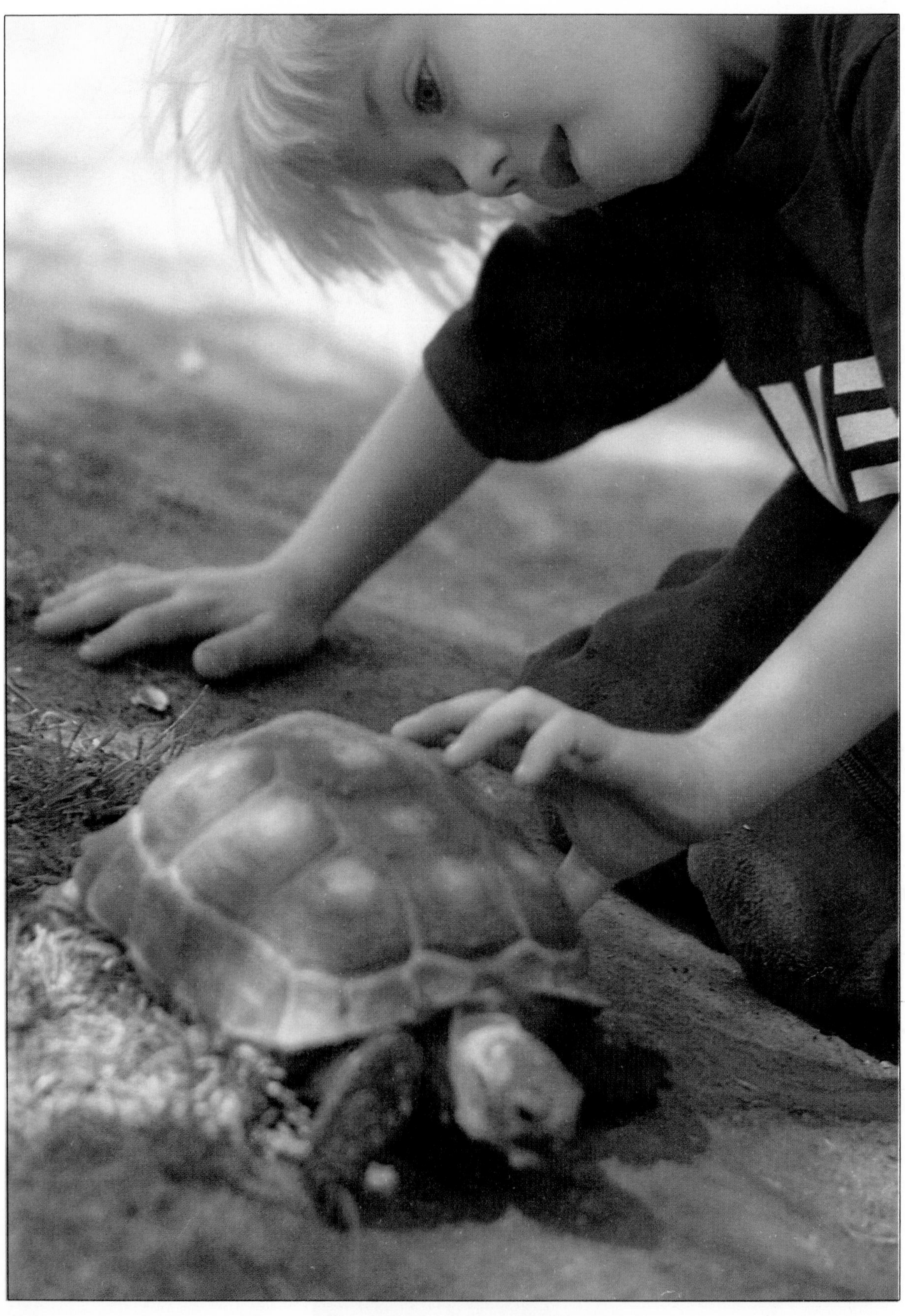

Unit 1

Life Science

The boy and the turtle are both living things. Yet, they are different in many ways. The turtle's hard shell protects its body. What type of covering protects your body? Work with a friend. Write three ways that the turtle and the boy are different.

Chapter 1

How Plants Are Different

What different plants can you find in the picture? People use plants in many ways. How do people use plants?

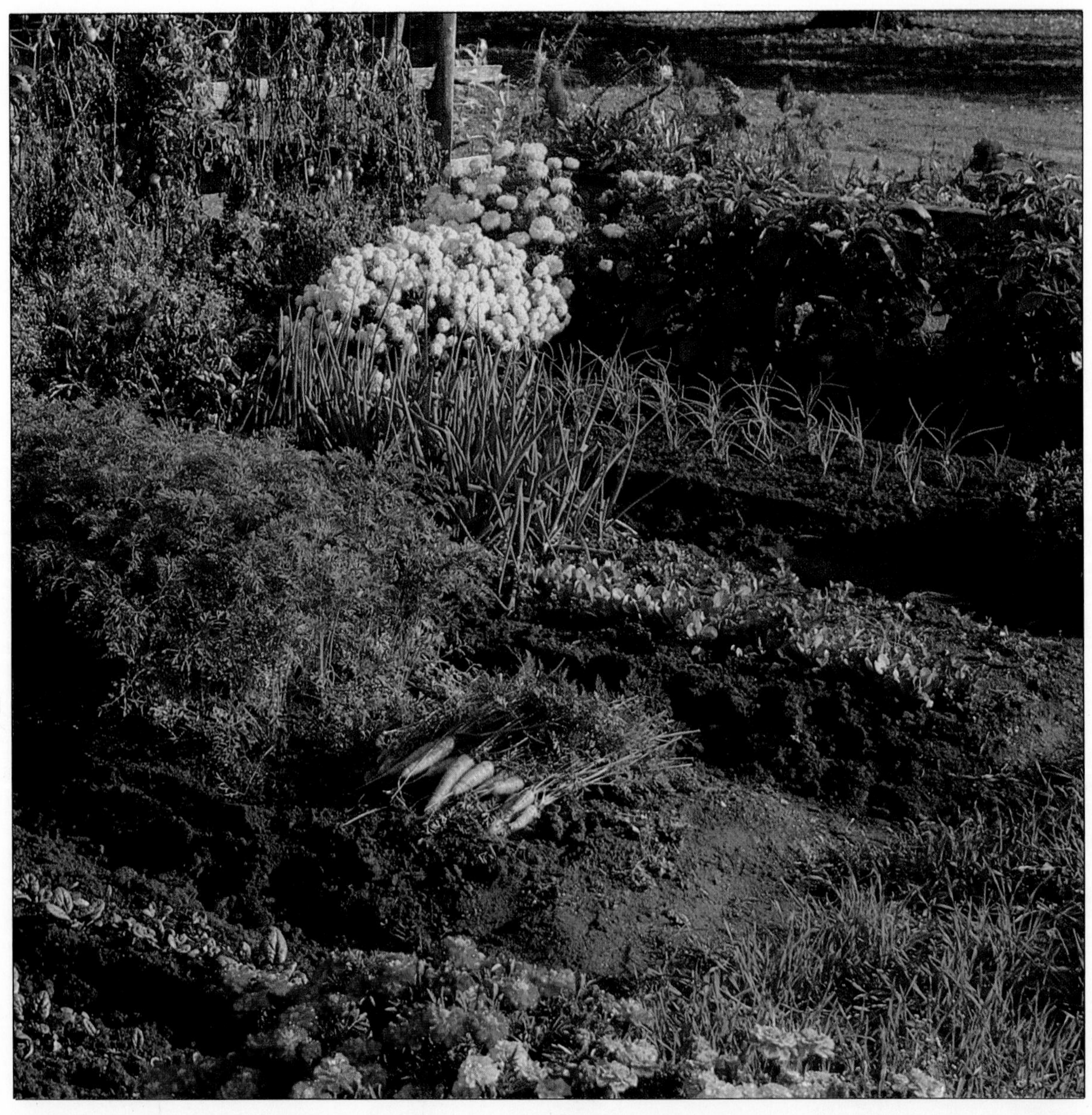

Starting the Chapter

You can group your toys by color and size. You can also group plant seeds in these ways. You will learn about other parts of plants as you read on.

TRY THIS

Grouping Seeds

Get some different seeds. Put the seeds in a line from smallest to largest. Then put the seeds in groups by color and shape. What other ways could you group the seeds?

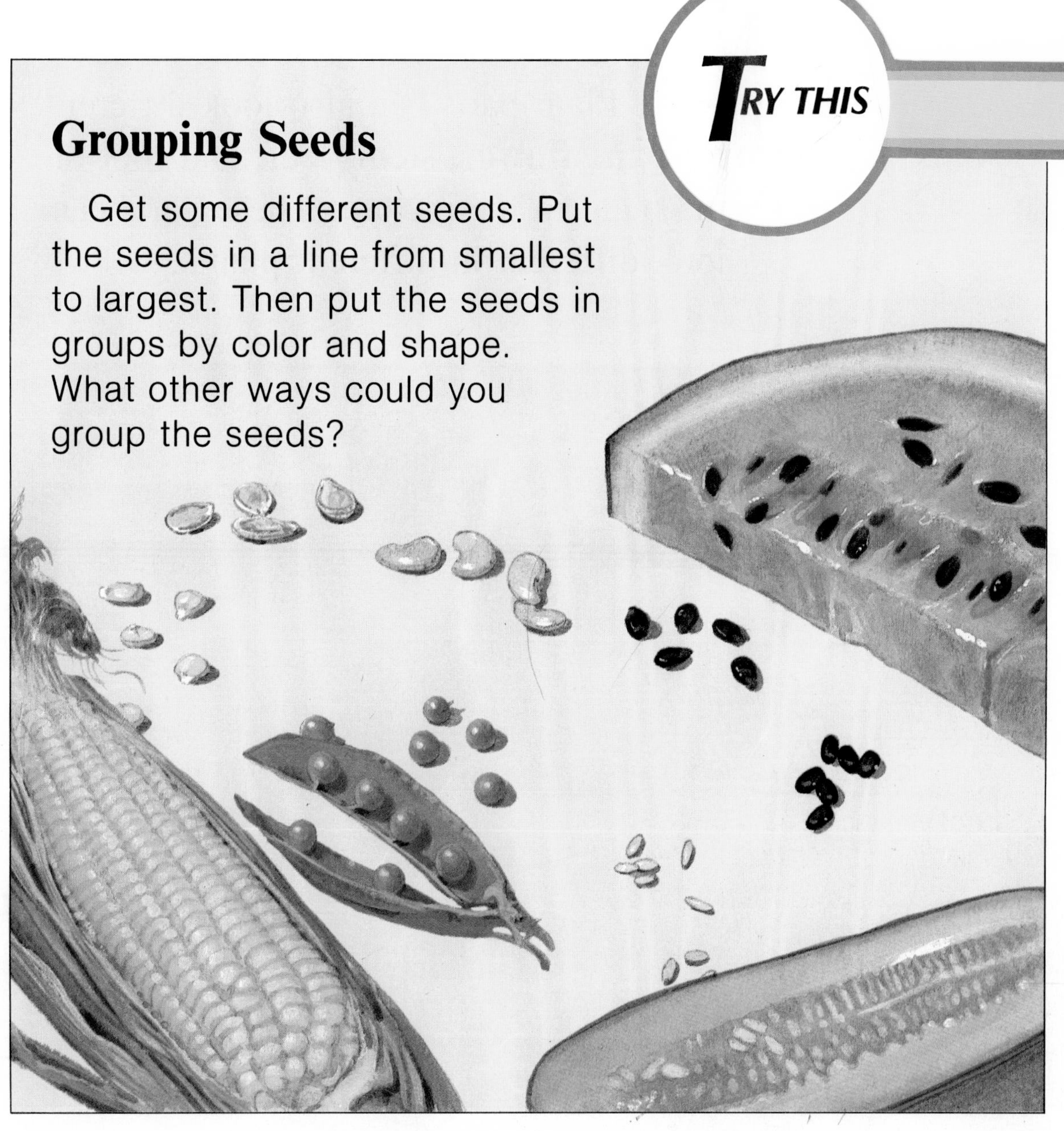

Lesson 1 How Can Plant Parts Be Different?

Look at the books in your classroom. How are they alike? How are they different? Books have many of the same parts. Sometimes these parts look very different.

Plants also have many of the same parts. Plant parts can also look different. Find the **flower,** stem, leaf, and root of the plant in the picture. These parts can look different in different plants.

Pretend you are walking through the field in the picture. What colors do you see? What do you smell?

Flowers have different shapes, sizes, colors, and smells. Some flowers grow at the top of a stem. Other flowers grow along the side of a stem. What different kinds of flowers have you seen?

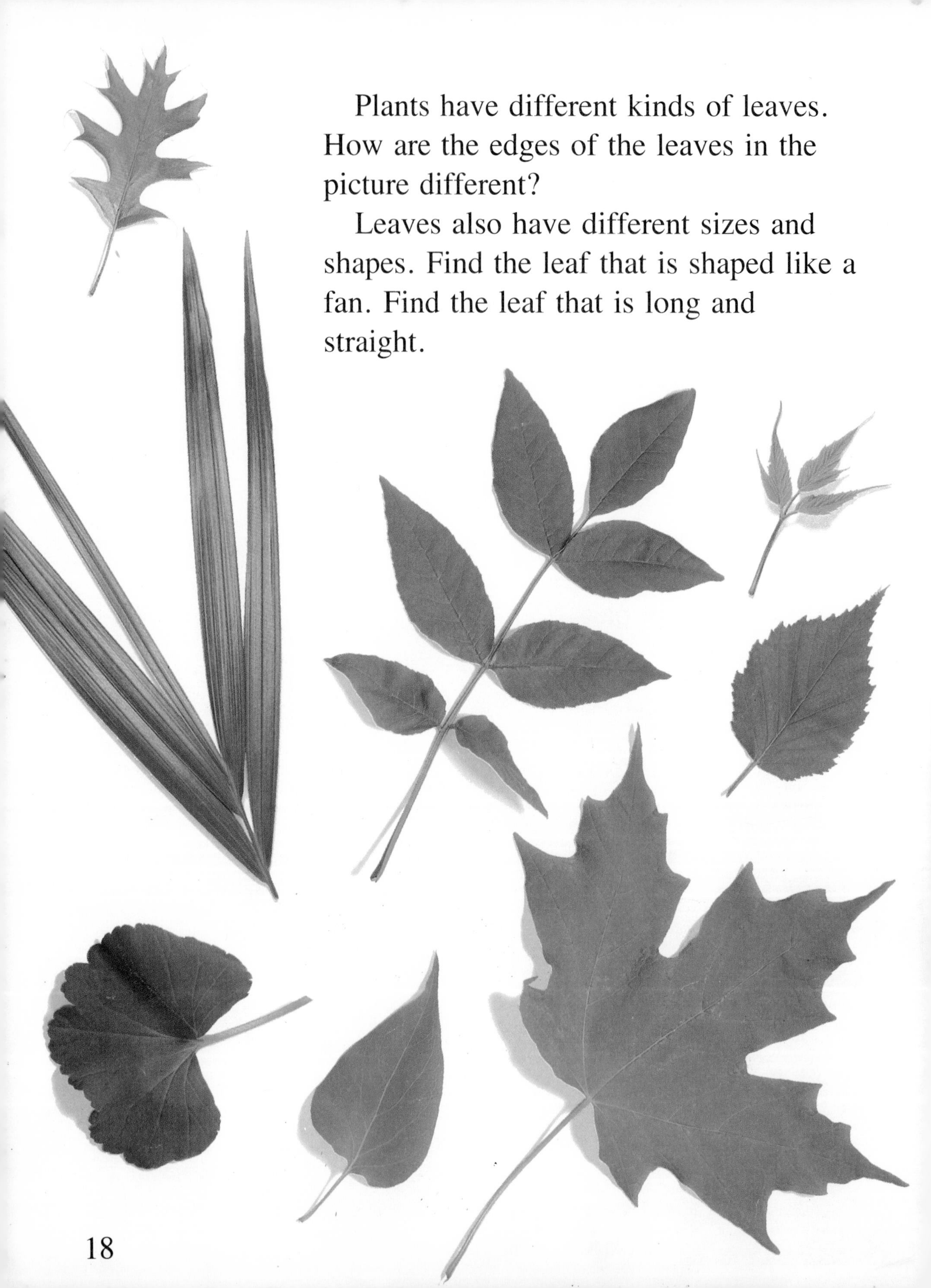

Plants have different kinds of leaves. How are the edges of the leaves in the picture different?

Leaves also have different sizes and shapes. Find the leaf that is shaped like a fan. Find the leaf that is long and straight.

What different plant stems do you see here? Plant stems can be thick or thin, rough or smooth. They can be soft or hard.

Plant roots grow in the soil. Roots grow longer as the plant grows and changes. Roots help plants get water from the soil. Plant roots can be short or long, thick or thin.

Lesson Review

1. What are the parts of a plant?
2. How can plant parts be different?

LIFE SCIENCE

Find Out

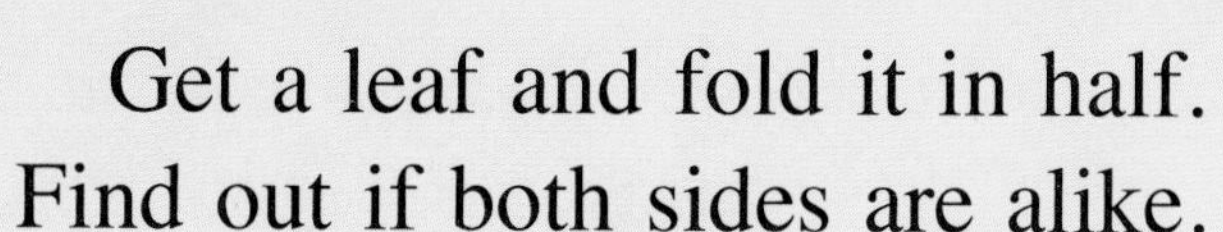

Get a leaf and fold it in half. Find out if both sides are alike.

Lesson 2 What Do Plants Use to Make Food?

Most plants need air, water, and sunlight to live and grow. They also need food. Most plants make their own food. They use sunlight, water, and air to make food. Many plants grow in soil. They use materials from soil to make food.

Plants make food in their leaves. Other green parts of plants can also make food. Find the green parts of the plant in the picture.

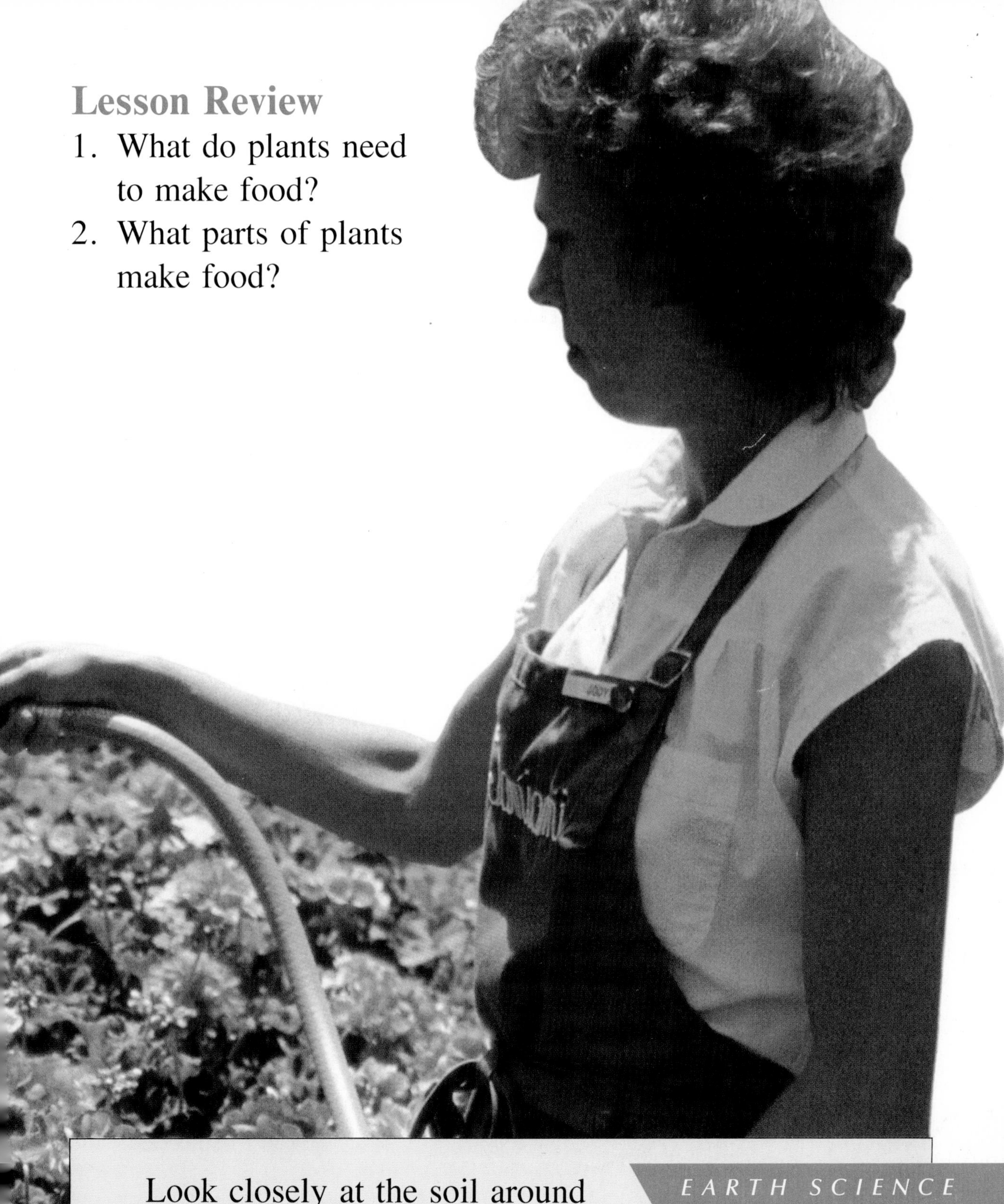

Lesson Review

1. What do plants need to make food?
2. What parts of plants make food?

EARTH SCIENCE
Find Out
CONNECTION

Look closely at the soil around a plant. Tell what the soil looks like. Also tell how it feels.

Learning What Plants Need

Follow the Directions

1. Cover two leaves of a plant with paper.
2. Put the plant in a sunny place.
3. Water the plant.
4. Take the paper off after four or five days.
5. Observe the two leaves that were covered.

Tell What You Learned

Tell what the two leaves looked like when you took the paper off. Tell what would happen if a plant did not get light for a long time.

Growing Plants in Space

Think about the different places you have seen plants growing. Then imagine growing plants in a spacecraft far away from earth.

These plants that grow in space do not need soil. They grow in holes in a large tube. Special lights help the plants grow. Machines spray water on the plants. The water has materials that plants usually get from soil.

What Do You Think?

How can growing plants in space help people?

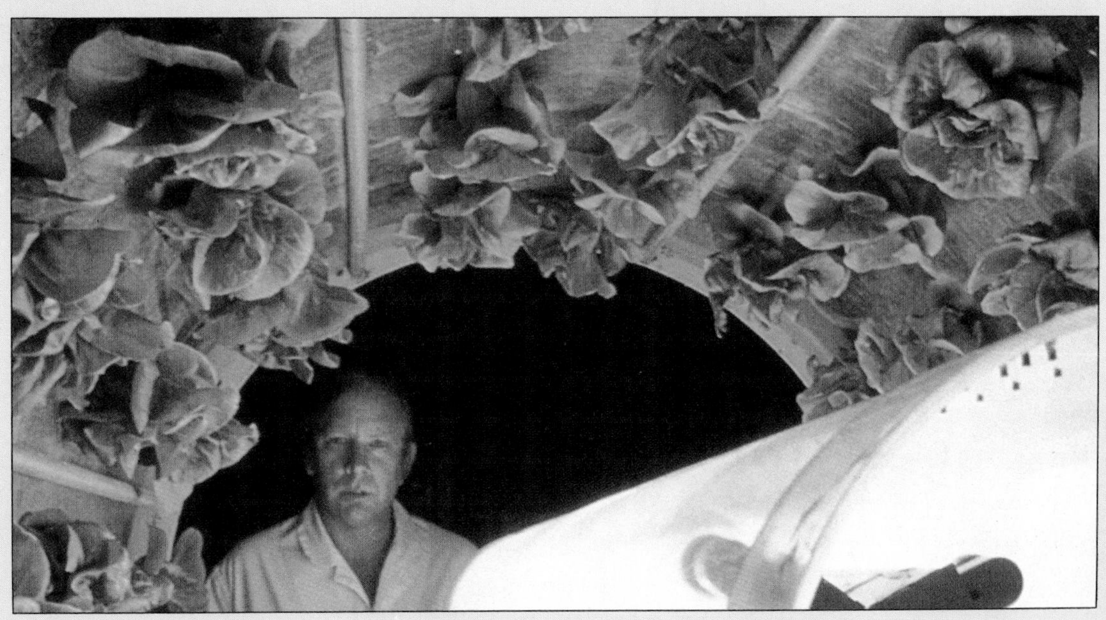

Lesson 3 What Different Ways Do Plants Grow?

Most new plants grow from seeds. Look at the picture to see how a new plant grows.

A seed has a tiny plant in it. A seed also has food for the tiny plant.

As the tiny plant grows, it uses food from the inside of the seed. The seed breaks open and the roots begin to grow down into the soil. Where do the stem and leaves begin to grow?

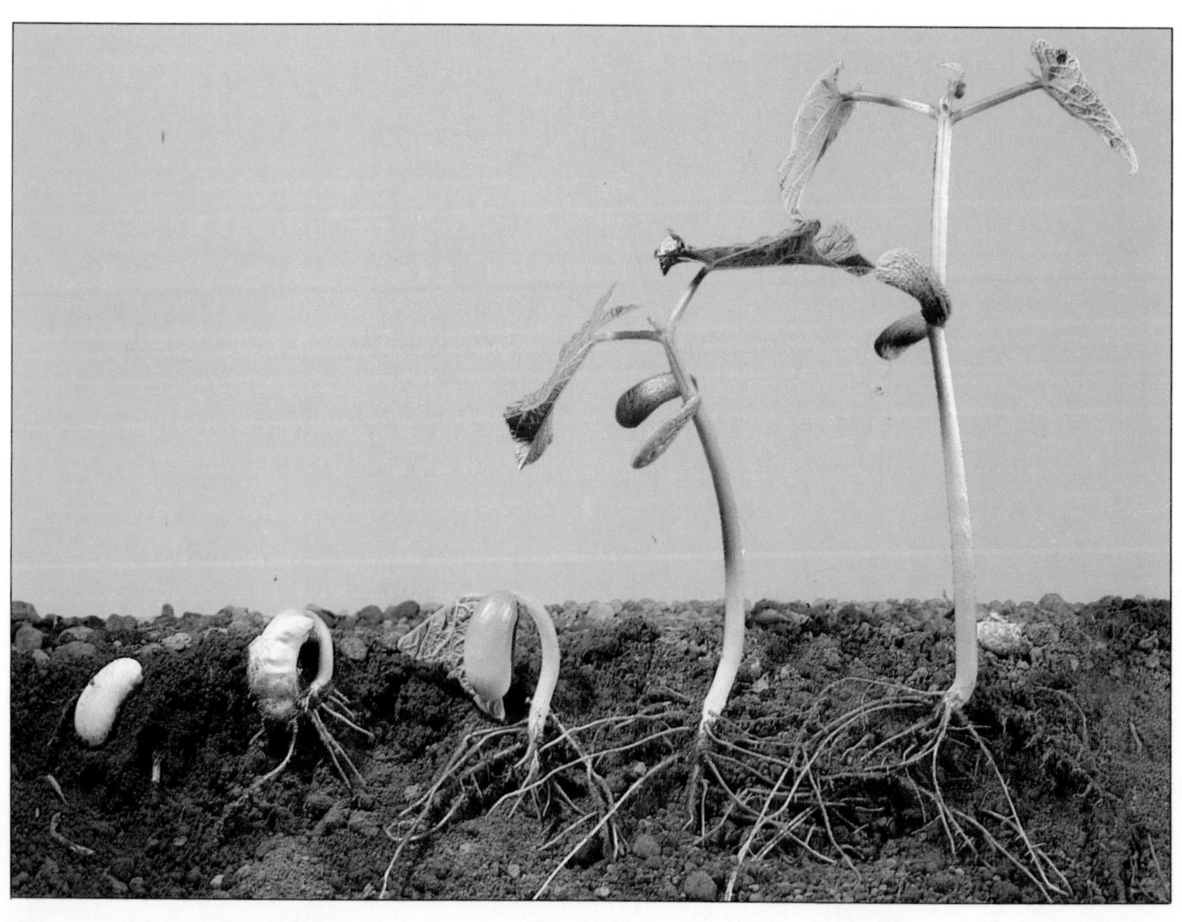

A new plant can start from other parts of a plant. New plants can grow from stems, roots, and leaves. A potato is an underground stem. A new potato plant can grow from a piece of potato with a **bud.**

Have you ever seen potatoes with buds like this? If you plant these potatoes in soil, new stems, leaves, and roots would grow. Finally, a new potato plant would grow from each potato.

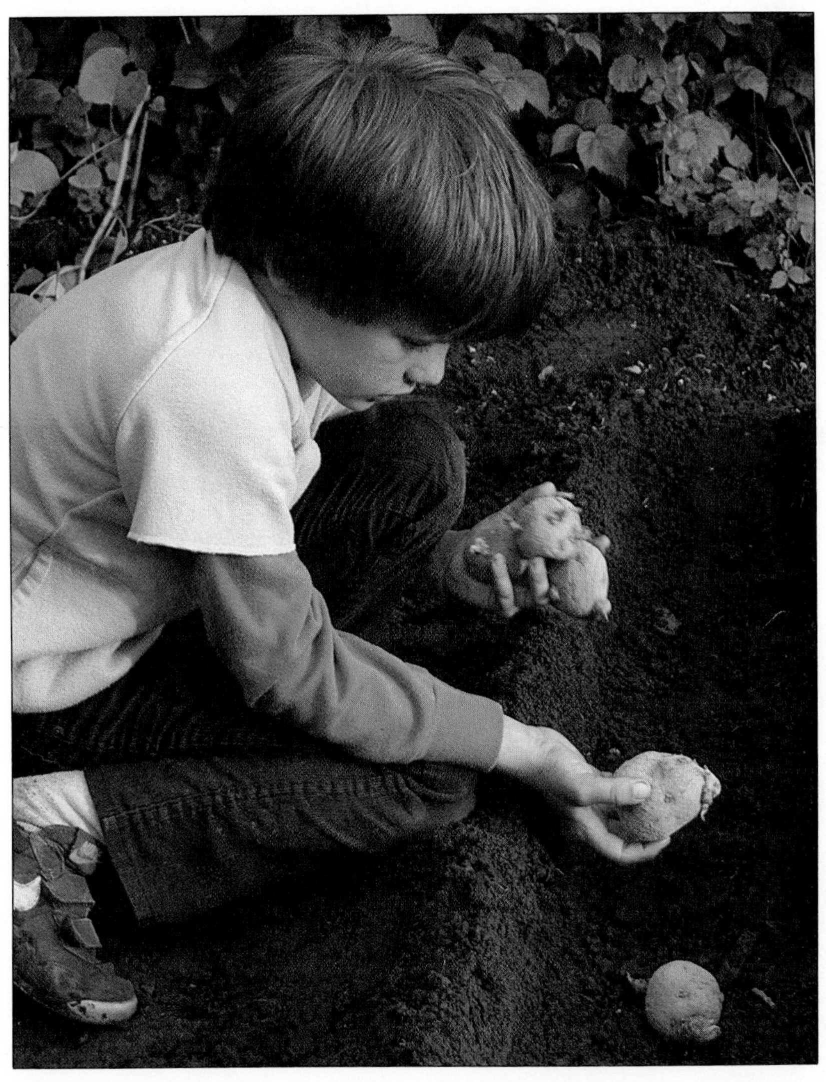

What happens if you take a leaf from this plant and keep it in water? A new plant will grow from the leaf and its roots.

Lesson Review

1. How does a plant grow from a seed?
2. What parts of a plant can grow a new plant?

LIFE SCIENCE

Find Out

Put a sweet potato in a glass of water. Find out how a new plant will grow.

Observing the Inside of a Seed

Follow the Directions

1. Take off the outside part of a seed.
2. Break the seed into two parts.
3. Observe the tiny plant inside the seed.
4. Find the root, leaf, and stem of the tiny plant.

Tell What You Learned

Tell what you observed when you broke open your seed. Tell what you learn from observing seeds.

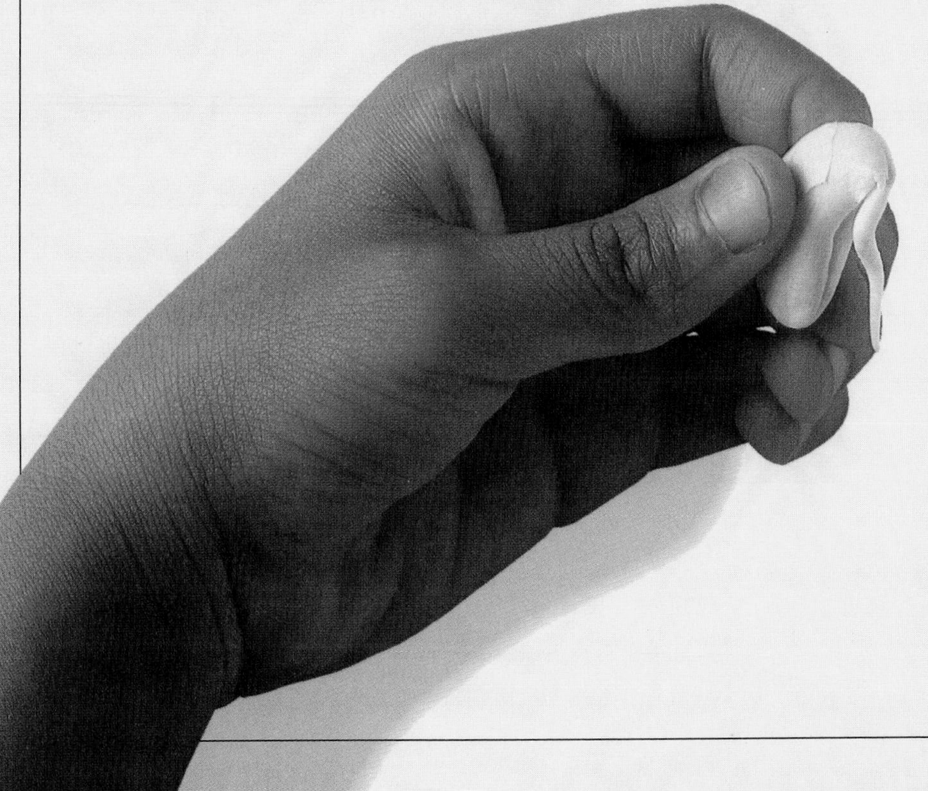

Lesson 4 Where Do Plants Grow?

Plants grow in different kinds of places or **habitats.** Cold habitats may have strong winds and very little rain. Plants in cold habitats are often small and grow near the ground.

A dry habitat is called a **desert.** Does a desert have much rain? The desert plants in the picture can hold water for a long time.

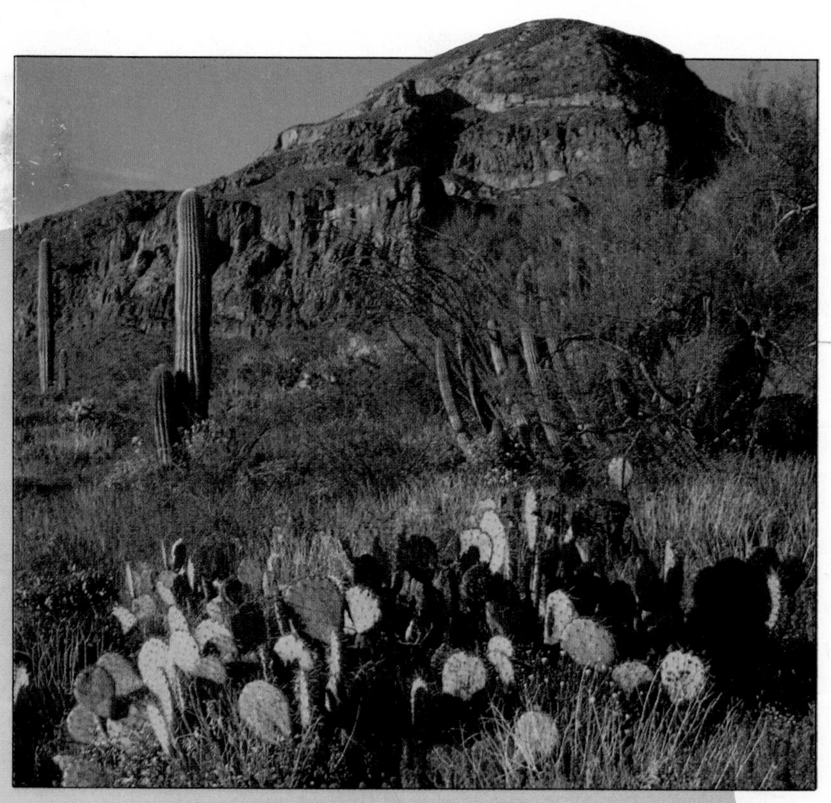

Wet habitats are places in or near oceans, rivers, and lakes. Plants also grow in wet habitats. The roots of this plant grow in the bottom of a **pond.** The stems grow up to the top of the water. What floats on top of the water?

Lesson Review

1. What habitats do plants grow in?
2. What kinds of plants grow in different habitats?

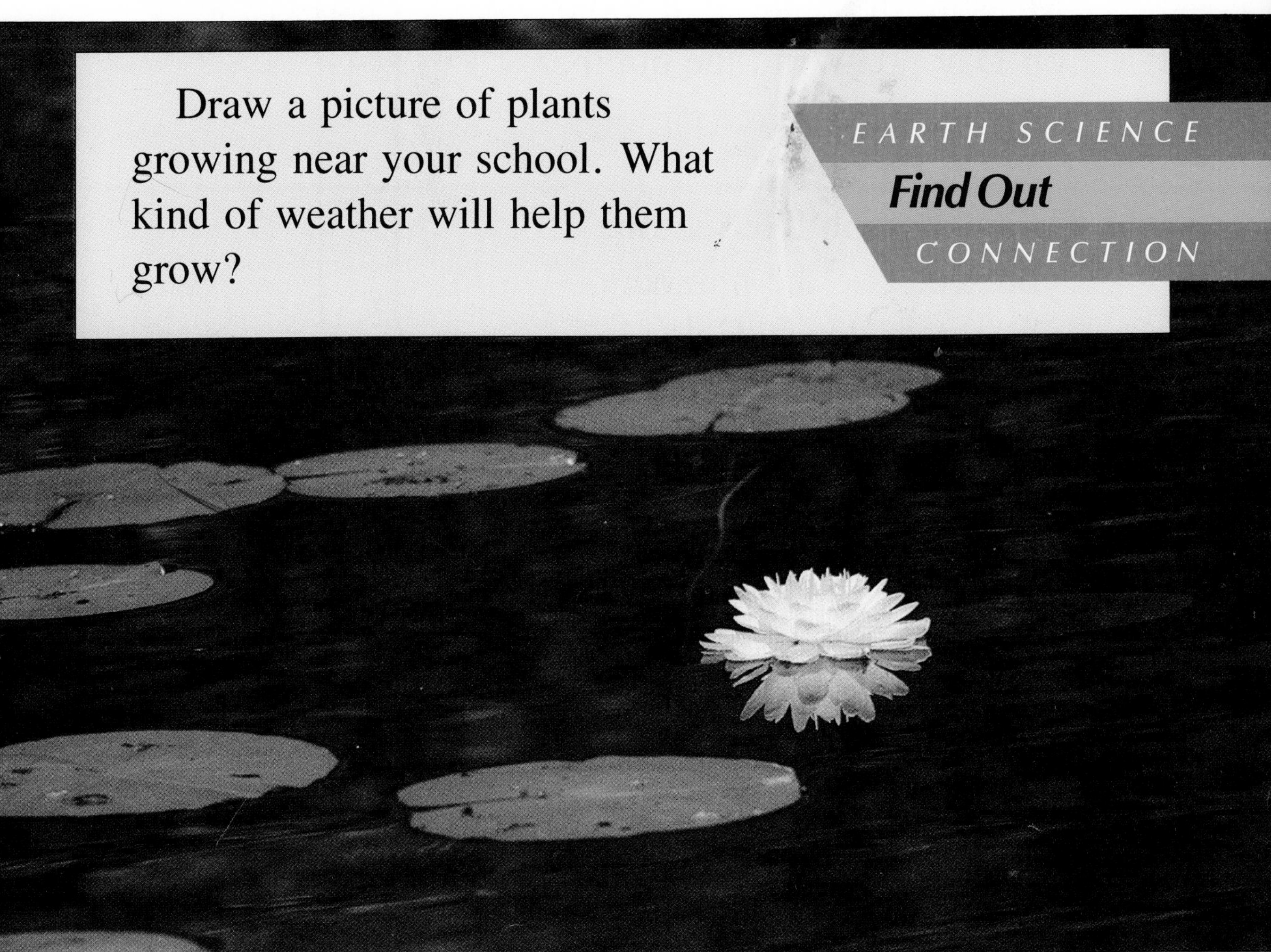

EARTH SCIENCE
Find Out
CONNECTION

Draw a picture of plants growing near your school. What kind of weather will help them grow?

Measuring a Plant and Making a Graph

How can you measure how much a plant grows in 30 days?

1. Look at the two pictures of the same plant. Use a metric ruler. Measure the plant as it looks on Day 1. Write the number on your own paper. Measure the plant as it looks on Day 30. Write the number on your paper.

2. Draw a graph like the one you see. Use the numbers you wrote down. Color in a square on the graph for each centimeter the plant measures.

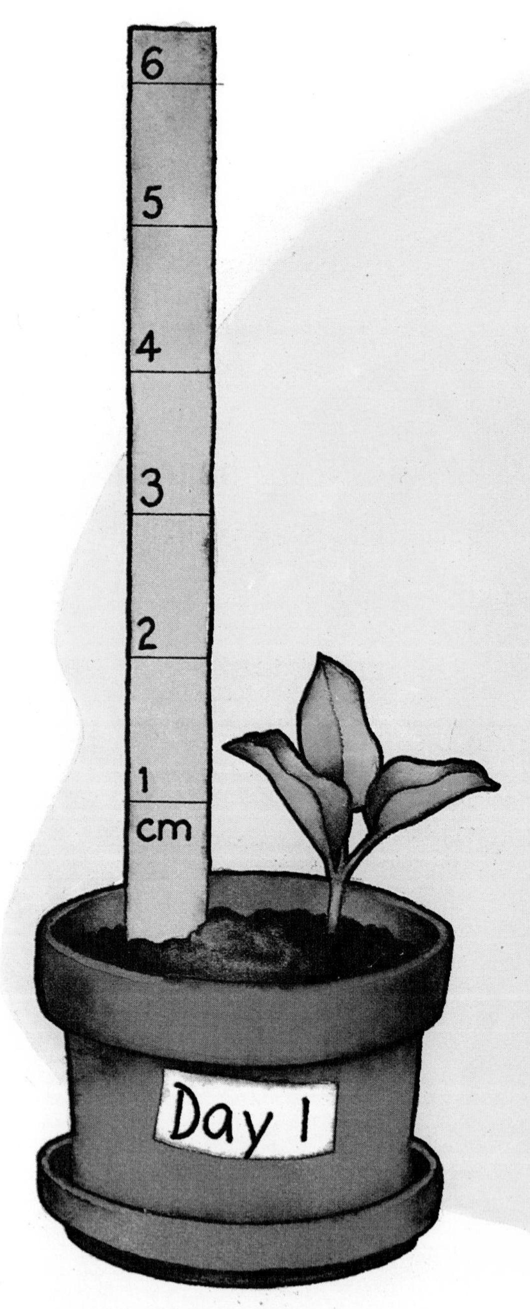

3. How many centimeters did the plant grow from Day 1 to Day 30?

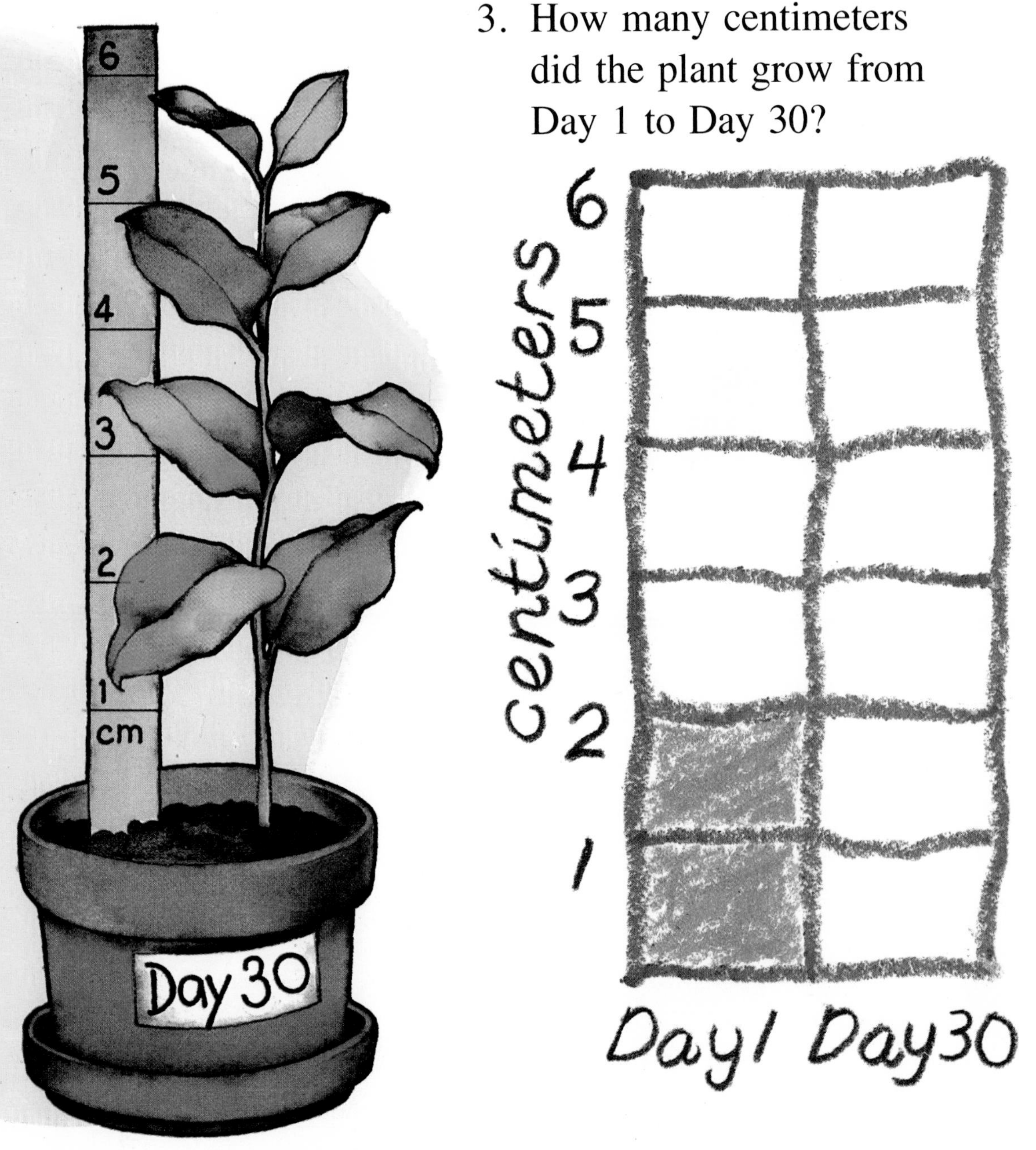

Chapter 1 Review

Review Chapter Ideas

1. Look at the picture below. Find the roots, stems, seeds, and leaves.
2. Tell what different kinds of flowers, leaves, roots, and stems plants can have.
3. Tell what plants need to make food.
4. Look at the picture below. Explain how a new plant grows from a seed.
5. Tell what parts of a plant can grow a new plant.
6. Name different habitats where plants grow.

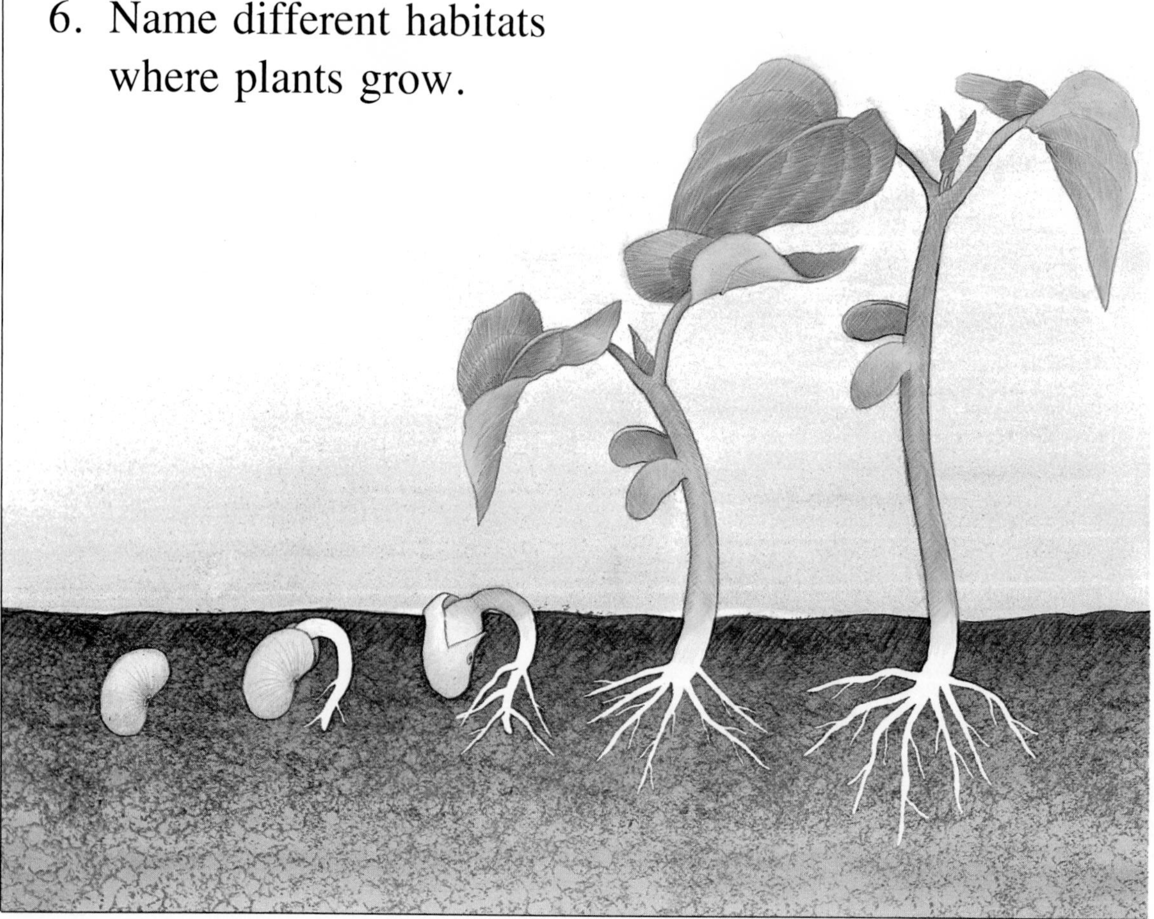

Review Science Words

Match the words and the pictures.

1. flower
2. bud
3. desert

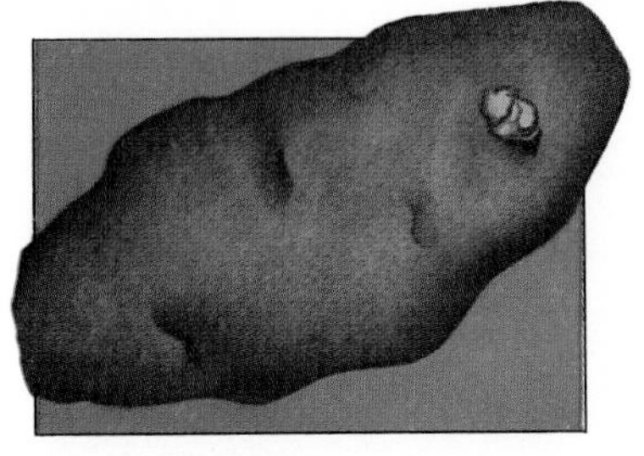

a.

b.

c.

Tell what the words mean.

4. habitat
5. pond

Use Science Ideas

Look at the plants in the pictures. Tell about the plants in each habitat.

Chapter 2

How Animals Are Different

The cat and the bird are different from each other. What is different about the places they live?

Starting the Chapter

Think about how some animals are different from each other. You can draw pictures of different animals. As you read on, you will learn about groups of animals.

TRY THIS

Drawing Differences in Animals

Fold a piece of paper into four parts. Next, draw a picture of a different animal in each part. How are the animals different from each other?

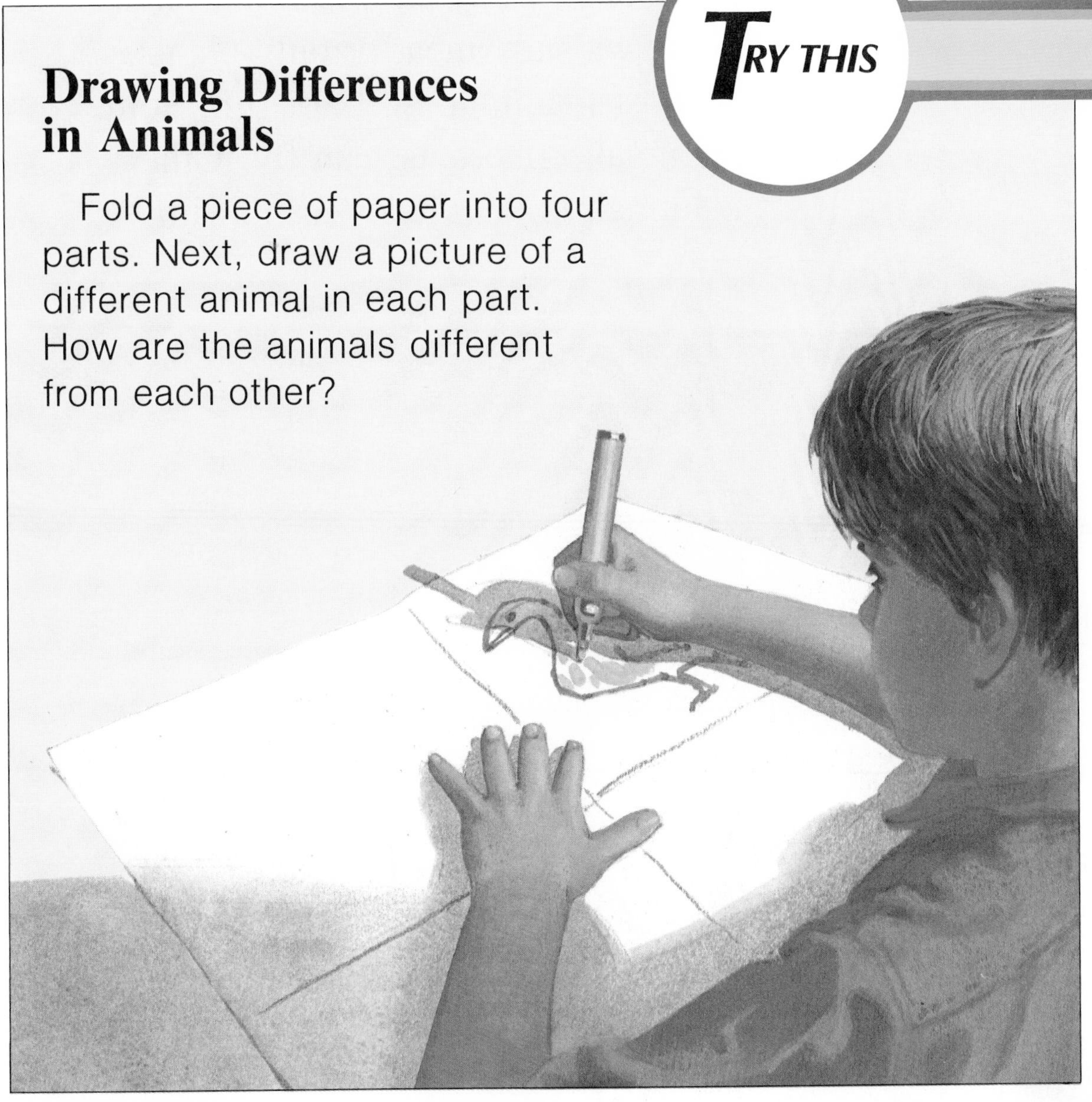

Lesson 1 What Are Some Groups of Animals?

One group of animals has many animals you know. The animals in this group are called **mammals.** What mammals do you see in the pictures?

Hair or fur covers the bodies of most mammals. Many eat meat and plants. Some eat only meat or only plants.

Most mammals walk or run. Some mammals, like bats, can fly. Other mammals, like whales, can swim.

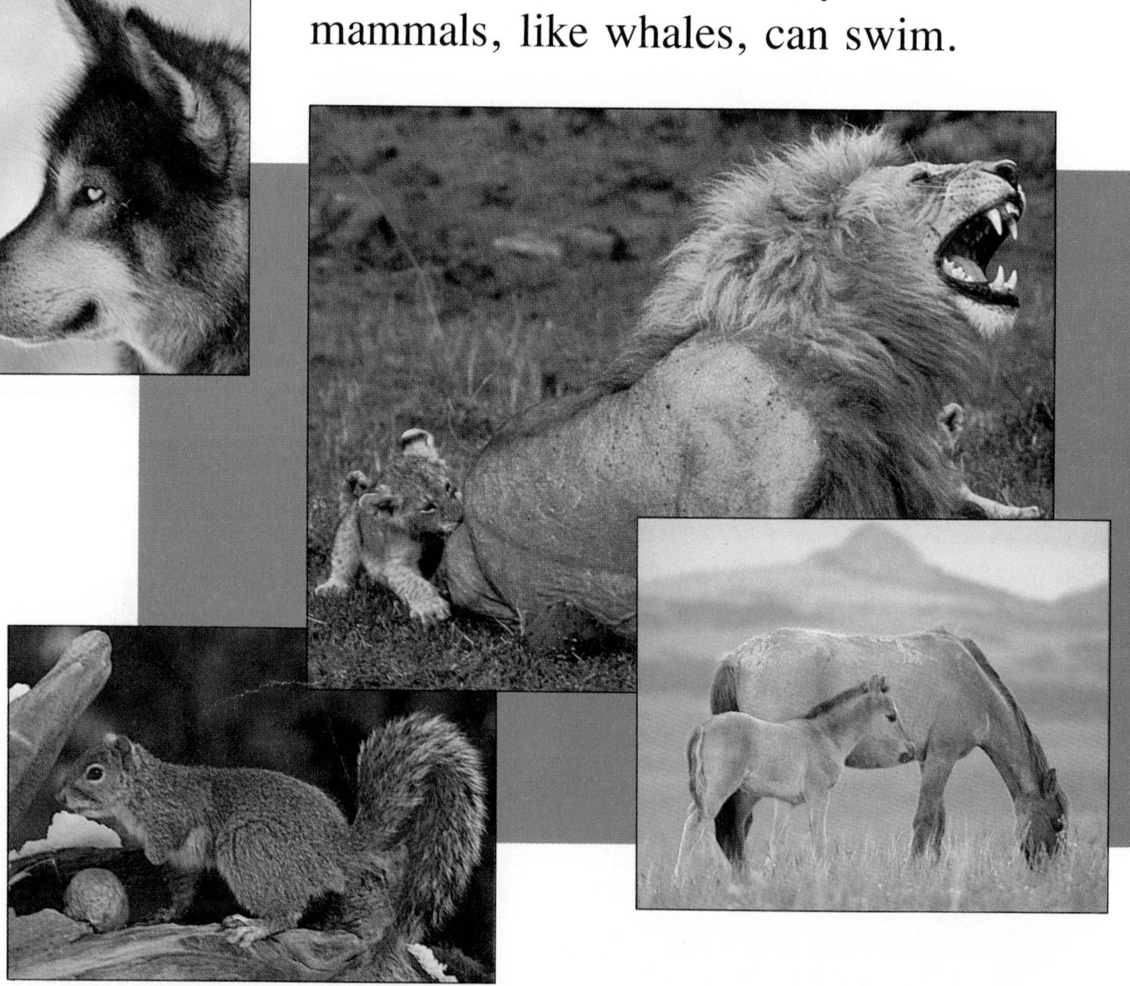

Feathers cover most animals in the bird group. Most birds can fly. Birds have wings.

Birds have different kinds of feet and beaks. Some birds eat small animals. Others eat seeds. How do these different kinds of feet help birds?

Most places in the world have a group of animals called **insects.** These animals have three main body parts. Find the parts in the picture.

Each insect has six legs. Many insects have wings and fly. Insects eat plants and other animals. Which of these insects have you seen?

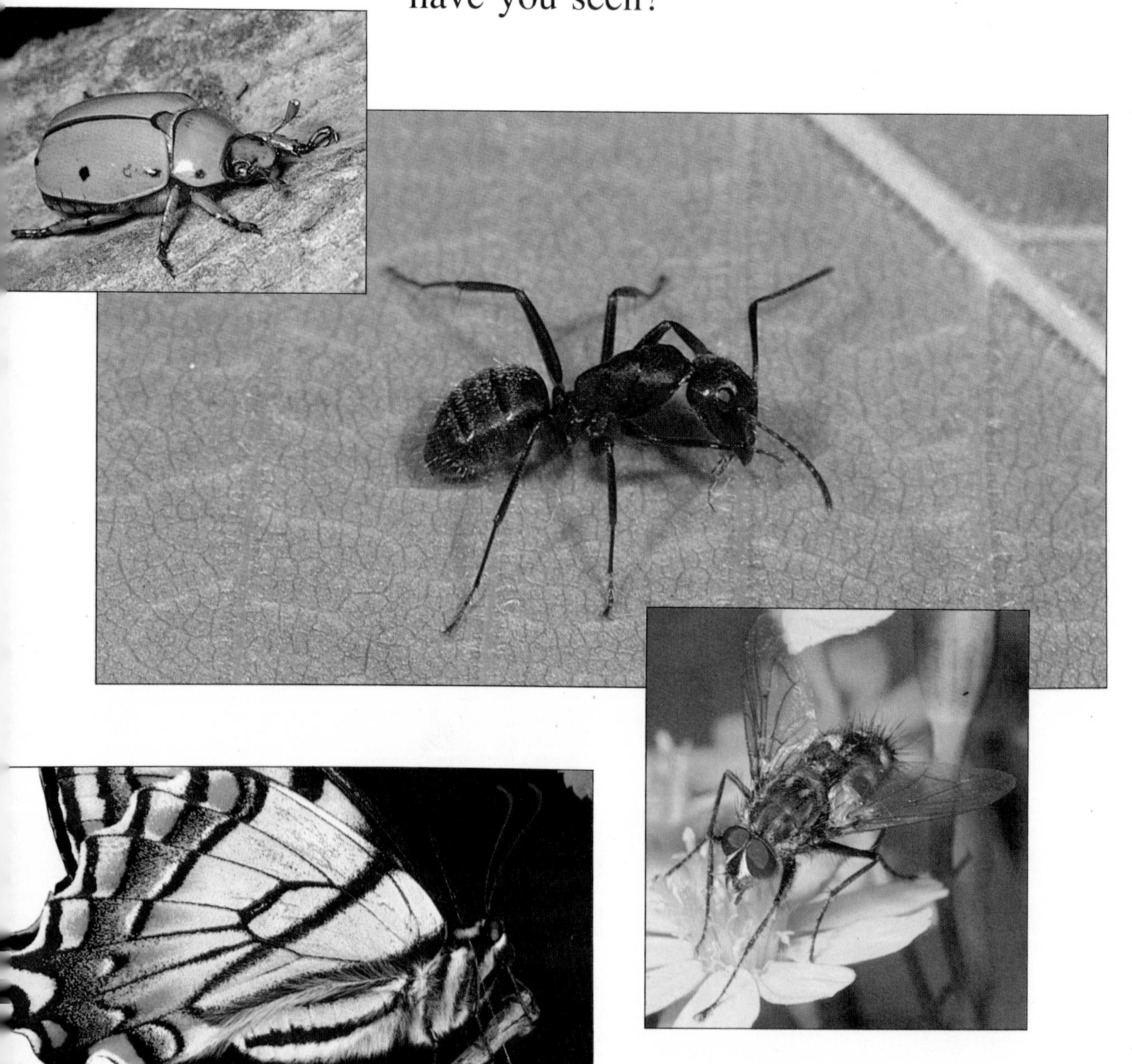

Another group of animals lives in water all the time. The animals in this group are fish. They have **scales** covering their bodies. Notice the fish in the picture.

Frogs belong to a group of animals called **amphibians.** They live some of the time in water and some of the time on land. Amphibians do not have scales. They have wet, smooth skin.

Another group of animals has snakes, turtles, lizards and alligators. These animals are **reptiles.** They have rough, dry skin. Some of these animals swim and some walk. Some reptiles eat animals, others eat plants. What animals from this group do you see here?

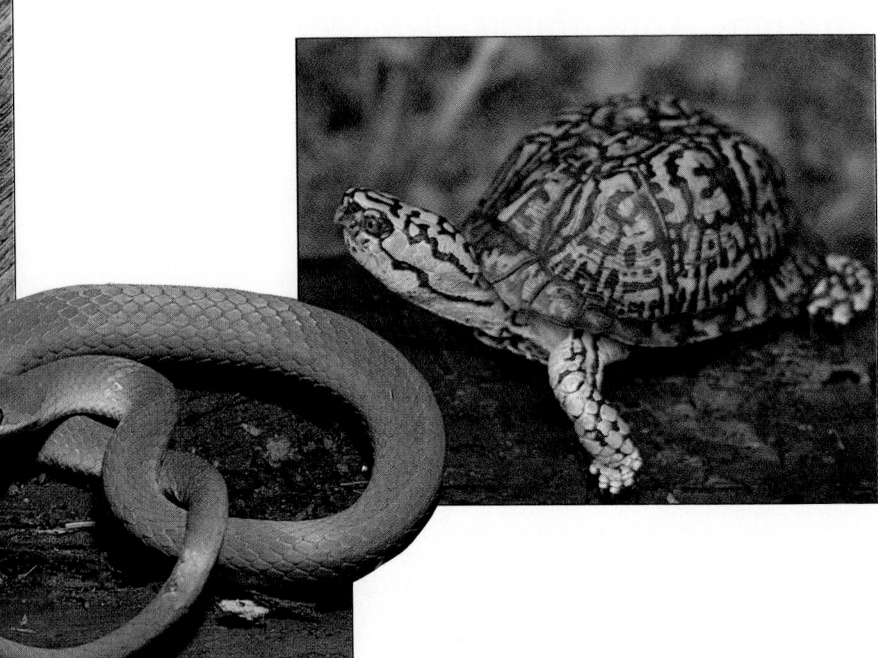

Lesson Review

1. What are six groups of animals?
2. What are animals in each group like?

LIFE SCIENCE

Find Out

What kinds of animals live in your neighborhood?

ACTIVITY

Learning About Animal Coverings

Follow the Directions

1. Touch the feather. Use a hand lens to observe it. Draw what you see inside a big circle.
2. Do the same with the fish scales and your skin.

Tell What You Learned

Tell how feathers, fish scales, and your skin are alike. Explain how your skin is different from an animal's covering.

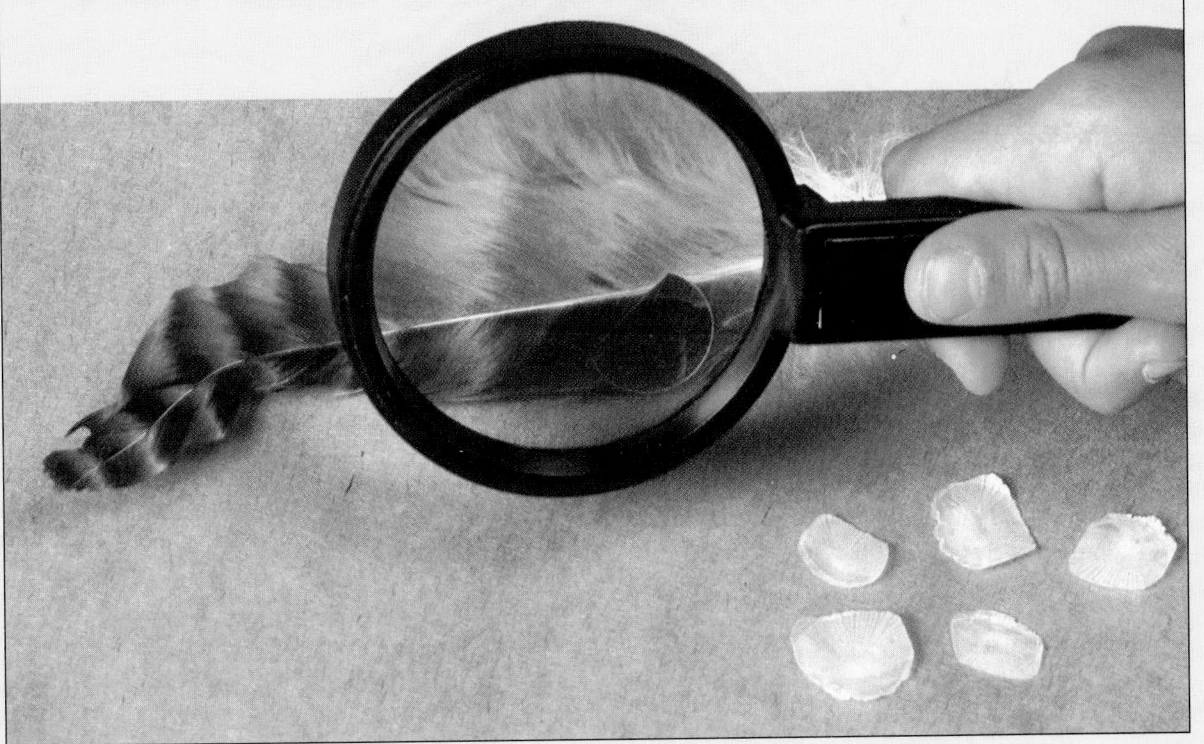

Lesson 2 Where Do Animals Live?

Animals live in different habitats. Some mammals, insects, and birds can live in water. Some live in oceans. Others live in rivers, lakes, and ponds. What animals do you see here?

Snakes, insects, and some small mammals can live in the desert. Animals that live in a dry habitat must work hard to find food and water.

Many kinds of animals live in the forest. Some live in trees. Some live on the ground. What forest animals do you see here?

A few animals can live in places that always have ice and snow. Most of these animals have thick fur to keep them warm.

Lesson Review

1. What are four habitats where animals live?
2. What animals can live in the desert?

EARTH SCIENCE *Find Out* CONNECTION

Very cold places have ice, snow, and strong winds. What animals live in these places?

Lesson 3 What Do Animals Need to Stay Alive?

All animals need food to stay alive. What do animals eat? Most animals get food on their own. Some animals need people to feed them.

Animals also need air, water, and shelter to stay alive. They get water from lakes and rivers. What animal do you see in the picture?

Many animals need protection from the cold to stay alive. Some animals live in caves or tree trunks for protection. Some live under the ground.

Some animals stay in sheltered places all winter. They **hibernate.** Their bodies work very slowly and they hardly move. They need very little food or water.

What else helps animals stay alive? Some animals have coverings that make them hard to see. How does a covering help keep this animal safe from other animals that could harm it?

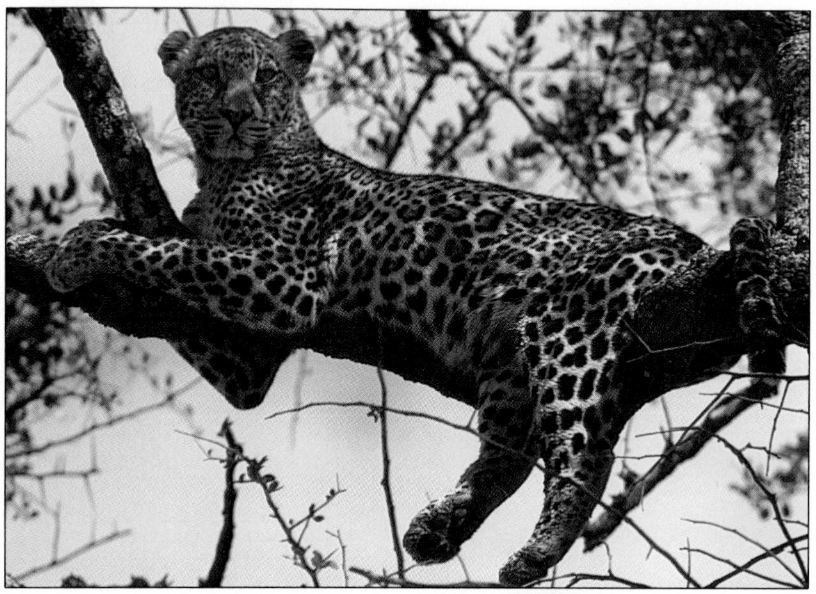

Some animals move to warmer places in winter to stay alive. Many birds leave cold places in winter and fly away.

Lesson Review

1. What do animals need to live?
2. What helps animals stay alive?

EARTH SCIENCE

Find Out

CONNECTION

Some geese fly south in winter. What is the weather like where they go?

Watching Animals Move

Follow the Directions

1. Watch a mealworm move.
2. Put a mealworm on paper. Watch how it moves.
3. Use a hand lens to watch it move.
4. Notice if the mealworm moves fast or slowly.
5. Draw the mealworm and how it moves.

Tell What You Learned

Tell how the mealworm moved. Describe three other ways animals move.

Lesson 4 How Do Animals Change as They Grow?

Baby mammals are born alive. They look like their parents. Some mammals stay with their parents for a long time.

Animals change in size and shape as they grow. Look at the animals in the picture. How will these animals change as they grow?

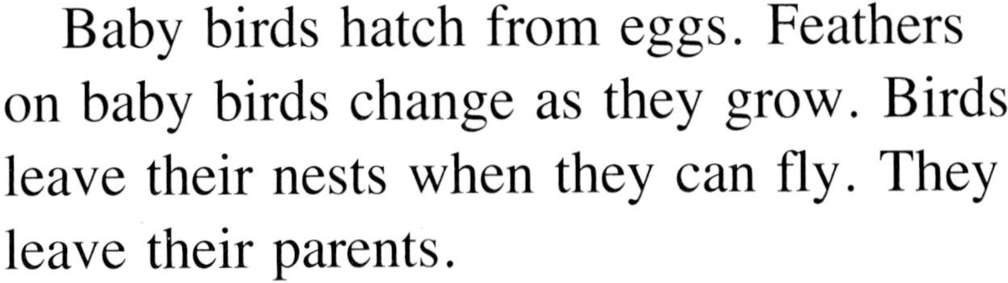

Baby birds hatch from eggs. Feathers on baby birds change as they grow. Birds leave their nests when they can fly. They leave their parents.

Young frogs are called **tadpoles.** They hatch from eggs. Tadpoles change in many ways as they grow. At first, they have tails and no legs. They look something like fish. What other changes do you see?

How do insects change as they grow? Some insects only change in size. Others change shape.

Beetles hatch from eggs. Notice that the young beetle looks like a worm. How does it change as it grows?

Lesson Review

1. In what ways do animals change as they grow?
2. How do frogs and beetles change as they grow?

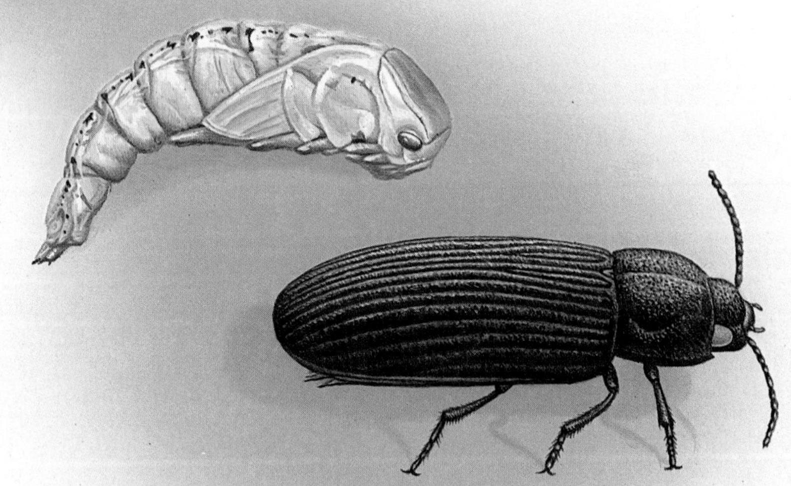

HUMAN BODY

Find Out

CONNECTION

Look at your baby picture. How have you changed and grown?

Learning Outside

Elizabeth Terwillager is a teacher who does not teach in a school. She teaches classes in forests, parks, and on beaches. She helps people learn about the plants and animals in these places.

Elizabeth Terwillager also works to start special parks where some plants and animals are protected. She cares about the living things in the world.

What Do You Think?

What might a young person learn from Mrs. Terwillager?

Using a Hand Lens and Making a Chart

What can a hand lens show about insects?

1. Look at the insect pictures. The small ones show how the insects really look. The others show insects as they look under a hand lens. Notice which pictures show insect legs clearly. Notice which pictures show insect body parts. Notice other differences.

2. Make a chart like this one. Draw a picture of each insect. Write what the hand lens lets you see better.

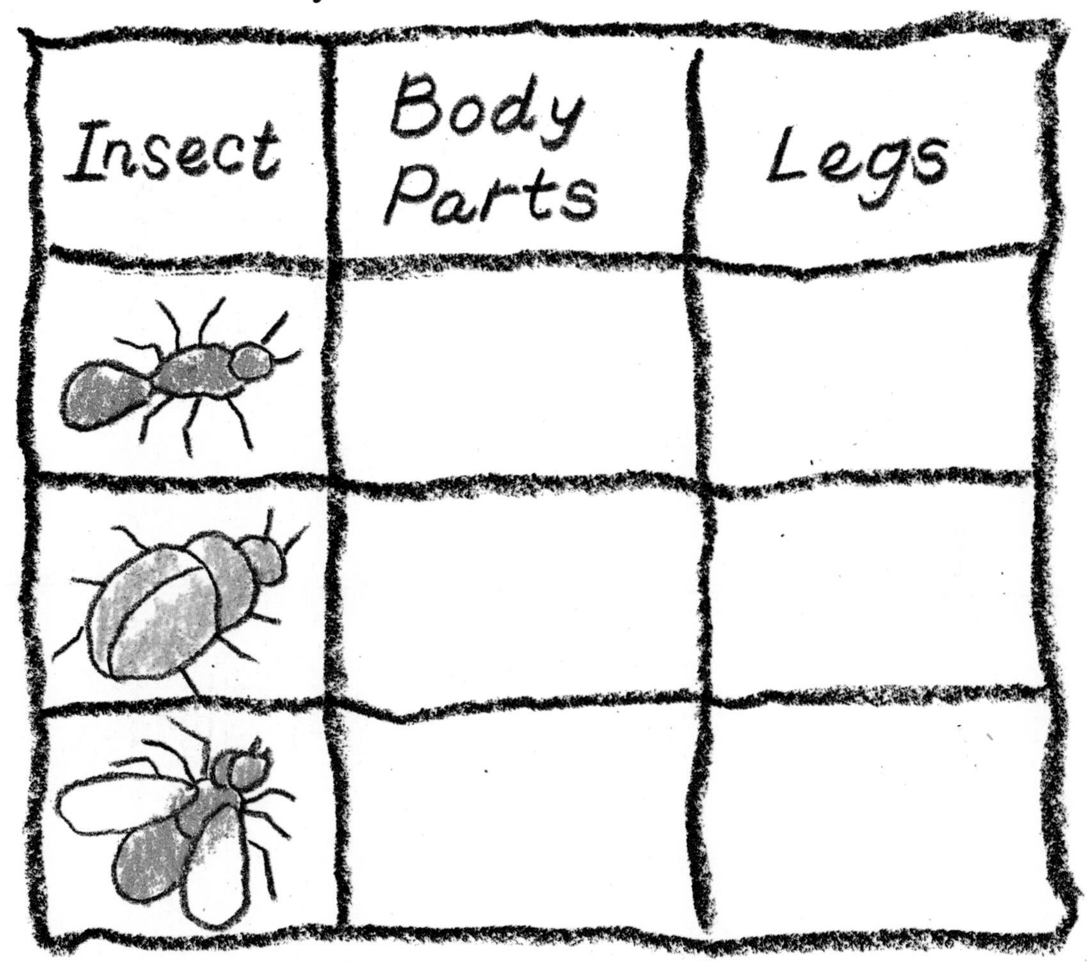

3. How does a hand lens help you learn about insects?

Chapter 2 Review

Review Chapter Ideas

1. Look at the picture. Tell about the group each animal belongs to.
2. Name four kinds of places where animals live.
3. Tell what animals need to live and what helps them stay alive.
4. Tell what animals do when they hibernate.
5. Name ways mammals and birds change and grow.
6. Tell how frogs and beetles change and grow.

Review Science Words

Match the words and the pictures.

1. mammal
2. reptile
3. insect
4. tadpole

a.

b.

c.

d.

Tell what the words mean.

5. hibernate
6. scales
7. amphibian

Use Science Ideas

Tell how the way a frog grows is like the way a beetle grows.

Chapter 3

Life on Earth Long Ago

This child is looking at bones from an animal that lived on earth long ago. What do you think the animal was like?

Starting the Chapter

Have you ever put together a puzzle? Make a picture puzzle of an animal. Then read about animals on earth long ago.

TRY THIS

Drawing Missing Parts of Animals

Draw a picture of an animal. Cut the picture into pieces. Give some pieces to a partner. Ask your partner to look at the pieces and draw a picture of the whole animal. How is your partner's picture like yours?

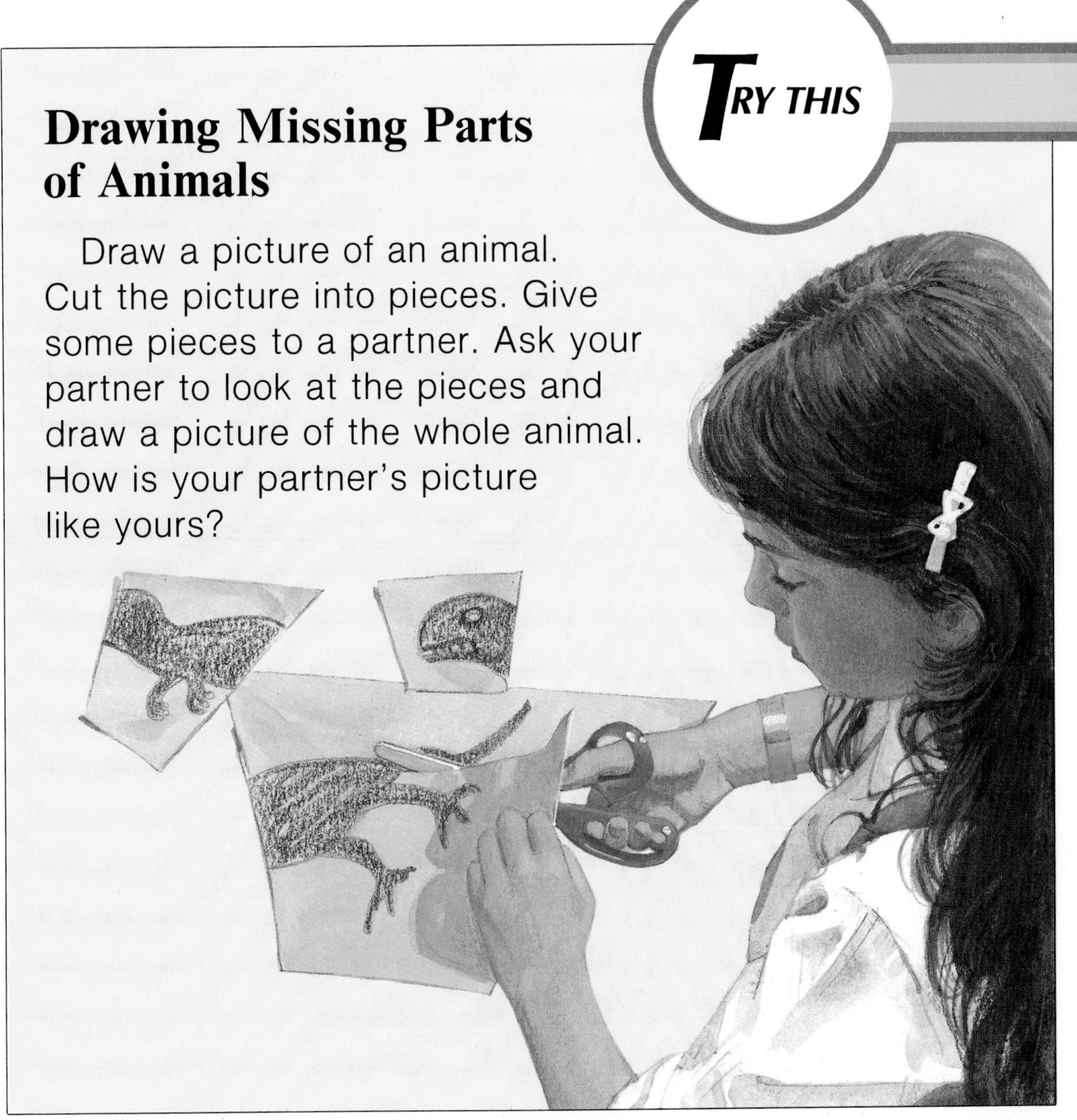

Lesson 1 What Tells About Life Long Ago?

What do you think each picture on these two pages shows? What do they tell you about plants and animals?

You see **fossils** in these pictures. Fossils tell about plants and animals of long ago. Fossils can be parts or marks of plants and animals. The parts or marks were often left in mud. The mud got hard and turned into rock after many years.

Fossils show what kinds of plants and animals used to live on earth. Fossils show the size and shape of plants and animals.

Fossils can also tell about what the **climate** was like long ago. The climate is the kind of weather a place has over a very long time. In a warm, wet climate, large plants with large leaves often grow. Find the large leaf fossils in the pictures.

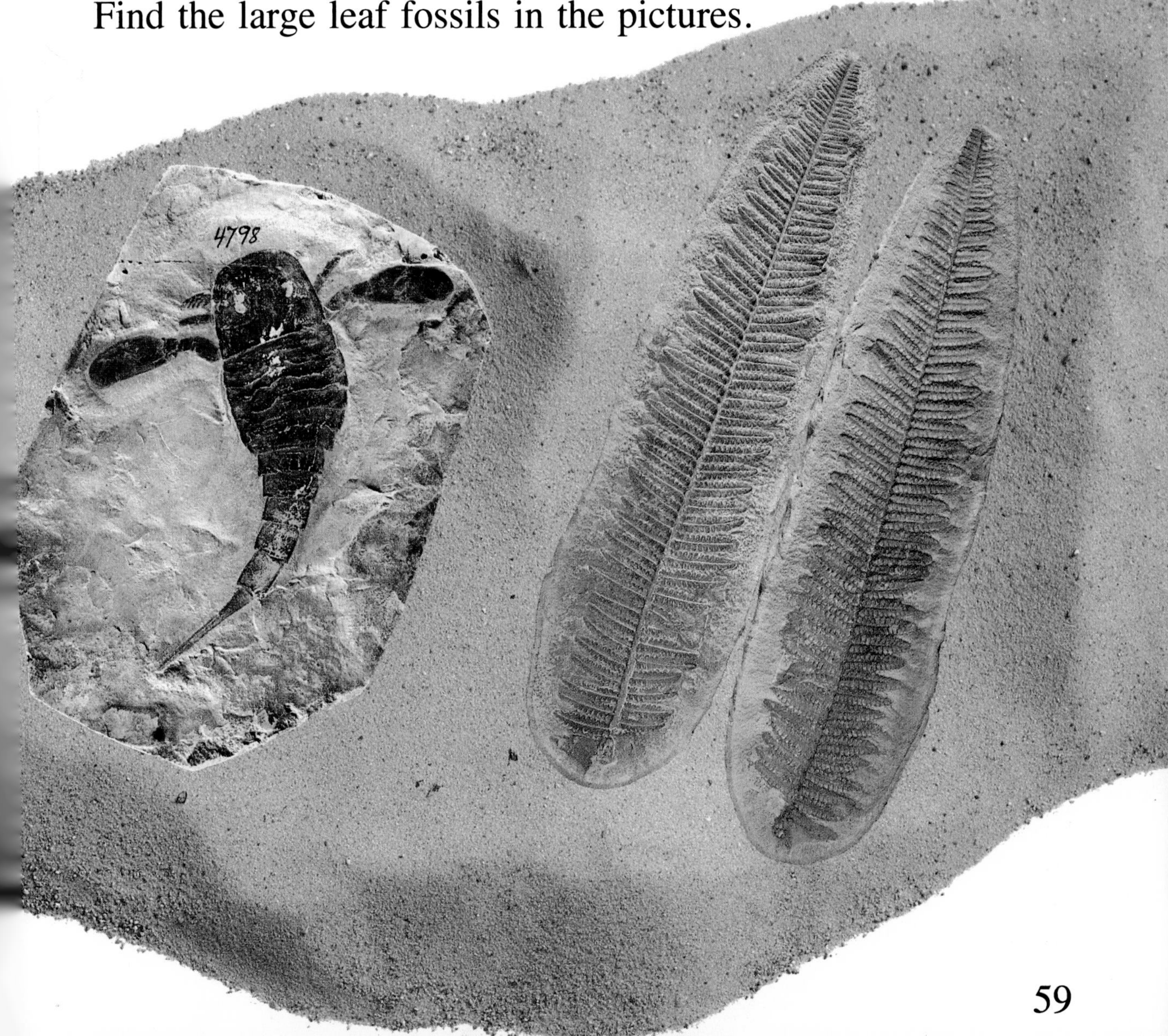

This person studies the teeth of an animal fossil. Pointed teeth like this tell that the animal ate meat. Animals with flat teeth ate mostly plants.

Suppose a person found a fossil of an animal with claws. What might the fossil tell about what the animal could do?

Lesson Review

1. What are some kinds of fossils?
2. What can people learn from fossils?

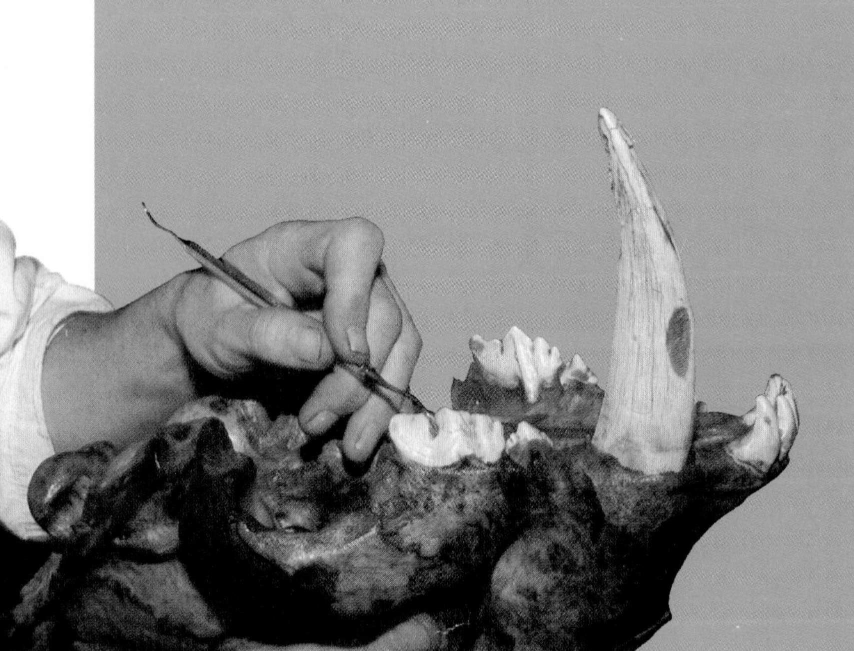

EARTH SCIENCE **Find Out** CONNECTION

Draw a picture of an animal fossil. Trade pictures with a classmate. Guess what animal the fossil picture shows.

ACTIVITY

Making a Fossil

Follow the Directions

1. Roll a piece of clay out flat.
2. Put a leaf on the clay.
3. Press the leaf into the clay the way you see here.
4. Take away the leaf.

Tell What You Learned

Tell what you saw when you took away the leaf. Explain what someone could learn from the marks of a leaf.

Lesson 2 What Were Dinosaurs Like?

When **dinosaurs** lived on earth, there were no people or buildings. What did the land look like?

Some dinosaurs were smaller than cats. Others were larger than elephants. This dinosaur was very large. It had long, sharp teeth for eating meat. It used its strong back legs to run after animals.

Tyrannosaurus Rex

Dinosaurs probably lived in a warm climate. The land was covered with big trees and other plants.

Some large dinosaurs moved very slowly. They ate plants. Smaller dinosaurs could run very fast. They ate small animals and eggs.

This dinosaur had a hard covering and spikes on its tail to help protect it.

Ankylosaurus

The different kinds of dinosaurs in the picture ate plants. Notice the flat teeth in the picture. They used their flat teeth to grind food.

The dinosaurs on this page had very thick skin. Look at their tails. How could their tails help protect them?

This giant dinosaur was one of the largest animals that ever lived. It was heavier than twelve large elephants. However, it had a very small head and mouth. The head was smaller than the head of a horse. It ate leaves from trees and other plants. Which part of this animal is very large?

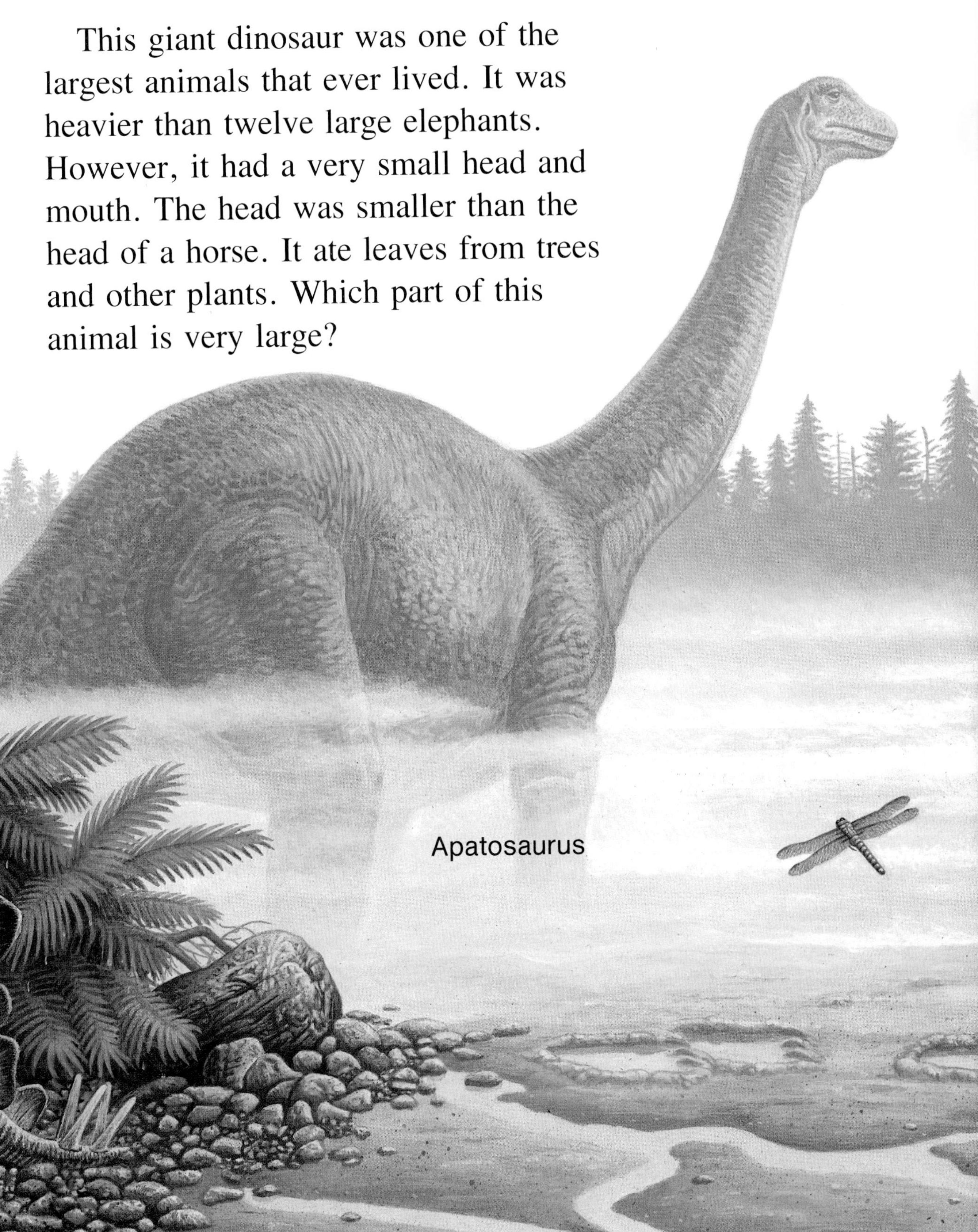

This dinosaur laid eggs like the ones shown in the small picture. Young dinosaurs hatched from the eggs.

After many years, dinosaurs disappeared from the earth. No one is sure why. Today, people study dinosaur fossils to learn more about dinosaurs.

Lesson Review

1. What did dinosaurs eat?
2. How did some dinosaurs protect themselves?

EARTH SCIENCE
Find Out
CONNECTION

Look in dinosaur books. Find out ideas about how dinosaurs disappeared.

ACTIVITY

Making a Model

Follow the Directions

1. Make a dinosaur from clay.
2. Make the dinosaur small or large.
3. Make the teeth show what the dinosaur eats.
4. Make a special covering and tail if it protects itself from other animals.
5. Name your dinosaur.

Tell What You Learned

Looking at your dinosaur, tell what it can do. Tell why it is important to study dinosaurs.

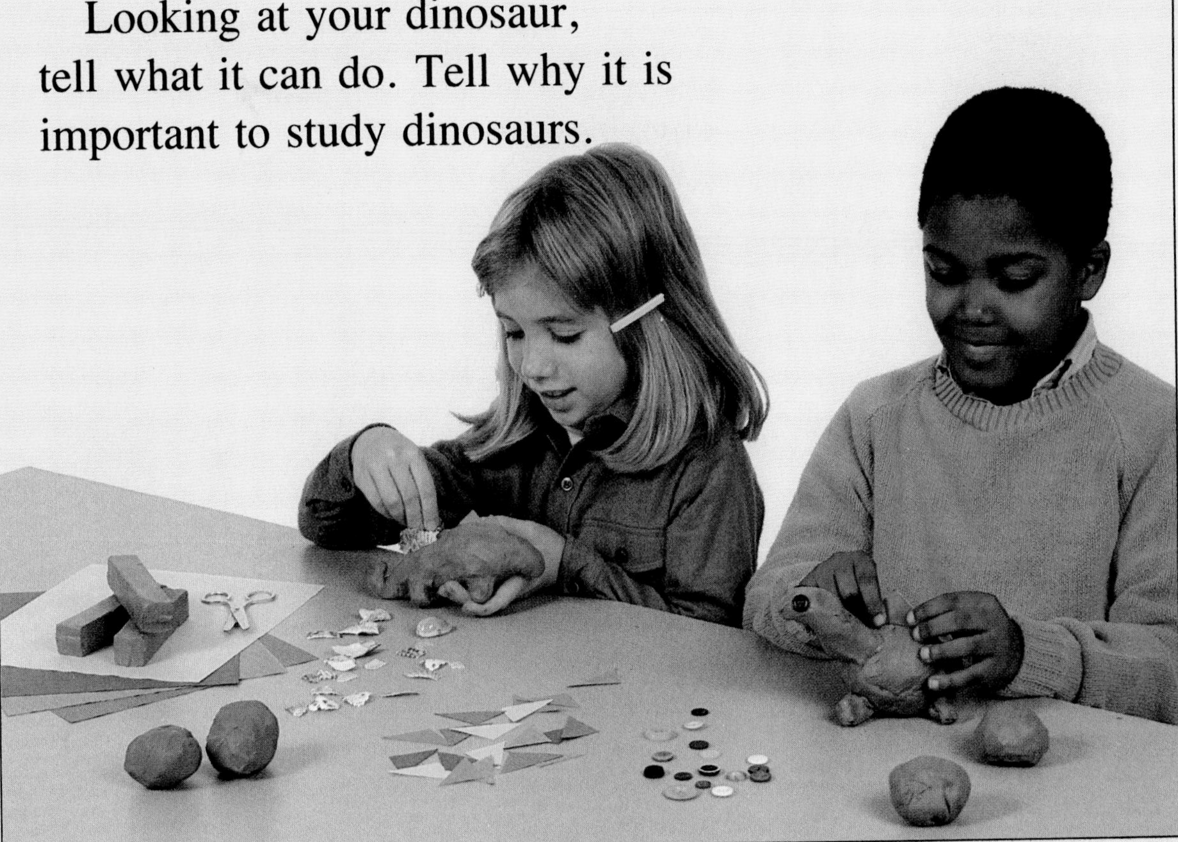

Lesson 3 What Other Animals Lived Long Ago?

The animals in the picture also lived when dinosaurs lived. The birds and mammals were different from the ones you know today. This **flying reptile** was very large. It ate small animals.

Fish and snails lived before dinosaurs. The climate was warm and wet. Large trees covered the land. Large insects lived in the forests. One flying insect was about your size!

After the dinosaurs disappeared, mammals lived everywhere on earth. Some of them looked like animals that live today. Which animal looks like a horse? Which animal looks like a cat? What does the other animal look like?

Lesson Review

1. What animals lived at the same time as dinosaurs?
2. What animals lived after dinosaurs?

Look for pictures of animal fossils. Find out how they are different from insects, birds, and mammals that live today.

EARTH SCIENCE **Find Out** CONNECTION

Lesson 4 What Can Change Plants and Animals?

The climate can change the kinds of plants and animals that live on earth.

Very many years after the dinosaurs lived, the climate changed. Some parts of the earth became very cold. Plants that needed warm, wet weather could not grow. The animals that ate the plants could not live. The earth had animals like the one in the picture. What helped this animal stay warm?

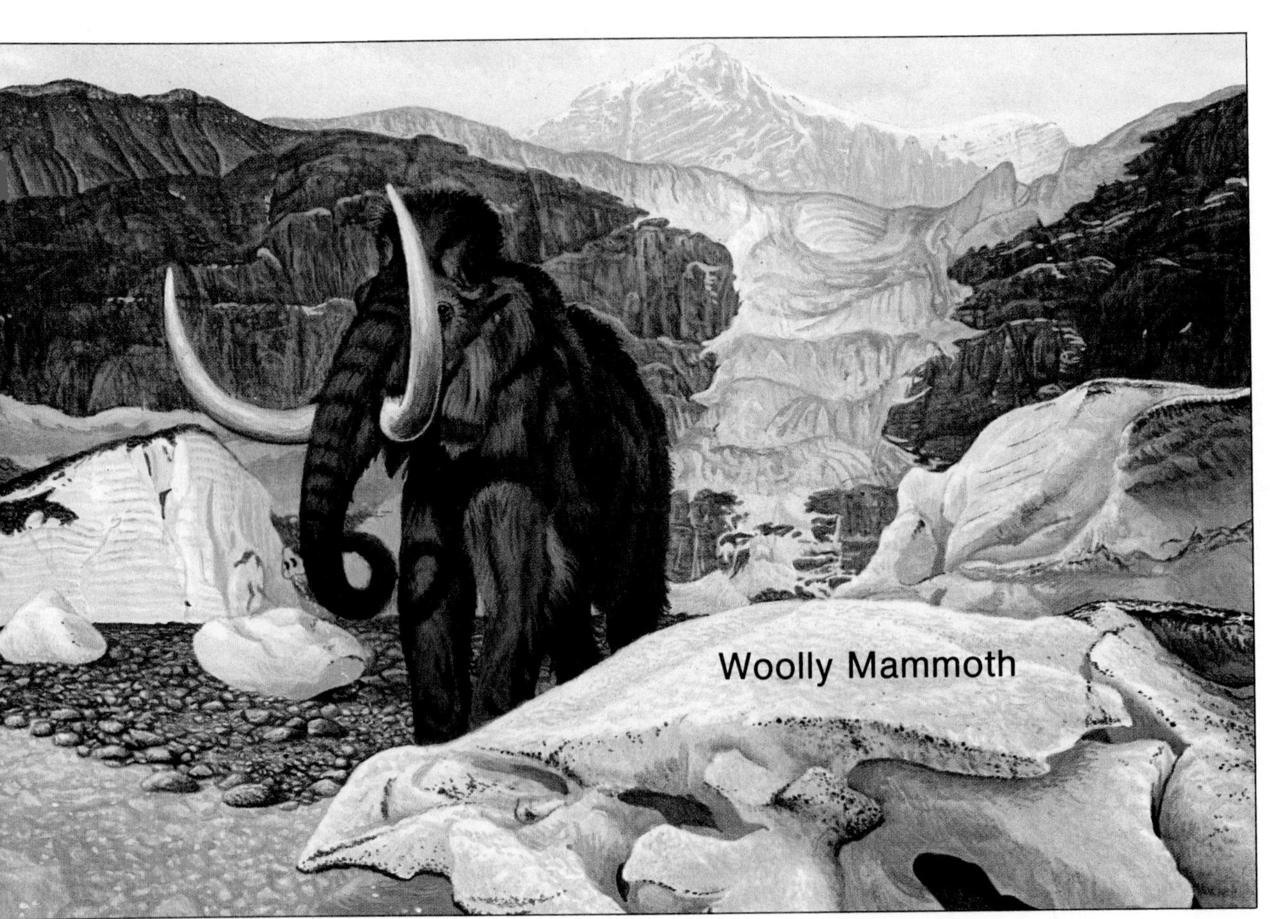

Plants and animals can change when water or land is changed. Harmful materials are sometimes put into rivers, lakes, and oceans. The fish and plants that live in the water die.

Sometimes people change the land where plants and animals live. Look at the picture. How has the land changed?

Today, many people protect plants and animals. They make parks where people cannot hunt animals or pick plants. This deer lives safely in a special park. People also make laws that protect plants and animals.

Lesson Review

1. What can change plants and animals?
2. How do people protect plants and animals?

LIFE SCIENCE

Find Out

What is one way you could protect plants and animals?

Dinosaur Jim

Jim Jensen is called Dinosaur Jim. He found a special way to put dinosaur bones together and make models of them. He has discovered many new fossils.

He gets dinosaur fossils for the museum where he works. People come to the museum to learn about the earth long ago.

What Do You Think?

Why do you think Jim Jensen is called Dinosaur Jim?

Lesson 5 What Comes From Life Long Ago?

Fuel is anything that can be burned to make a fire. People use **coal,** oil, and gas for fuel. These materials come from plants and animals that lived long ago.

Coal comes from plants. Oil and gas come from living things in oceans. Sand and soil covered the plants and animals after they died. The plants and animals slowly changed into coal, oil, and gas after millions of years. How do people get oil from the earth?

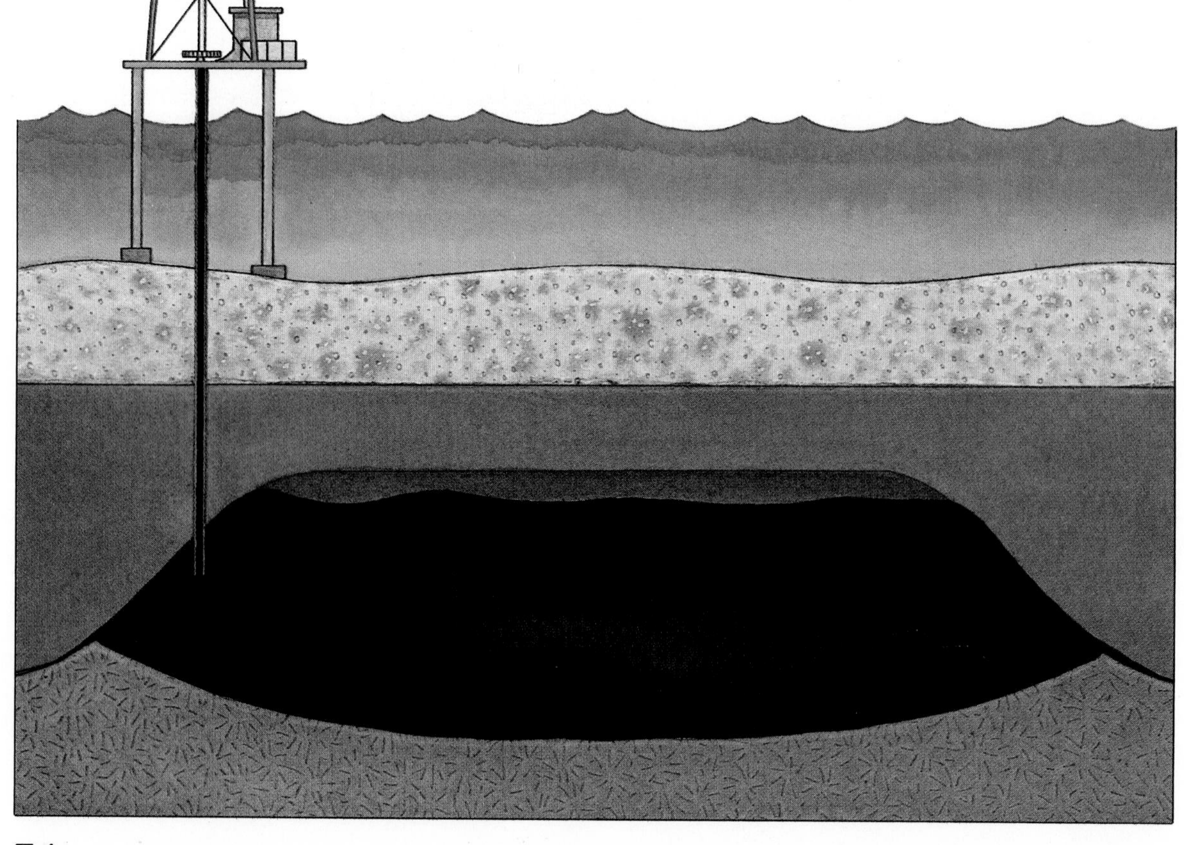

Someday coal, oil, and gas will be used up. People can save fuel. They can use less fuel in homes. Coal and oil can be used to make electricity. You can save fuel by using electricity carefully. How do these people save fuel?

Lesson Review

1. What fuels come from life long ago?
2. How can people save fuel?

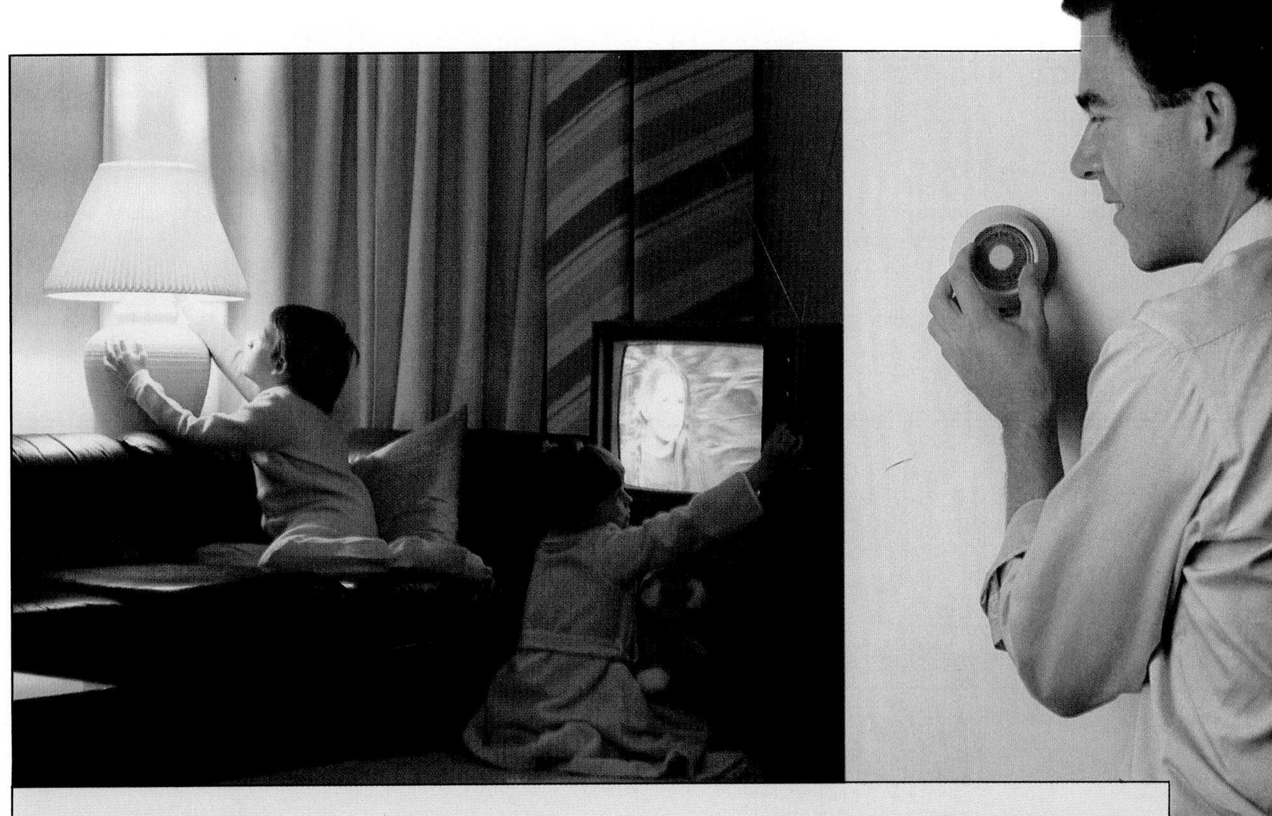

PHYSICAL SCIENCE **Find Out** CONNECTION

How do you use electricity where you live? Make a list.

Using a Ruler and Making a Graph

How long are the fossils?

1. Measure each fossil in the picture using a metric ruler. Measure to the longest part of the leaf the way you see here. Write down the number of centimeters for each fossil on your own paper.

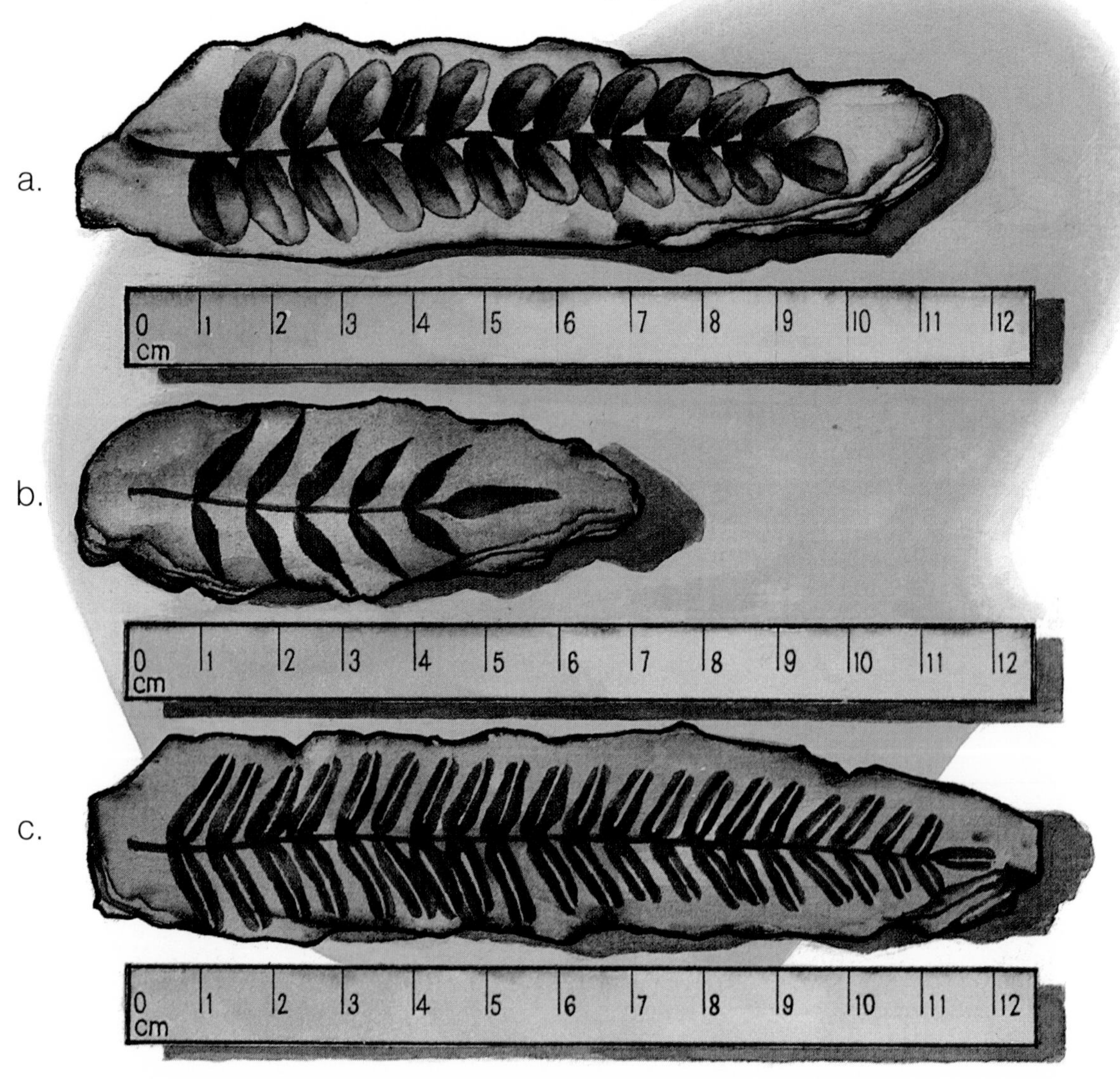

2. Draw a graph like this one on your own paper. Color up to the number of centimeters each fossil measured. Use a different color for each row.

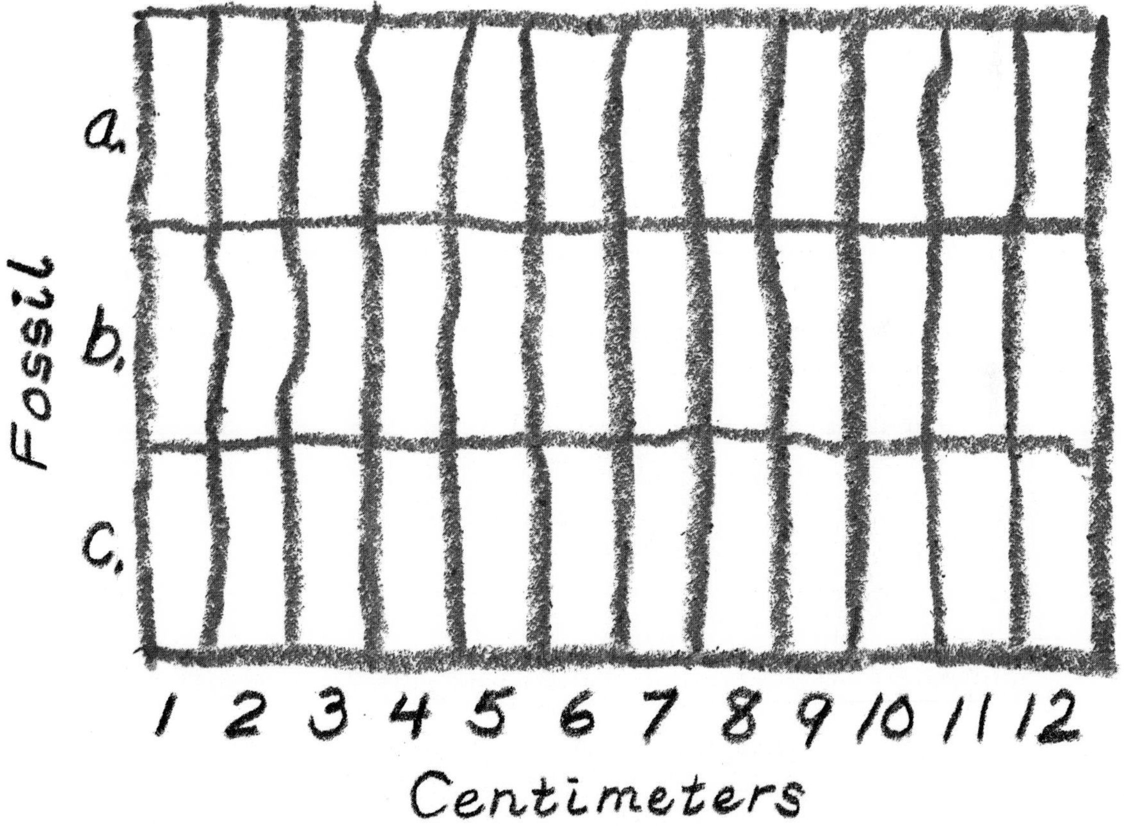

3. Look at your graph. Which fossil is the longest?

Chapter 3 Review

Review Chapter Ideas

1. Tell what people can learn from fossils.
2. Tell what two different kinds of dinosaurs looked like.
3. Look at the pictures. Tell what lived on earth long ago.
4. Tell how climate and people can change plants and animals.
5. Tell what fuels come from living things of long ago.
6. Tell what people can do to save fuel.

Review Science Words

Match the words and the pictures.

1. fossil
2. coal
3. dinosaur
4. flying reptile

a.

b.

c.

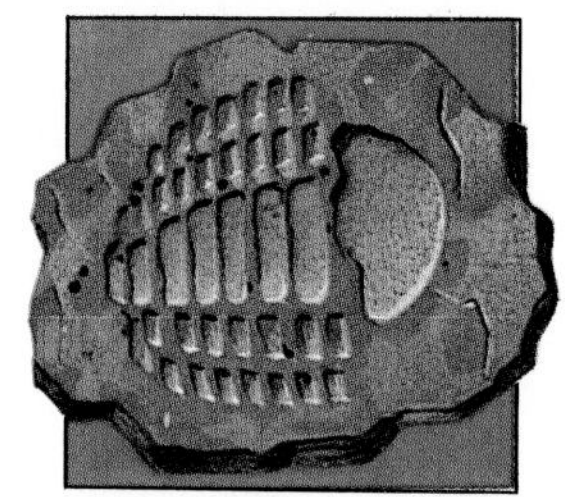

d.

Tell what the words mean.

5. climate
6. fuel

Use Science Ideas

Tell what animals lived before dinosaurs and after dinosaurs.

Careers

Farmers

Farmers often grow plants that people use for food. They choose plant seeds that can grow well on the land. They plant the seeds when the weather is right. They try to protect their plants from insects.

Farmers water their plants if the plants do not get enough rain. Farmers also use machines to help them with their work.

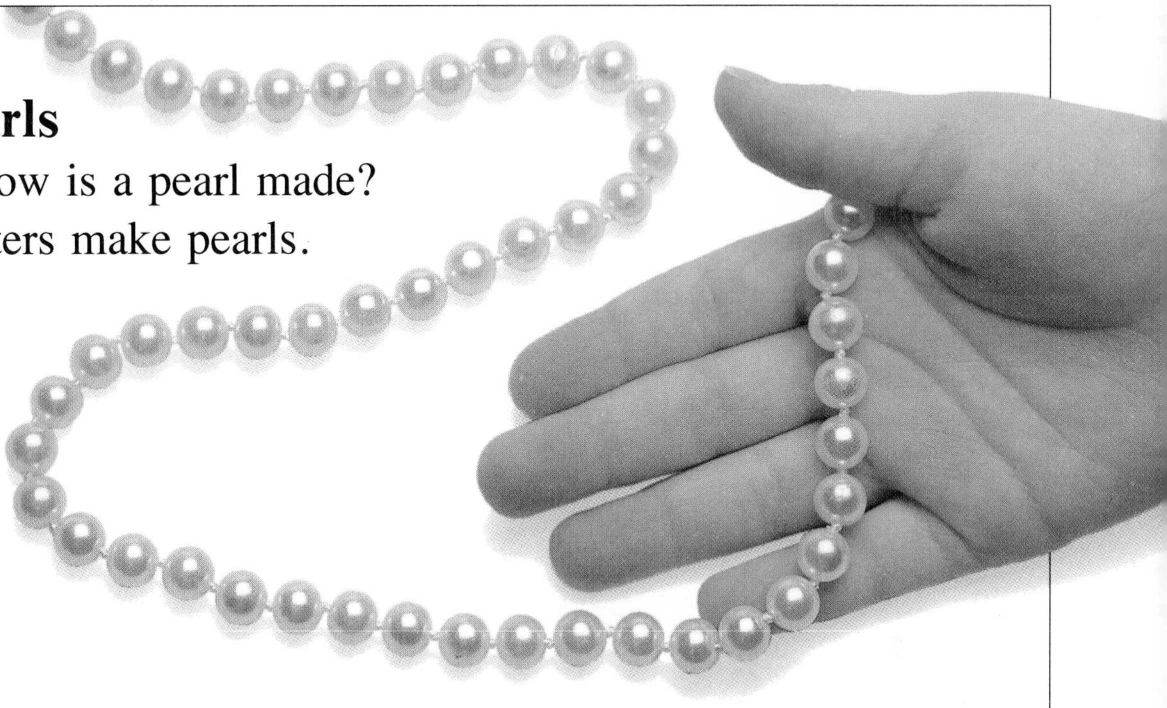

Pearls

How is a pearl made? Oysters make pearls.

Sometimes a grain of sand gets inside the oyster's soft body. Layers of a special material begin to form around the sand. The special material makes a smooth covering around the grain of sand. After the grain of sand is wrapped in many layers, a ball forms. The ball is a pearl.

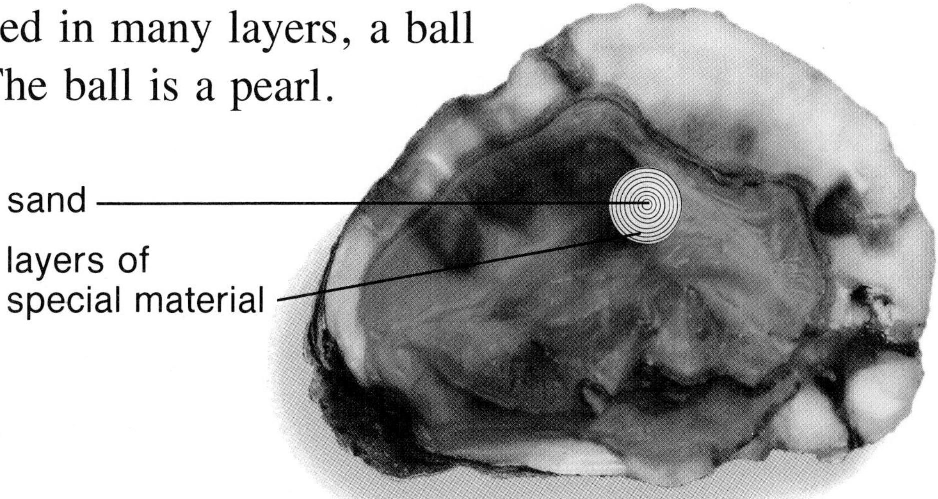

sand

layers of special material

Unit 1 Review

Answer the Questions

1. How can plants be different from each other?
2. Where do plants grow and what ways do they grow?
3. What group does each animal belong to?

4. How do animals change as they grow?
5. What can people learn from fossils?
6. What can change plants and animals?

Study the Picture

How do you know these animals could not have lived at the same time?

What to Do

1. Guess how many centimeters high a plant is that grows near your school. Measure it with a ruler.
2. Make a nest. Put one cup of grass, ¼ cup of soil, and ¼ cup of white glue in the bowl. Mix everything together. Press the mix against the sides of the bowl. Let the mix dry for more than one hour. Lift your nest out of the bowl. Draw a picture of an animal that might use your nest. 
3. Write a story about a dinosaur. Tell where the dinosaur lived, what it ate, and what it could do.

K-LINEVILLE

Unit 2

Physical Science

Look at the picture. It shows a toy train set. Electricity runs the train and the bright lights. The train's engine is a machine. What colors and shapes do you see? Tell what you might hear when the train is running. Draw a picture of a train you have seen.

Chapter 4

Matter Around You

You can describe everything in this picture. How would you describe what you see?

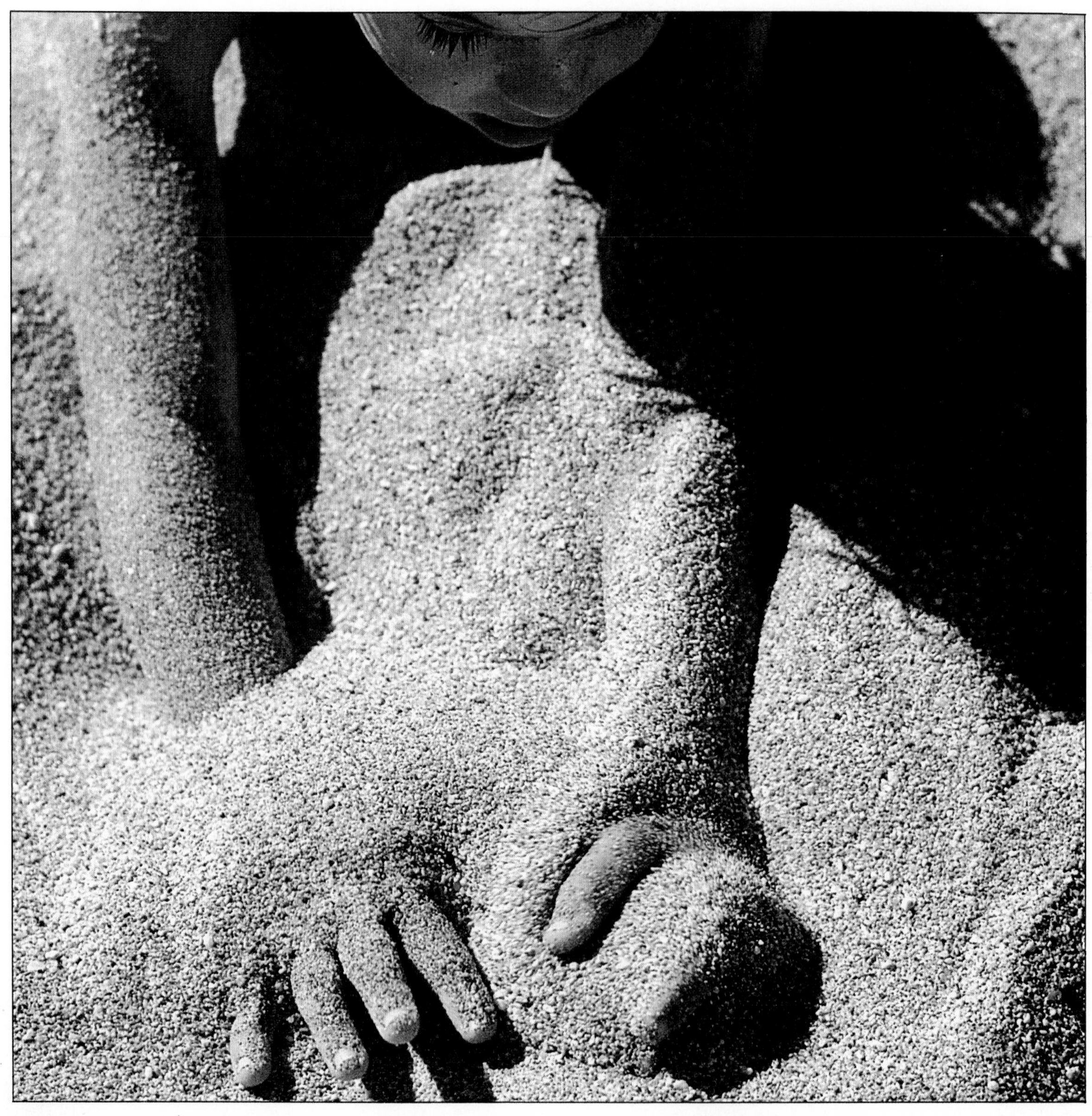

Starting the Chapter

How much do you weigh? You and everything around you has weight. Some large things weigh more than some small things. Some small things weigh more than some large things. As you read on, you will learn more about weight.

TRY THIS

Weighing Different Objects

Find eight small objects to weigh. Use a balance and blocks. Which object is the heaviest? Which is the lightest?

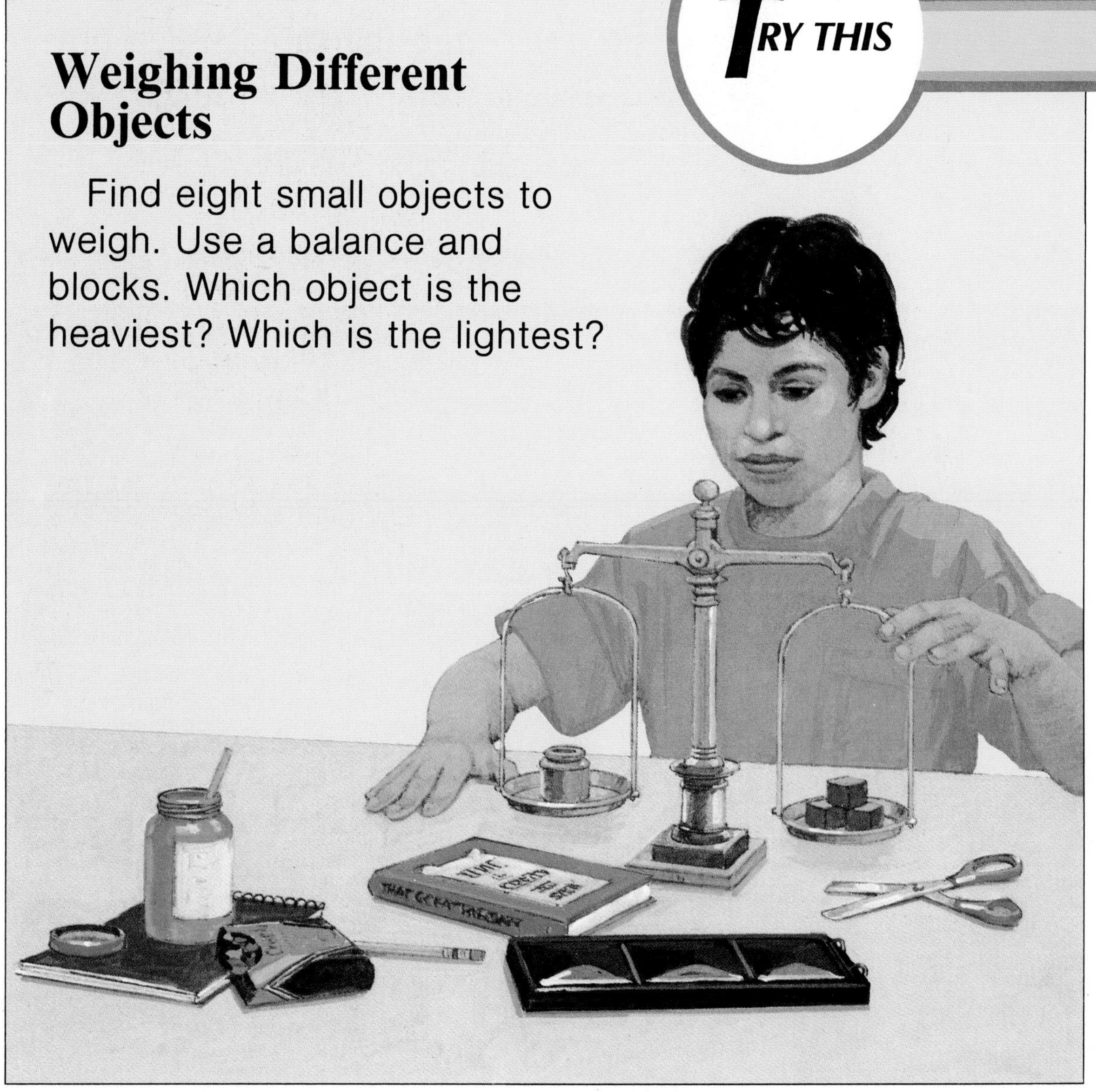

Lesson 1 What Is Matter?

Most **matter** takes up space and has weight. A book takes up space on a shelf. The air inside a balloon takes up the space inside the balloon. The milk inside a glass takes up the space inside the glass.

Look at the objects in the picture. They do not weigh the same. Each object has a different weight. How do you know that the objects have weight?

How can you describe matter? You can tell about what matter is like, or what **properties** it has. Shape, color, and size are properties of matter. Floating and sinking are also properties of matter. What properties do these objects have?

Lesson Review

1. What is matter?
2. What are three properties of matter?

Find a ball and a block. Guess how many grams each weighs. Then weigh each on a scale.

PHYSICAL SCIENCE

Find Out

Grouping Objects by Properties

Follow the Directions

1. Collect many different kinds of lids.
2. Group the lids by size.
3. Group the lids by color and by shape.
4. Group the lids by other properties you think of.

Tell What You Learned

Tell what properties you used to group your lids. Name other objects you could group by their properties.

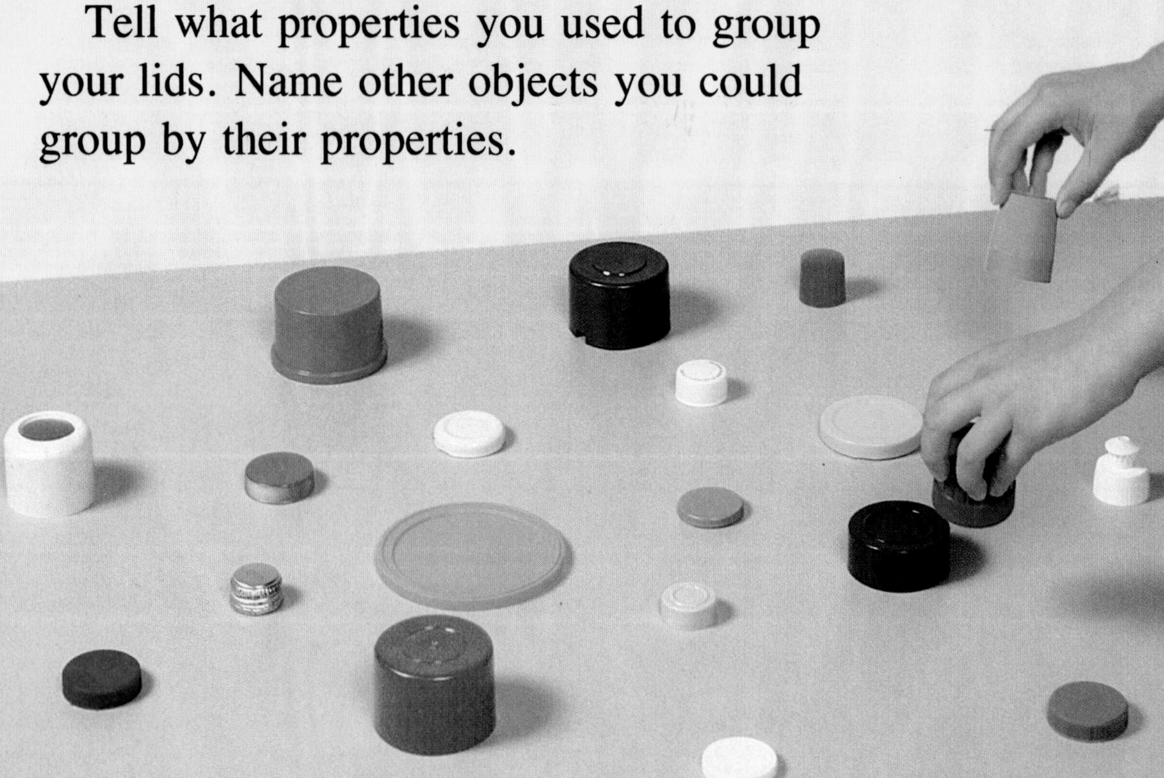

Using Matter Again

People sometimes throw away matter they have used. Some of the matter could be changed and used again. When people use matter again, they recycle it.

People can recycle glass, paper, and metal. People collect these kinds of matter and bring it to places like this. Machines will change the matter so people can use it again.

What Do You Think?

Why do people want to recycle matter?

Lesson 2 How Can You Group Matter?

You can group matter three ways. Matter can be a **solid,** a **liquid,** or a **gas.** The objects in the picture are solids.

What are properties of solids? They have a certain size and shape. They take up space.

Suppose you could touch the solid objects in the picture. How would the objects feel?

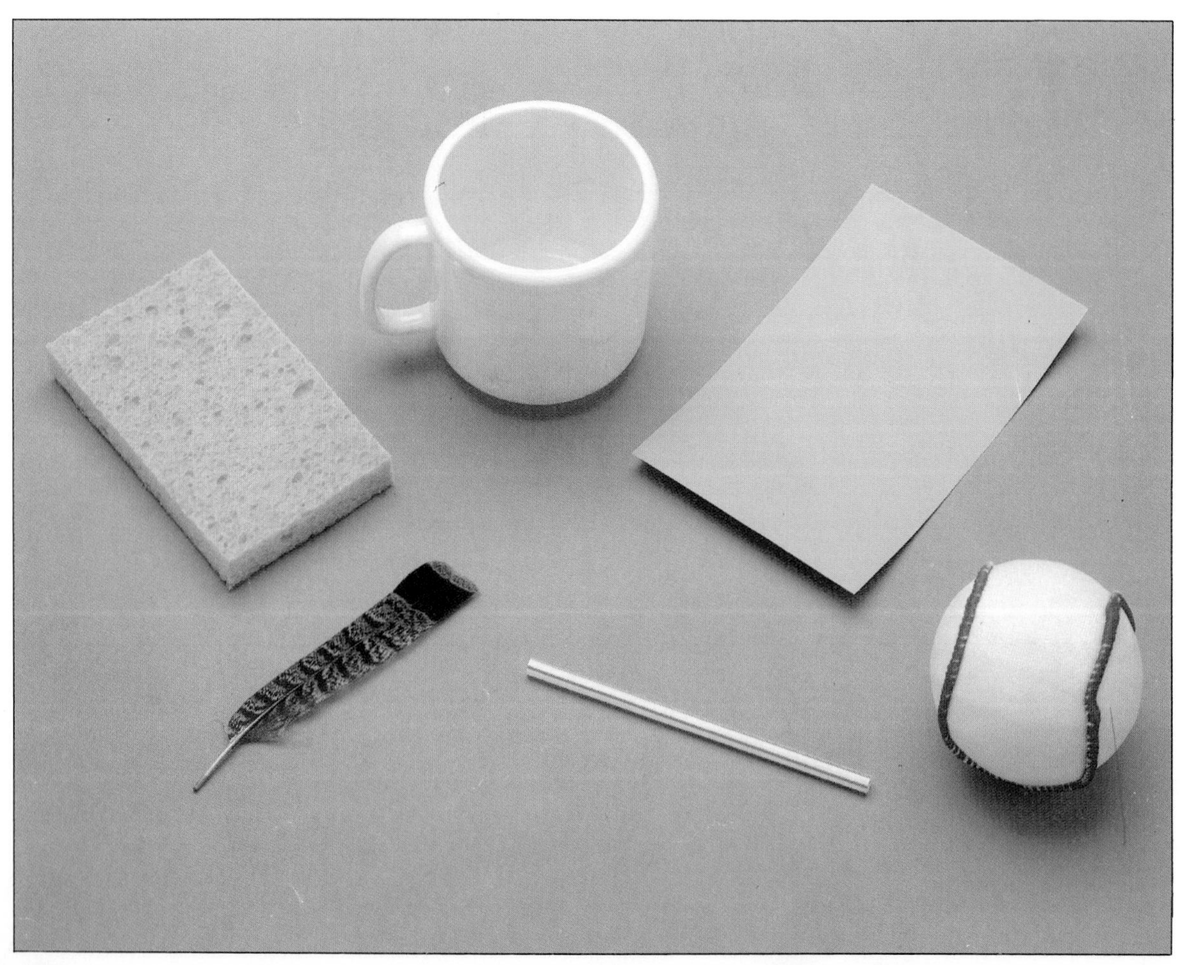

What are some properties of liquids? They take up space. They do not have their own shape. Liquids have size and weight. What liquids can you name?

What happened to the milk after it left the pitcher? The milk changed shape in the air. Then it changed again as it filled the glass. When you pour a liquid, what shape does it take?

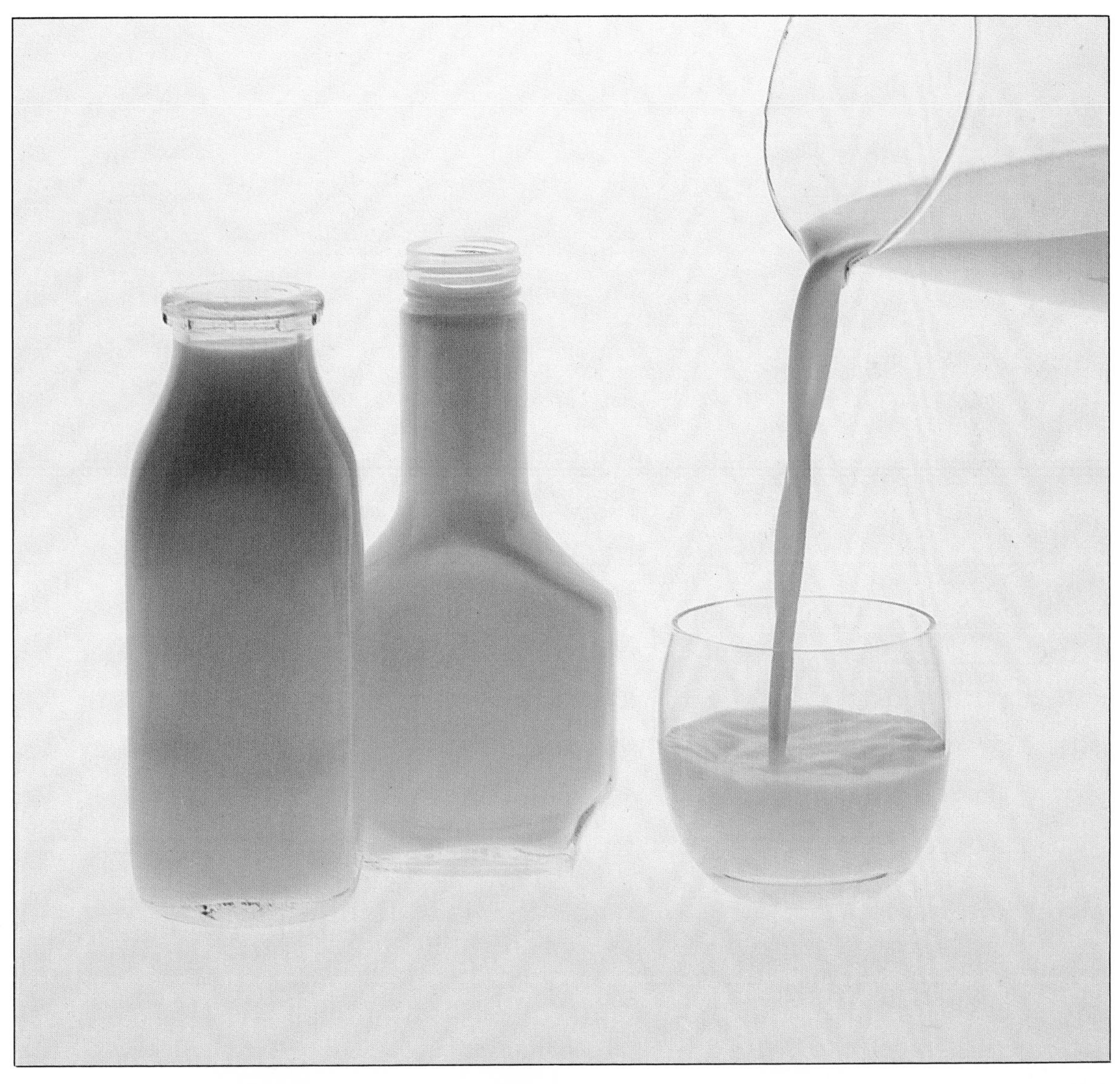

How are the liquids in the picture different? Notice the colors of the liquids. Think of how the liquids would feel to touch. Which liquids do you think will pour easily?

Light liquids will float on top of heavy liquids. Find the bottle that shows one liquid floating on another. Which liquid is heavy? Which is light?

Gases make up another group of matter. What are some properties of gases? Gases take up space. They have no shape of their own. You cannot see most gases. Air is one kind of gas.

What shapes does the gas take in these balloons? Suppose the girls let the air out. The gas would spread out and fill a larger space.

Some gases weigh more than other gases. These balloons are filled with a special gas. This gas weighs less than the air outside the balloons. What would happen if the gas inside the balloons were heavier than the air?

Lesson Review

1. What are three groups of matter?
2. What are two properties of solids, liquids, and gases?

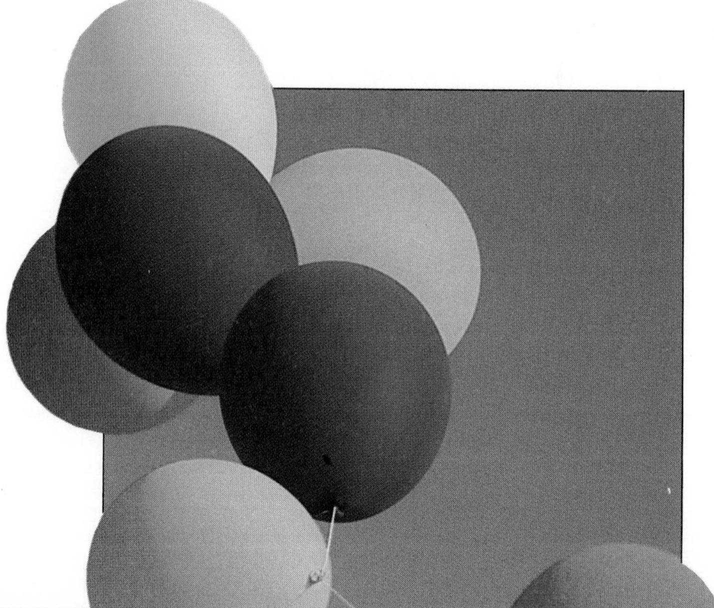

HUMAN BODY
Find Out
CONNECTION

You need to drink water every day. How does this liquid help keep your body healthy?

Using Matter to Make Bubbles

Wear cover goggles for this activity.

Follow the Directions

1. Use air and liquid.
2. Blow a bubble.
3. Observe the outside of the bubble.
4. Observe the bubble break.

Tell What You Learned

Tell what kind of matter makes up the outside and the inside of a bubble. Name two other things that can be filled with a gas.

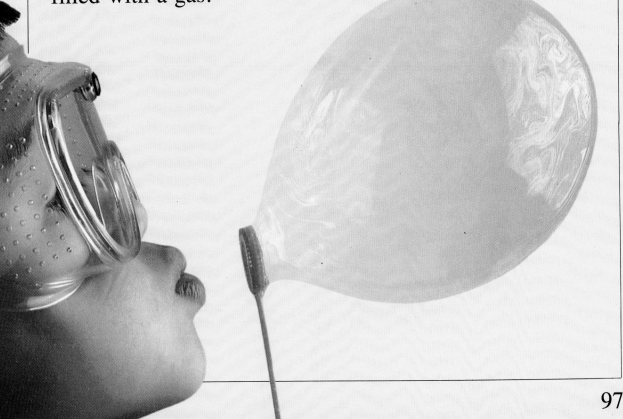

Lesson 3 How Can Matter Change?

Matter can change from one kind to another. A solid can change to a liquid. Heat makes this change. What changes this ice into water?

Solid butter can become a liquid. Heat from a stove can change the butter. What other foods can change this way? What makes a candle change to a liquid?

Liquids can change to solids. Notice the hot liquid in the picture. A machine pours the liquid into a shape. The liquid changes to a solid when it cools. What does the solid matter look like?

Freezing changes liquids to solids. Freezing changes water to ice. What are some ways to use ice?

A liquid can change to a gas. Heat can make this change. These towels and sheets have water in them. What happens to the water as they dry?

The light from the sun heats the water. It changes to a gas called **water vapor.** When water changes to a gas, it **evaporates.** The gas goes into the air.

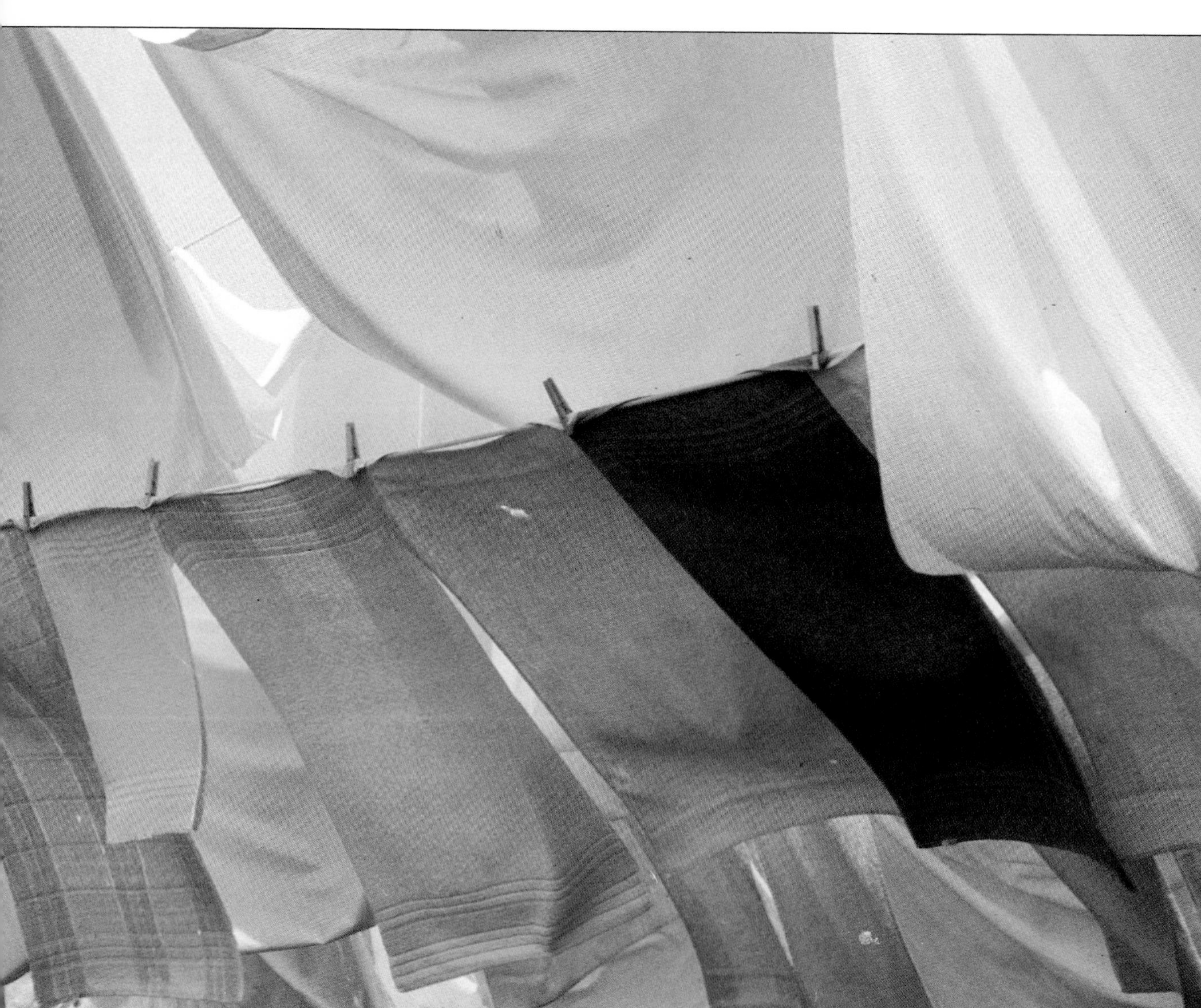

Gases can change to liquids. Water vapor is a gas that can change to drops of water. Cold changes water vapor in the air to a liquid. Where is liquid from water vapor in this picture?

Lesson Review

1. What are four ways matter can change?
2. What happens when water evaporates?

PHYSICAL SCIENCE

Find Out

Watch a small amount of water on a dish for a few days. See what happens to the water.

Measuring Liquid and Making a Graph

What can a graph show about measuring liquid?

1. Find the lines and numbers on the three beakers shown below. Notice that beaker **1** has 50 milliliters of colored water in it. Milliliters are marked mL.

2. Find the number that shows how much water is in beaker **2.** Write that number on your paper. Do the same for beaker **3.**

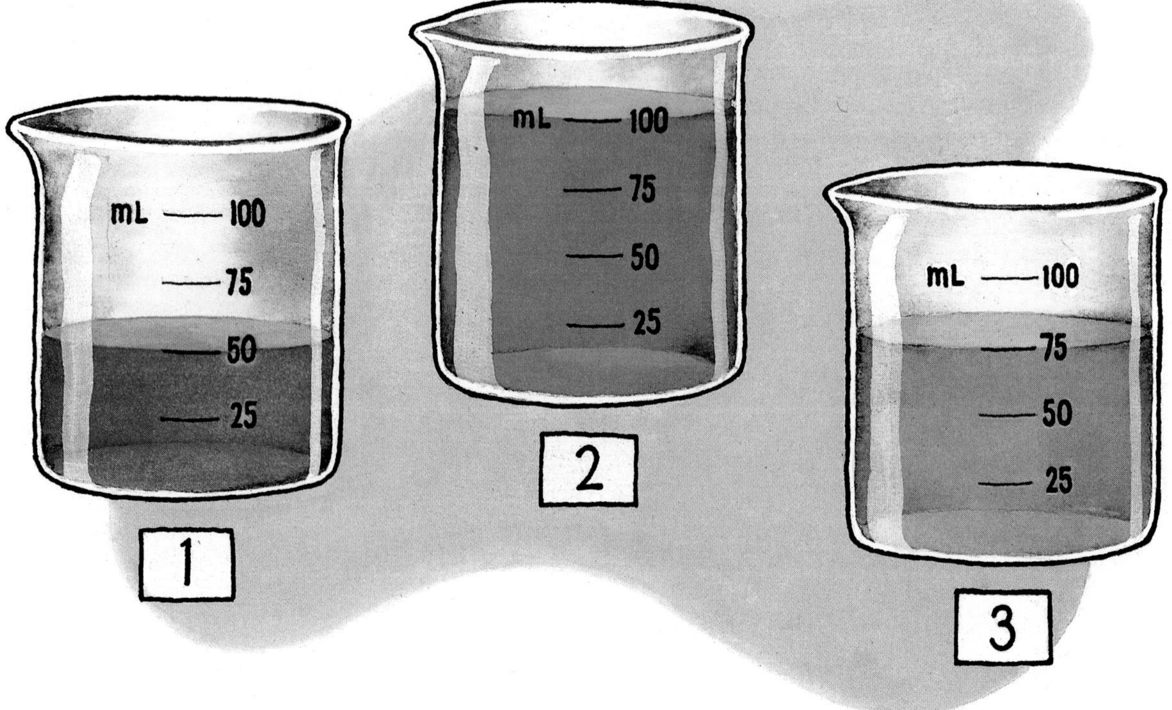

3. Make a graph like this one. Make a dot on the correct line to show how much water is in beakers **2** and **3.** Use a different color crayon for each dot. Draw a line to connect all three dots.

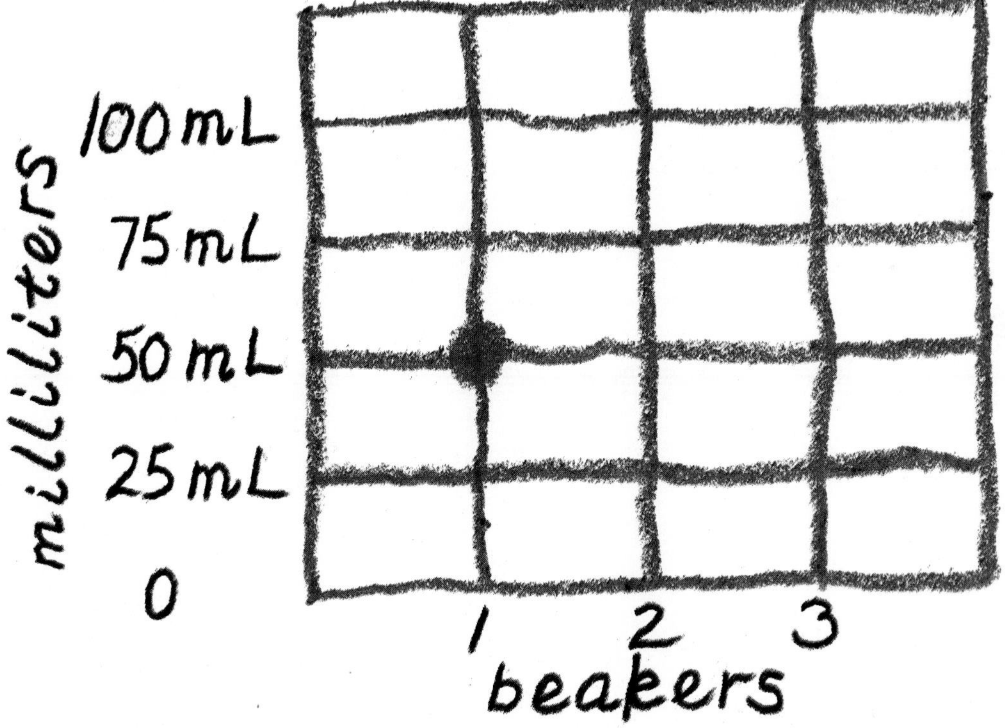

4. Look at your graph. Which beaker has more water than beaker **3**? Which beaker has less water than beaker **3**?

Chapter 4 Review

Review Chapter Ideas

1. Tell what matter is.
2. Name three ways to group matter.
3. Name two properties of a solid, a liquid, and a gas.
4. Look at the pictures. Tell how the solid changed.
5. Tell what can change a liquid to a gas.
6. Explain what makes water vapor change to drops of liquid water.

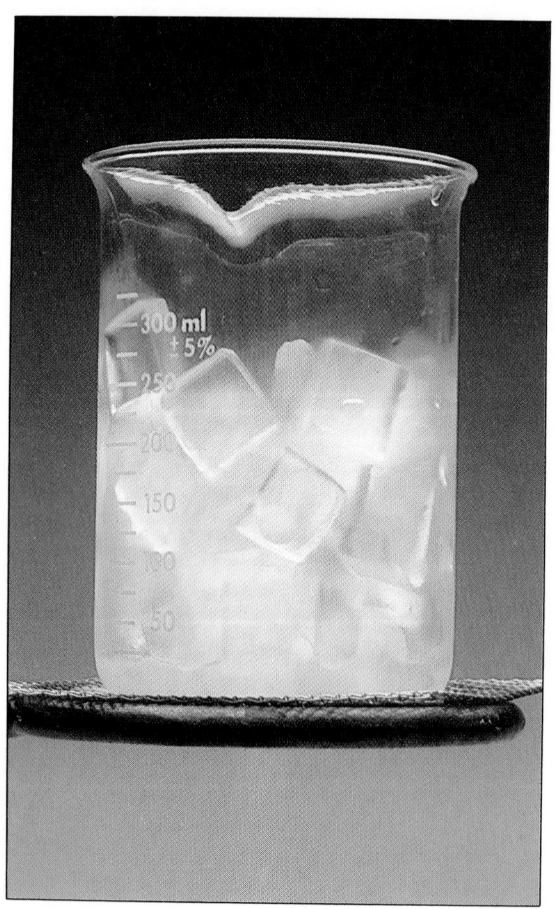

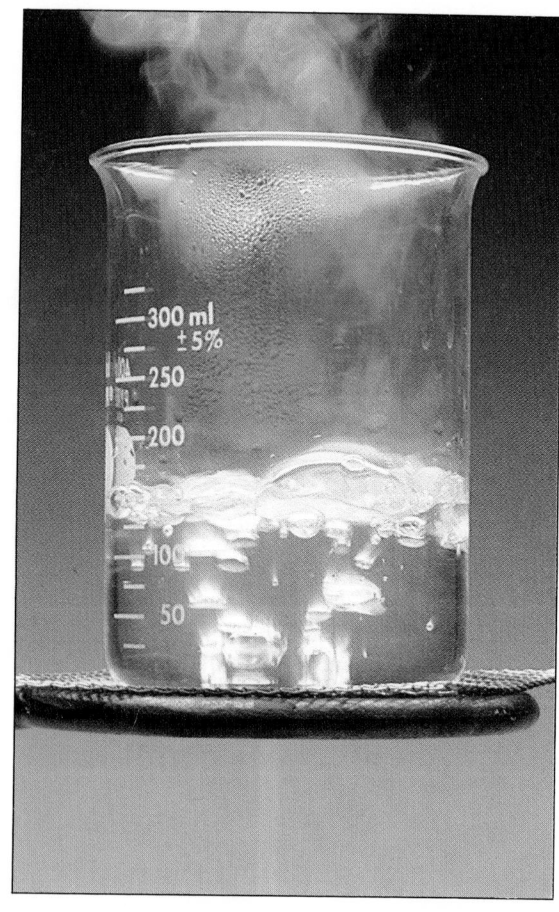

Review Science Words

Match the words and the pictures.

1. liquid
2. solid
3. gas

a.

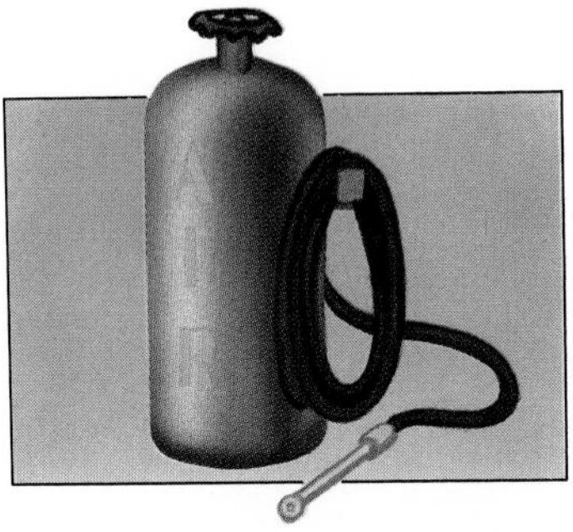

b.

c.

Tell what words mean.

4. matter
5. properties
6. evaporate
7. water vapor

Use Science Ideas

Tell what would happen next.

Chapter 5

Heat, Light, and Sound

Pretend you are sitting around this campfire. What do you see? What do you feel?

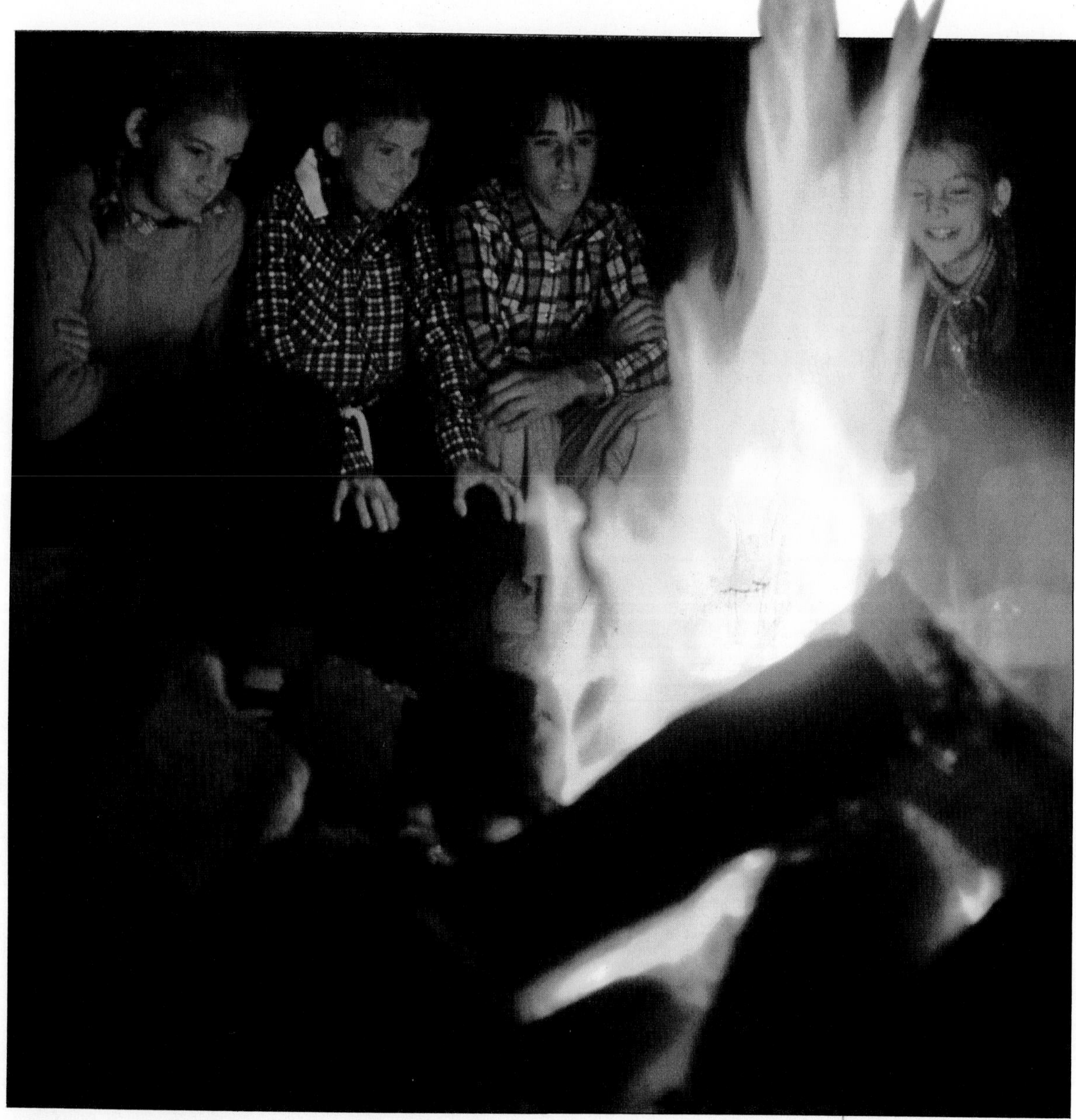

Starting the Chapter

Think of the kinds of food you like to eat. Think of washing your hands with warm water. You need heat for cooking food and warming water. You can see how heat changes clay. Then read on, to learn more about heat.

TRY THIS

Describing Changes In Clay

Hold a piece of clay. Does it feel warm or cold? Roll and squeeze a small piece of clay for 2 minutes. Feel the clay again. Does it feel warm or cool? Where did the heat come from?

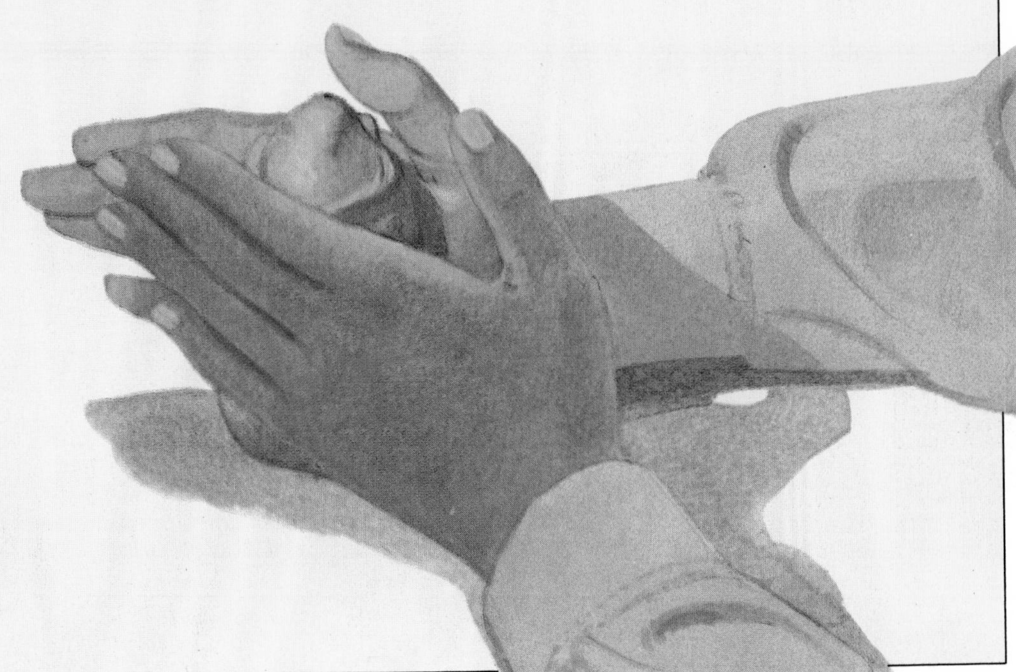

Lesson 1 What Is Heat?

This person uses heat to cook food. **Heat** is **energy** in motion. First, the heat moves from the stove to the pan. Then the energy moves to the food.

Where do you think the heat energy moves next? It moves into the air around the pan. Where could you feel the heat?

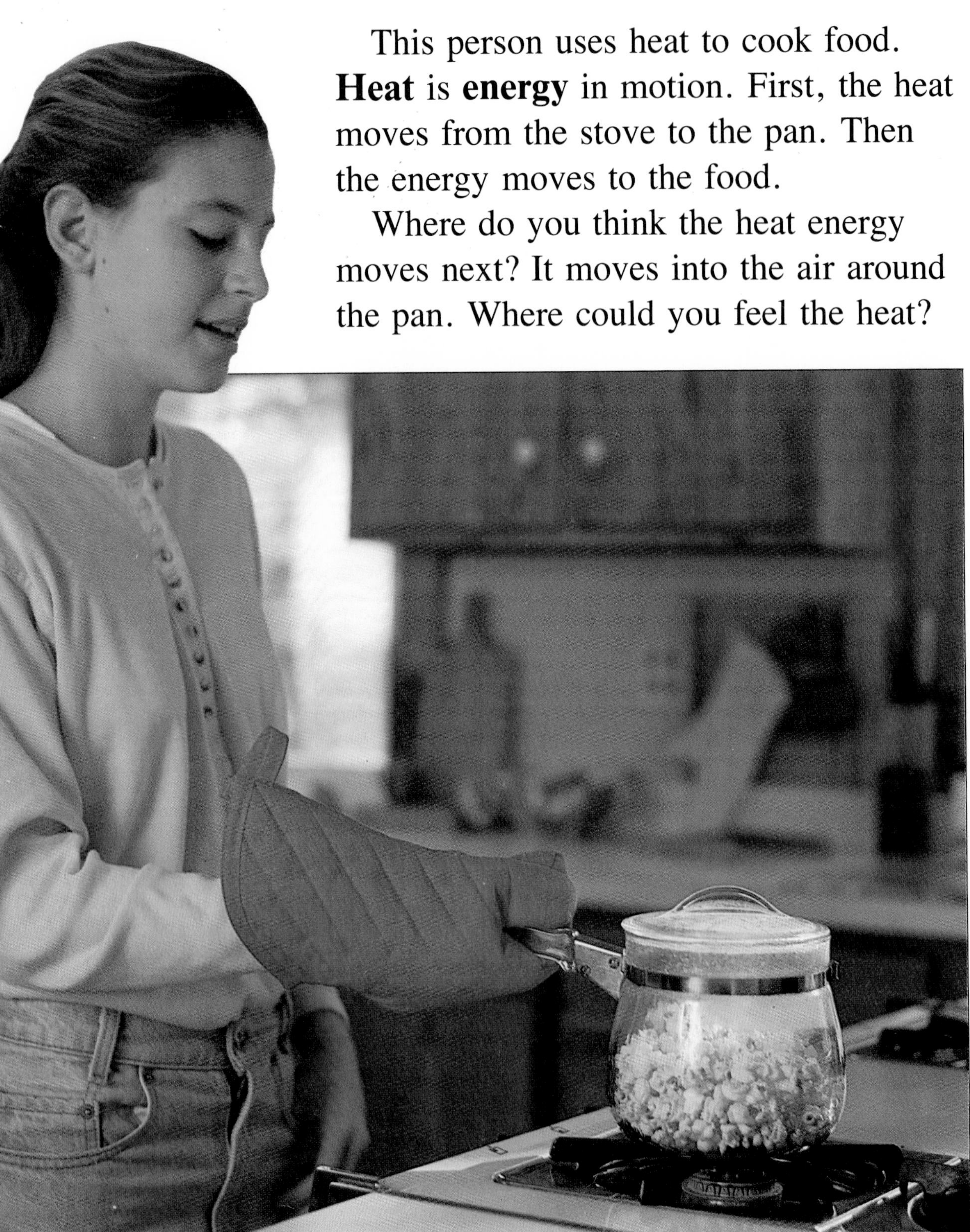

Heat comes from fires. It also comes from the light of the sun. You can feel the light from the sun as heat.

Many objects in a home give off heat. Toasters give off heat. Most people have heaters in homes to keep the homes warm. What kinds of heaters do you know about? What gives off heat in this room?

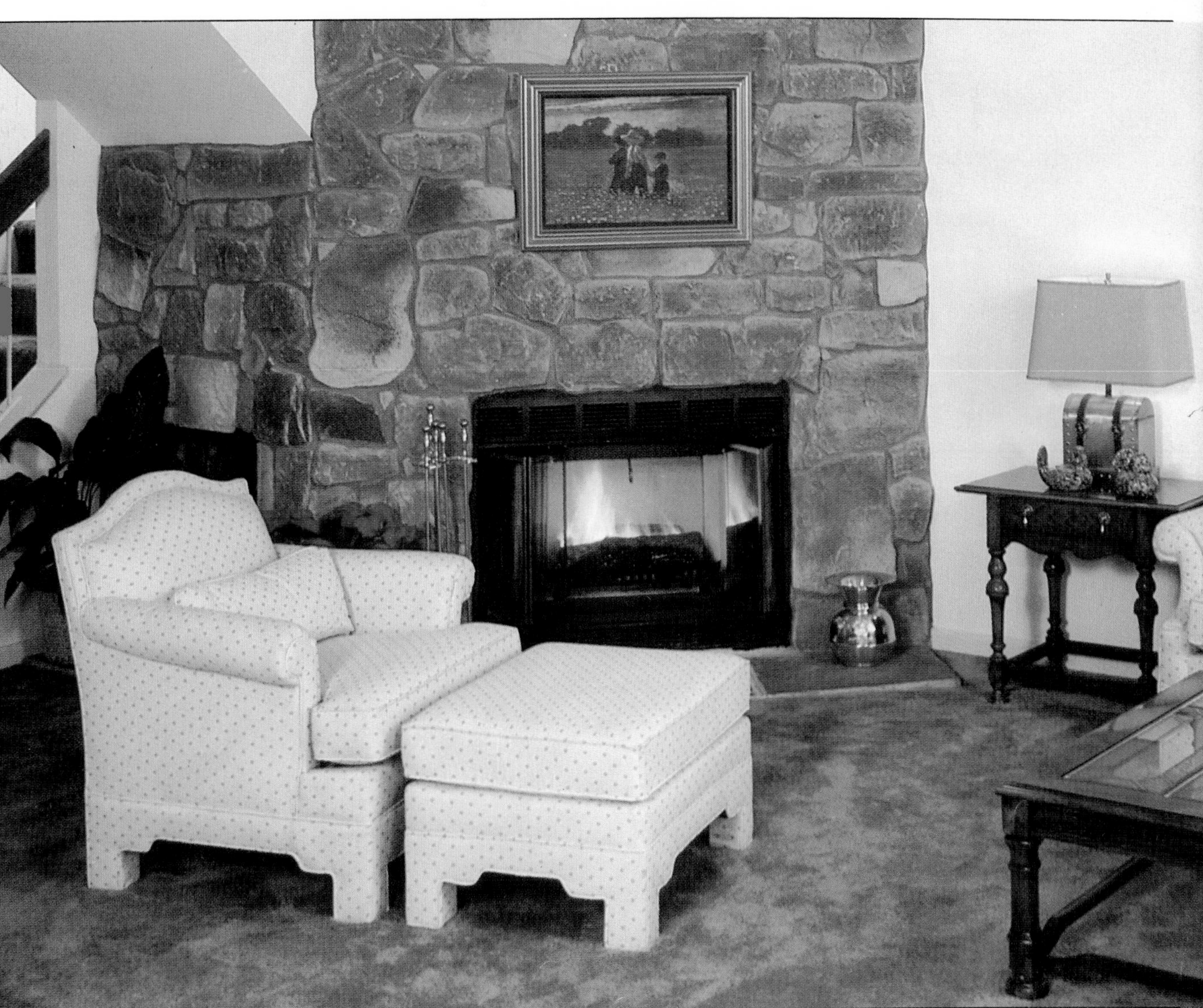

Heat moves through metal well. Heat does not move well through cloth and wood. What kind of spoon would stay cool in a hot metal pan? What cloth could you use to keep heat from a hot pan away from your hand?

People who work in kitchens often use objects like these. They keep heat from moving to other objects.

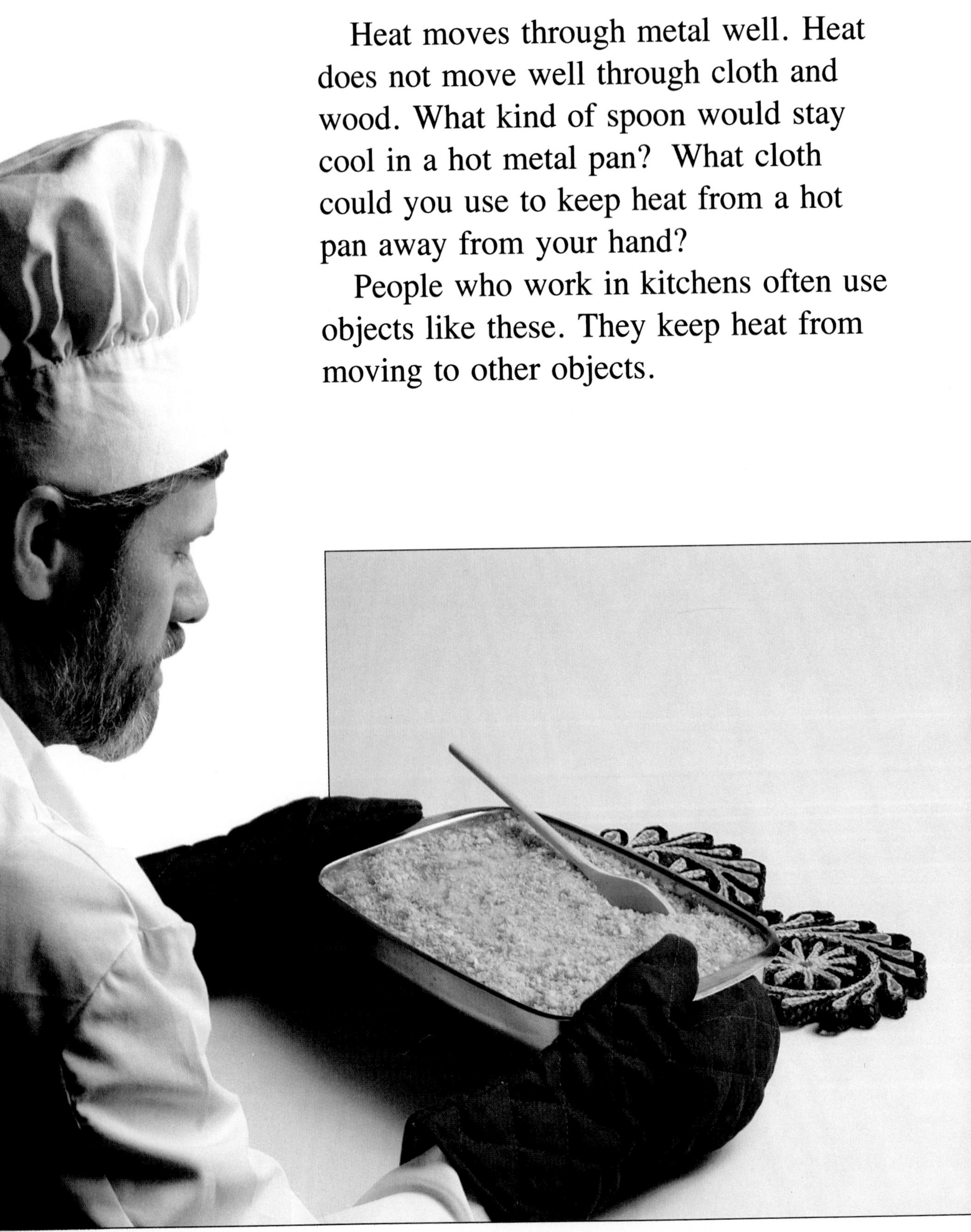

Temperature is a measure of how hot something is. You can use a **thermometer** to measure temperature. All thermometers have numbers. The numbers show temperature. Some thermometers measure the temperature of food. Other thermometers measure the temperature of air.

Lesson Review

1. What gives off heat?
2. How does heat energy move?

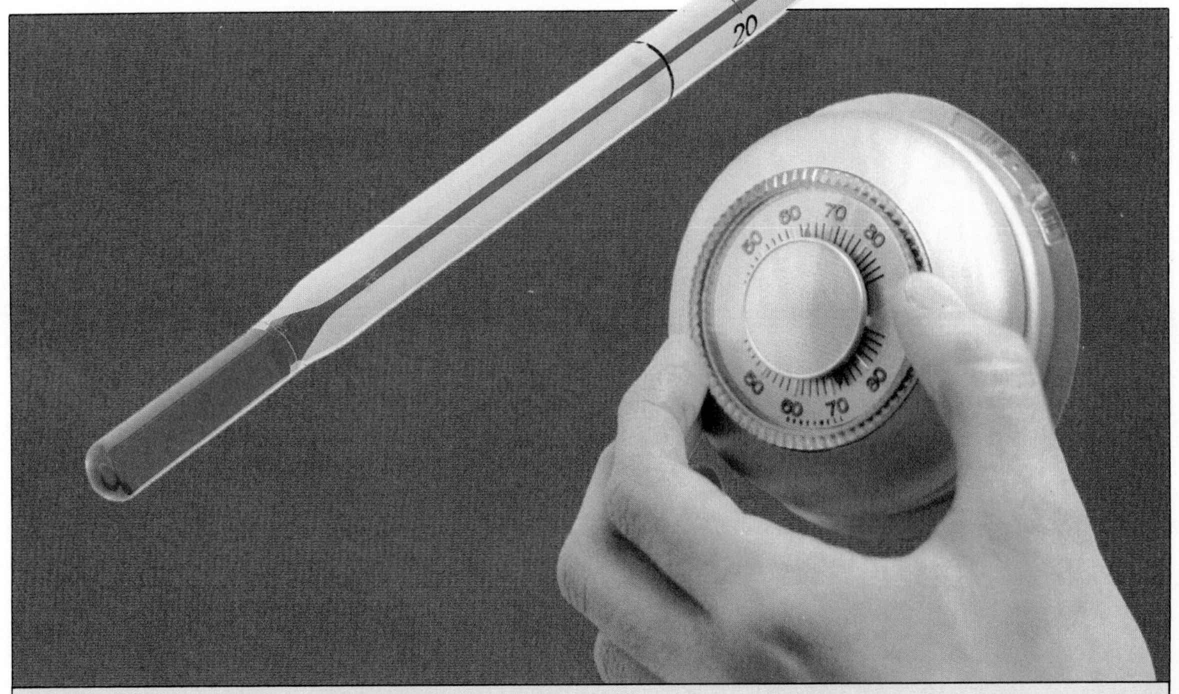

LIFE SCIENCE
Find Out
CONNECTION

Cooking foods can make them safe to eat. What are some foods that people cook?

Lesson 2 What Is Light?

Light is a kind of energy. You need light to see. Suppose you were reading a book. Would more or less light help you see the words and pictures better?

The sun gives off light. You can see the light from the sun. Fires give off light. Light bulbs give off light. A wire inside a bulb heats up. Then light comes from the wire. What gives off light in this picture?

Most things you see do not give off their own light. This girl can see her book because the light from the lamp shines on it.

Light moves to objects in a straight line. The light in the picture goes straight to the book the girl is reading. Then the light bounces from the page to the girl's eyes. What does she see?

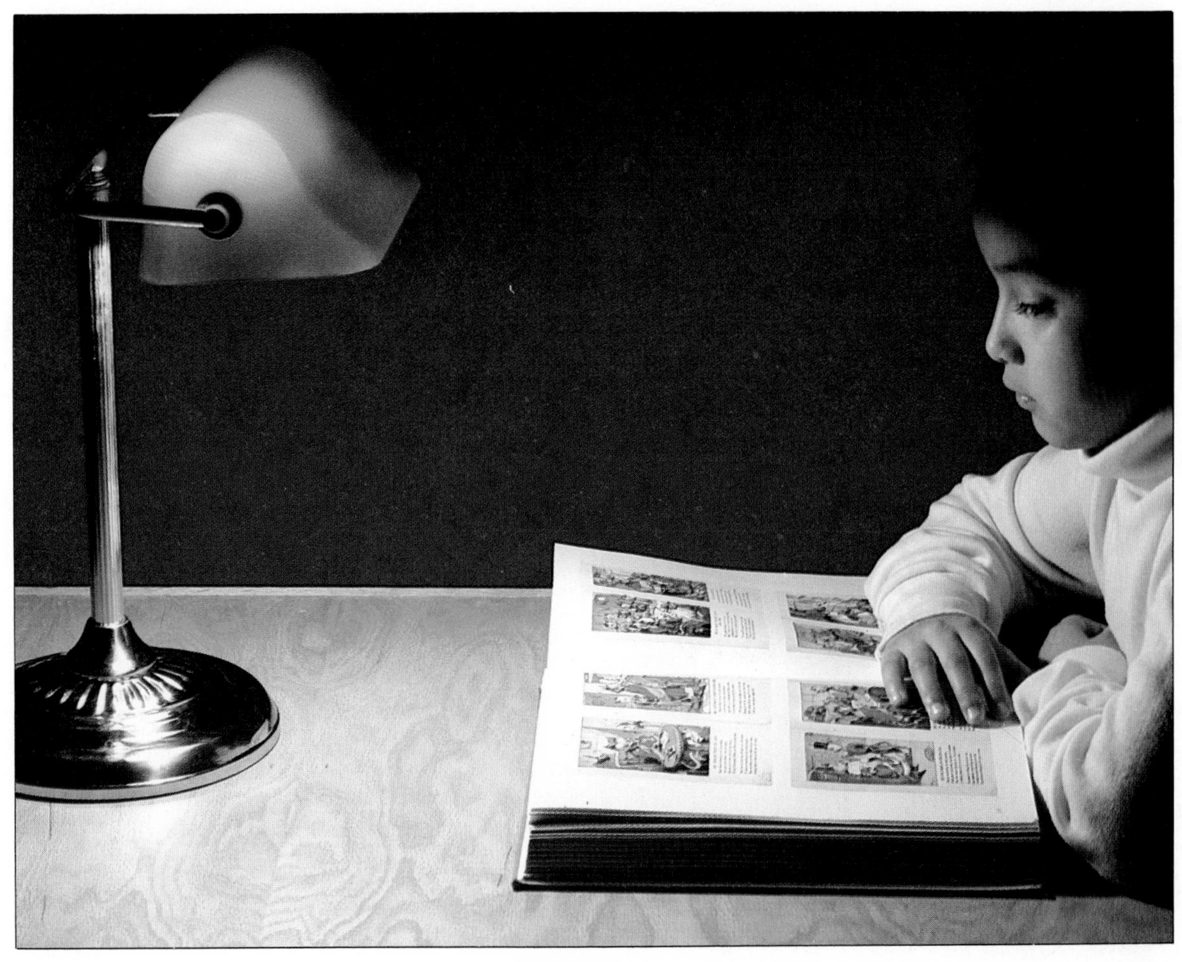

More light bounces off light colored objects than dark colored objects. Suppose you were in a room with very little light. Could you find a white object or a black object more easily?

Light can pass through some objects. Other objects stop light and make shadows. What makes shadows here?

Lesson Review

1. What gives off light?
2. How does light move?

PHYSICAL SCIENCE

Find Out

Shine a flashlight on a mirror in a dark room. See how the light moves.

ACTIVITY

Letting Light Through

Follow the Directions

1. Turn on a flashlight.
2. Put different things in front of the flashlight.
3. Find out what stops light.
4. Find out what lets light through.

Tell What You Learned

Tell which things let light through. Name two things people use that let light through.

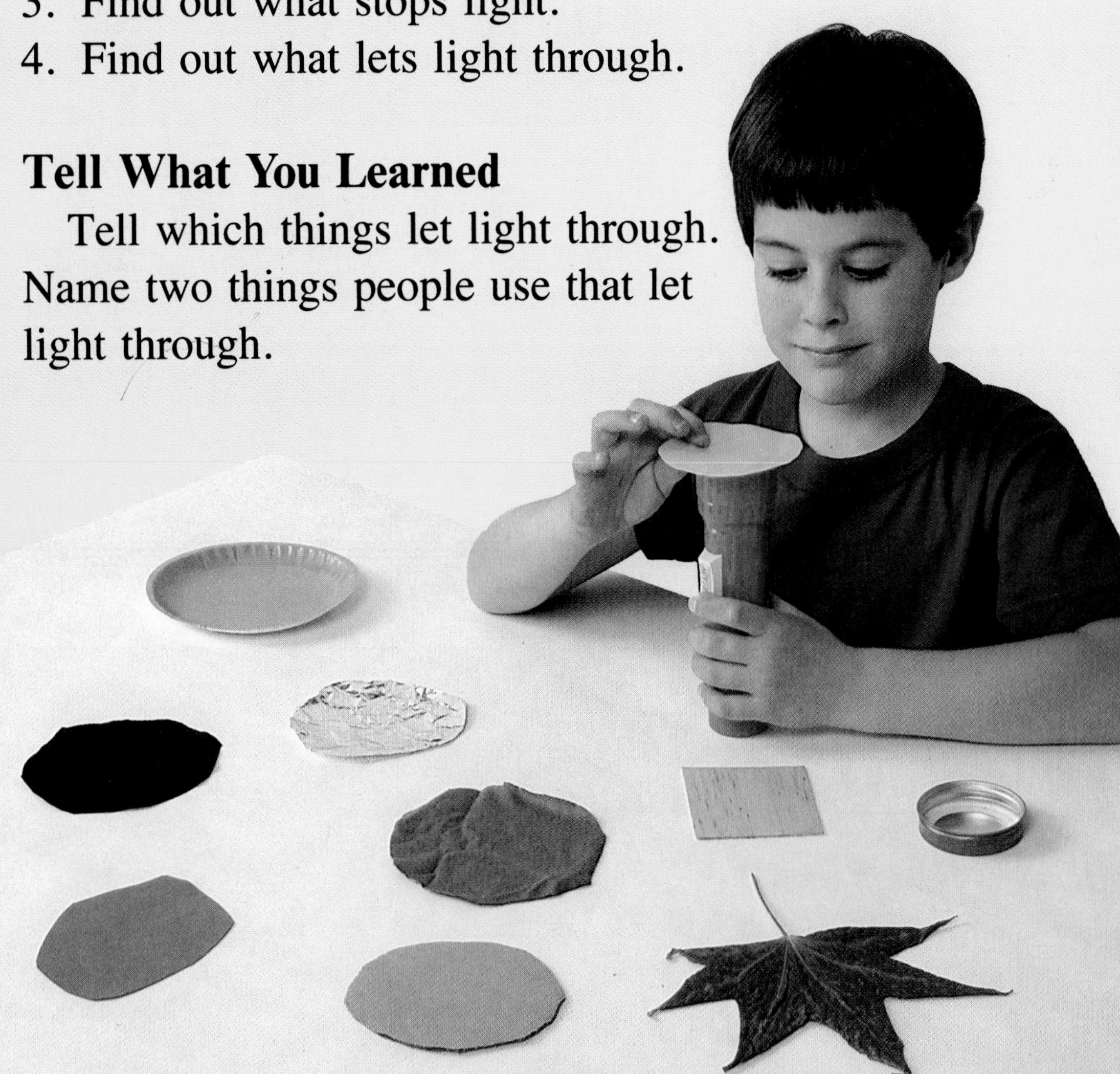

Lesson 3 How Can You Use Heat and Light Safely?

People use heat in different ways. Heat keeps you warm and helps cook your food.

This family uses heat carefully in the kitchen. They use potholders when handling hot pans. How did the boy use the toaster safely?

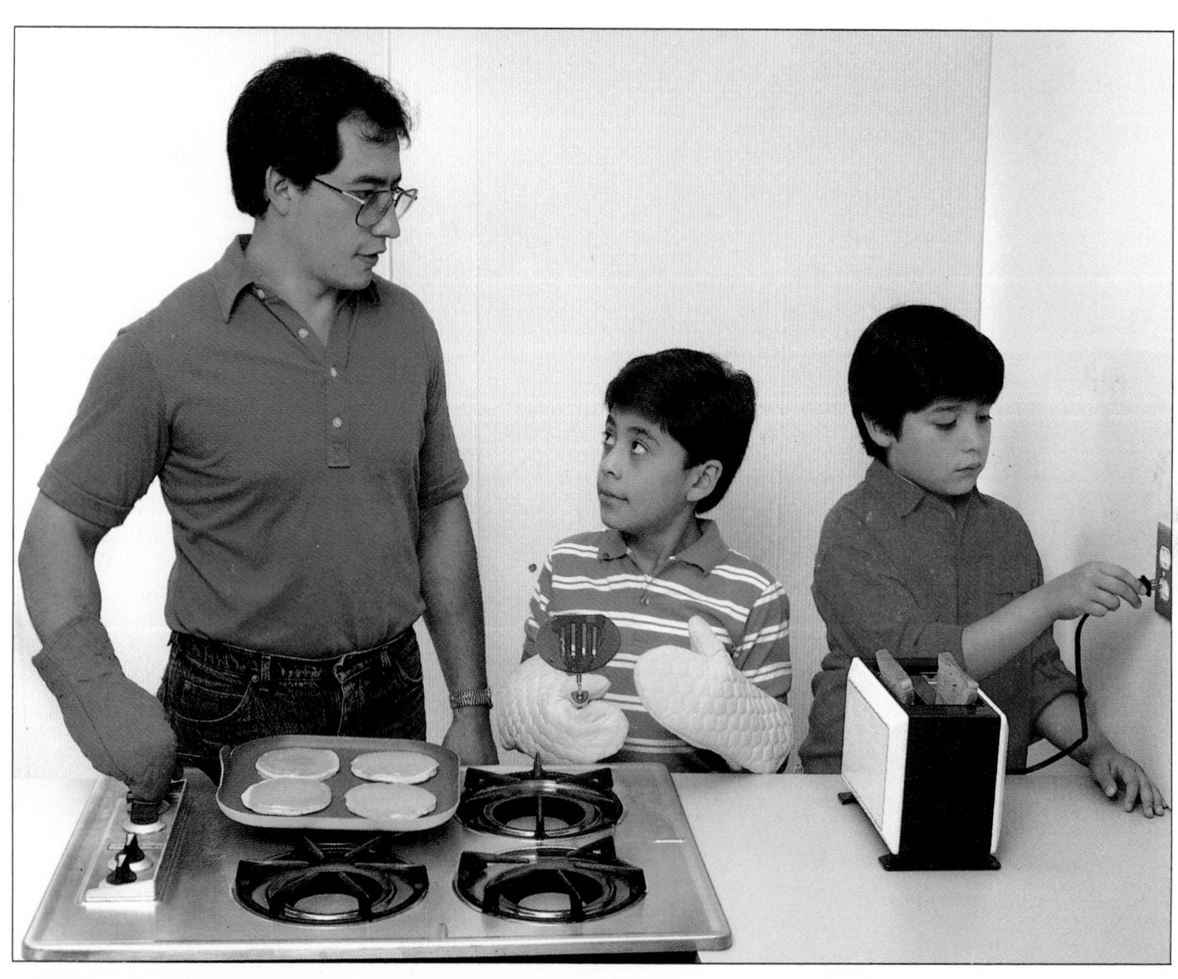

The family also uses heat safely in other parts of their home. An adult helps a child dry her hair. How does the family use heat safely when ironing clothes?

Matches can start fires. Heat from fires can be very harmful. What does the child do to be safe with matches?

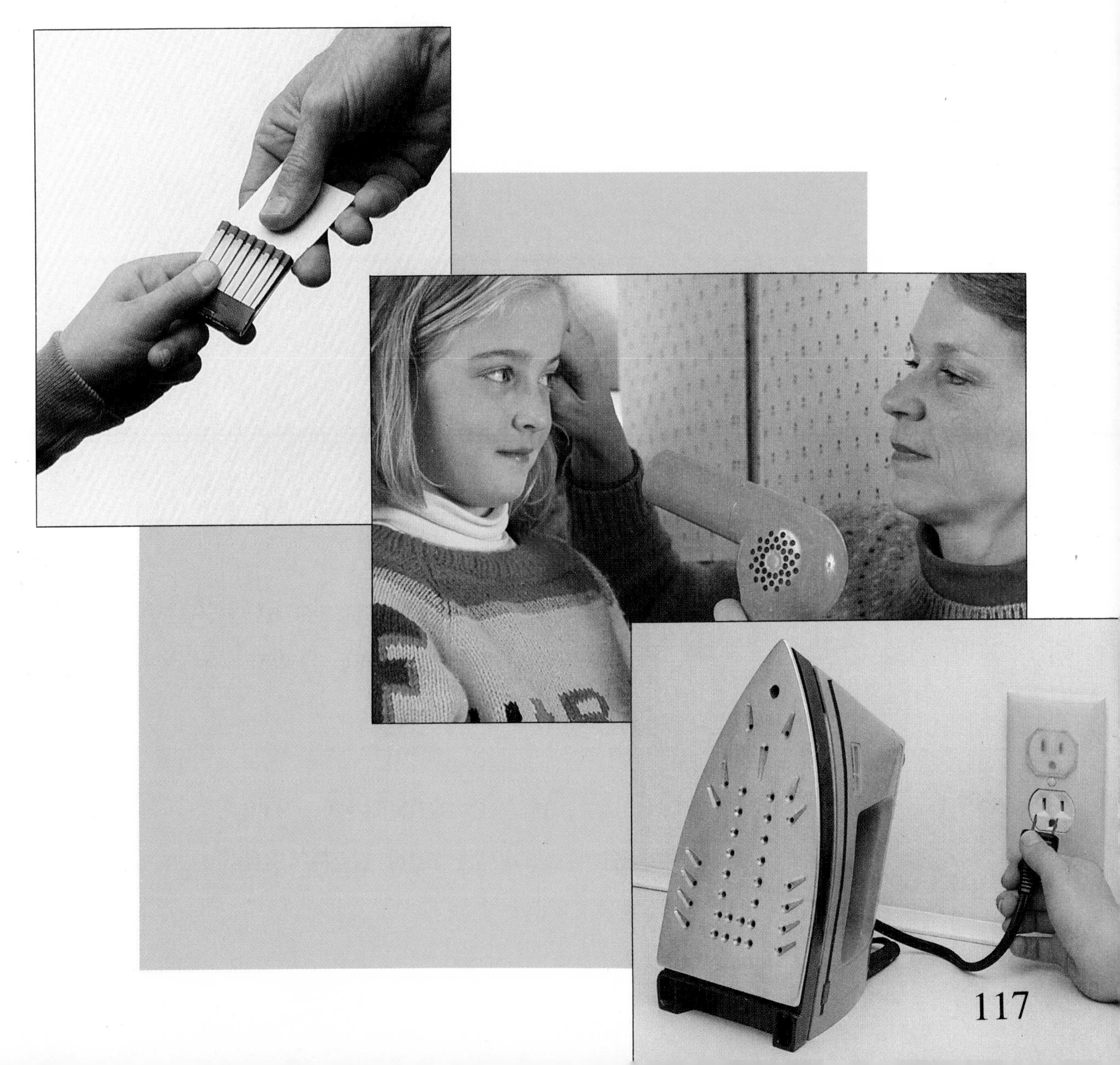

How can you use light safely? Using a lamp like the one in the picture could start a fire. Do not use any lamp that has a broken cord.

You can protect your eyes and skin from bright sunlight. Wearing hats and sunglasses can help. What are other ways to be safe in the sun?

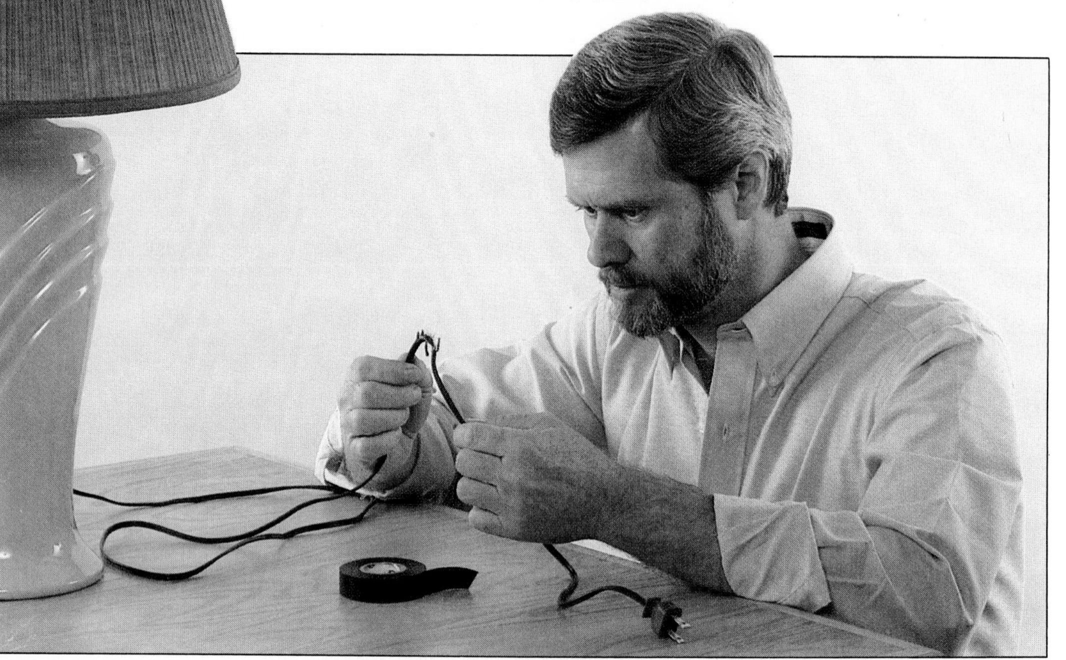

Lesson Review

1. How can people use heat safely?
2. How can people use light safely?

PHYSICAL SCIENCE

Find Out

What are two ways you can use heat and light safely at school?

Microwave Ovens

Most ovens get hot when they are used to cook food. What keeps this oven cool? It uses a kind of energy called microwaves. Microwaves bounce off the inside of the oven. The oven does not get hot.

Microwaves pass through paper, plastic, and glass. Microwaves pass into food. They heat the food very quickly. They can cook food much faster than other ovens.

What Do You Think?

How are these ovens useful to people?

Cooking Time
Minutes
Eggs 2
Soup 3
Corn 6
Peas 4
Carrots 6
Potatoes 7
Fish 12
Lamb 16
Chicken 14
Meat Loaf 16

Lesson 4 What Is Sound?

Sit very still. What sounds do you hear? **Sounds** are a kind of energy. All the sounds you hear come from objects that **vibrate.** When an object vibrates, it moves back and forth very quickly.

When you make sounds, your throat vibrates. When some animals make sounds their throats vibrate. What kind of sound does a horse make?

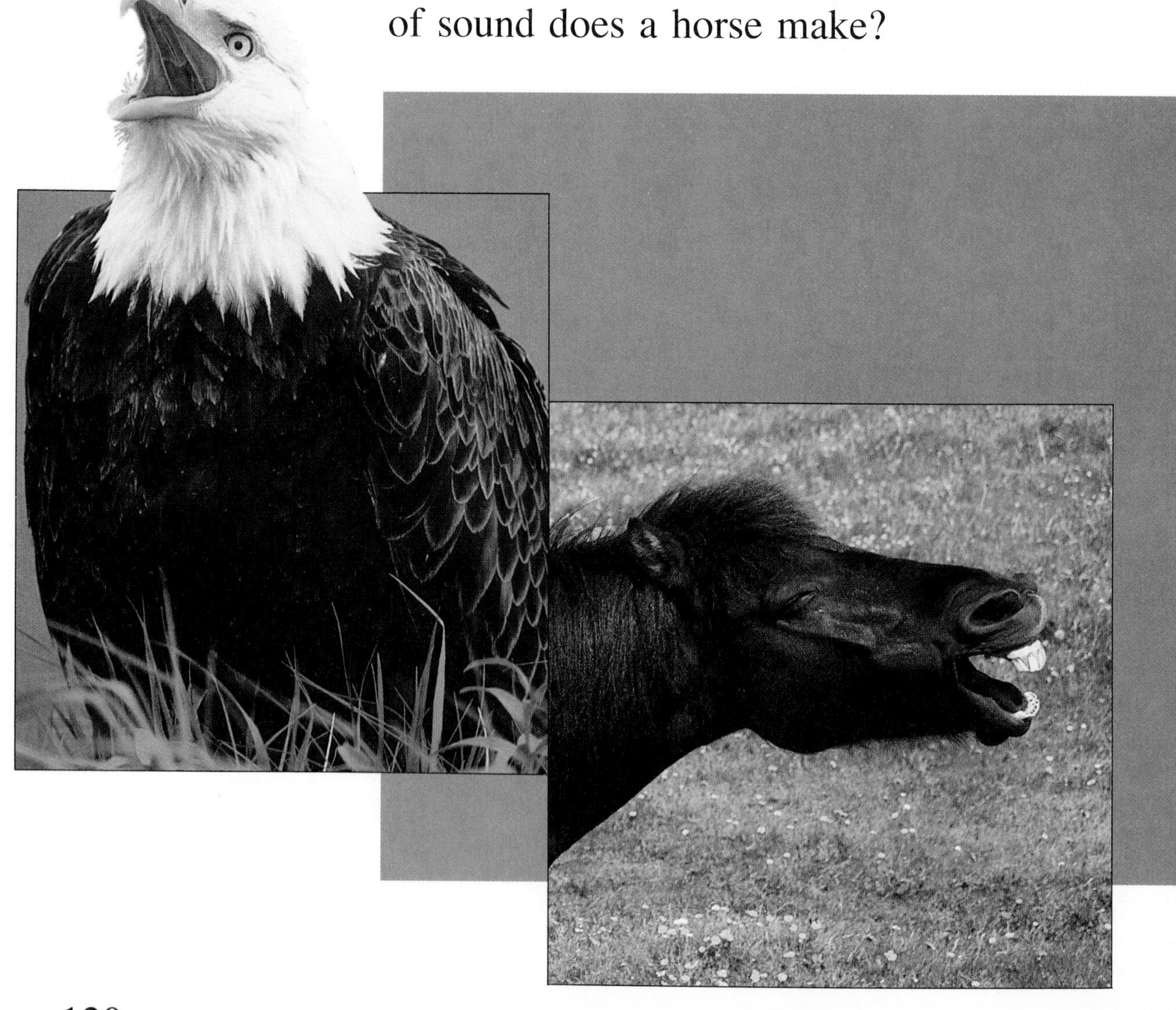

You hear when sounds move to your ears. The triangle vibrates when it is tapped. The air around the triangle also vibrates. Sounds then move through the air to your ears. A small part inside your ear called an **eardrum** begins to vibrate. Then you hear the triangle ring.

Sounds can change from high to low and from loud to soft. Most birds make high sounds. Cows make low sounds. Music has different sounds. Some are loud. Some are soft.

The sounds your voice makes can change. Other objects make sounds that change. How do the sounds this truck makes change?

Lesson Review

1. How do objects move to make sound?
2. How can sounds change?

PHYSICAL SCIENCE

Find Out

Slowly fill a glass with water as you tap on it with a spoon. Find out how the sound changes.

ACTIVITY

Making Sounds Change

Wear cover goggles for this activity.

Follow the Directions

1. Work with a partner. Hold your hanger as the child in the picture is.
2. Ask your partner to tap the hanger with a pencil. Listen to the sound.
3. Bend your hanger into a different shape.
4. Ask your partner to tap the hanger again. Listen to the sound.

Tell What You Learned

Tell how the sound changed each time. Name different ways sounds change.

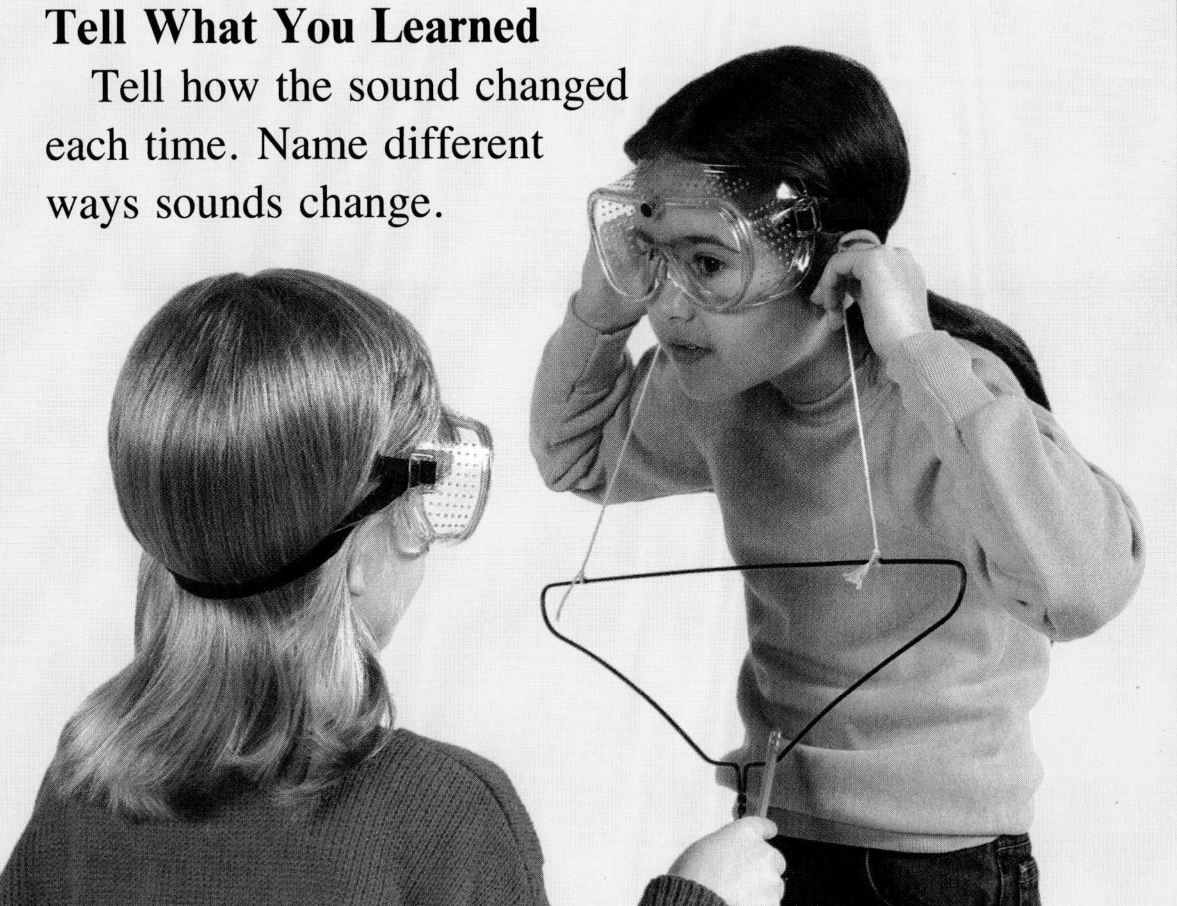

Lesson 5 How Does Sound Help You?

You get information from sound. You get information from listening to the radio and TV. Some sounds warn you of danger. How does the sound of a railroad crossing warn you?

People enjoy many sounds. People like music, the sound of ocean waves, and birds singing. What sounds do you like?

Protect yourself from very loud sounds. They can hurt your ears and harm your hearing. Try not to listen to very loud sounds that last for a long time. How can you listen to music safely? How does this worker protect his ears?

Lesson Review

1. How can sound help you?
2. What should you do to protect your ears from loud sounds?

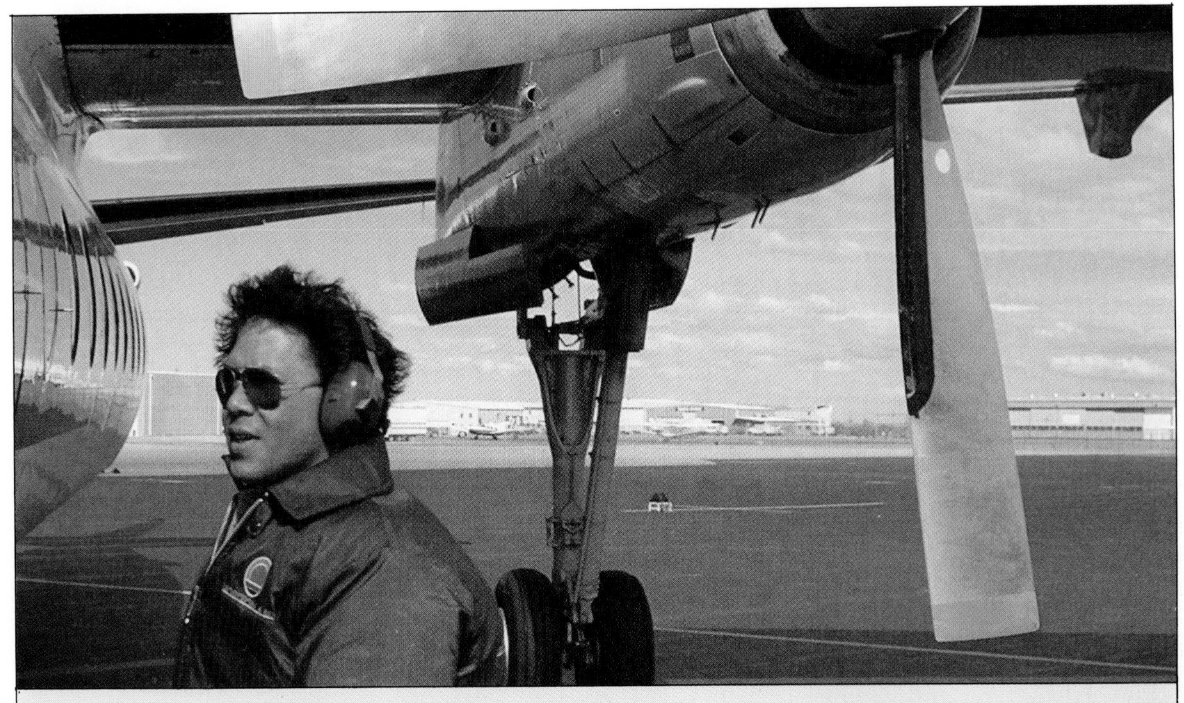

Some neighborhoods have a siren to warn for storms. Find out if your neighborhood has one.

EARTH SCIENCE
Find Out
CONNECTION

Using a Thermometer and Making a Chart

What different temperatures can you measure?

1. Look at the three glasses of water. Find the numbers on each thermometer. Notice how the temperature of glass **a** is 5°C. Find the temperature of glass **b** and glass **c.**

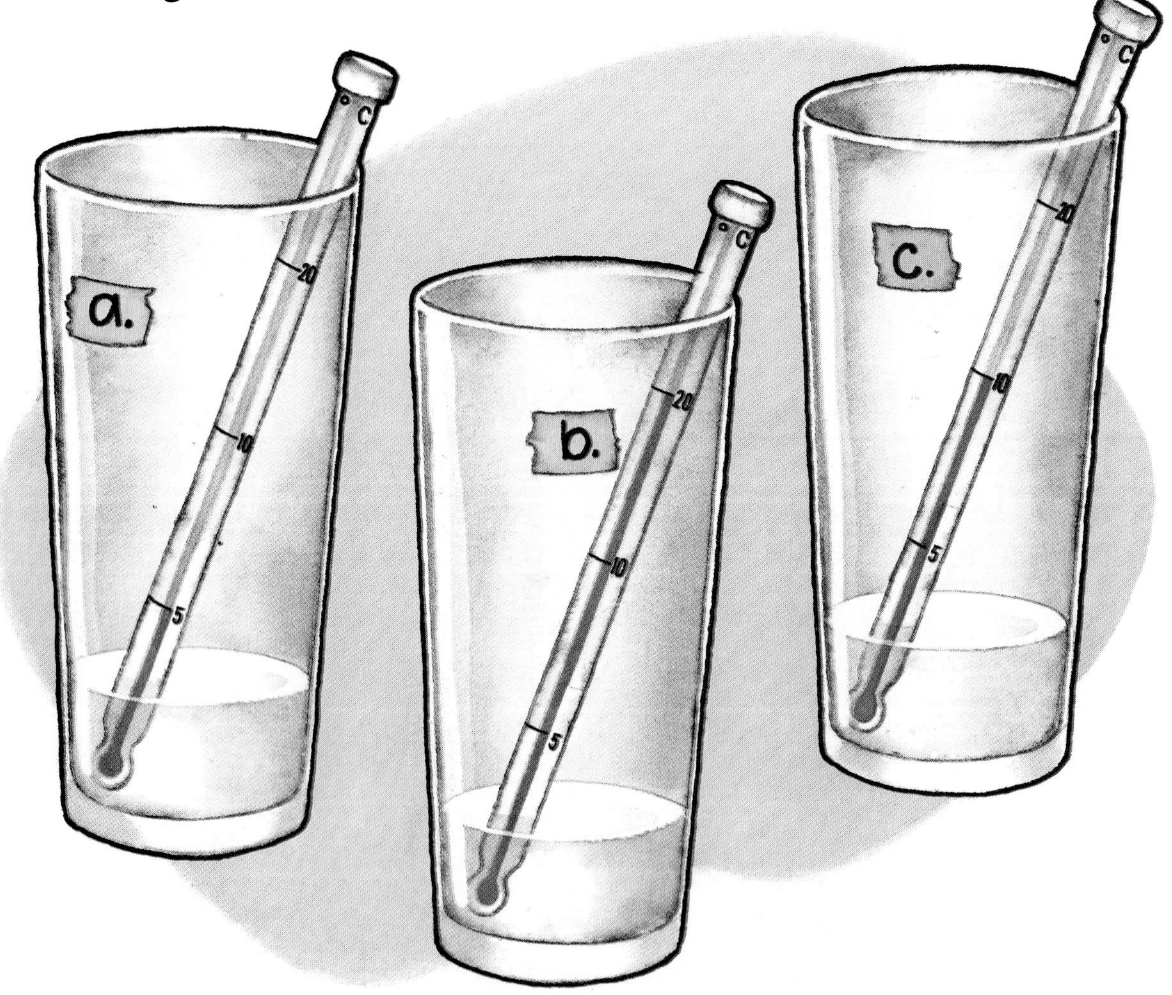

2. Make a chart like this one. Write down each temperature you measured.

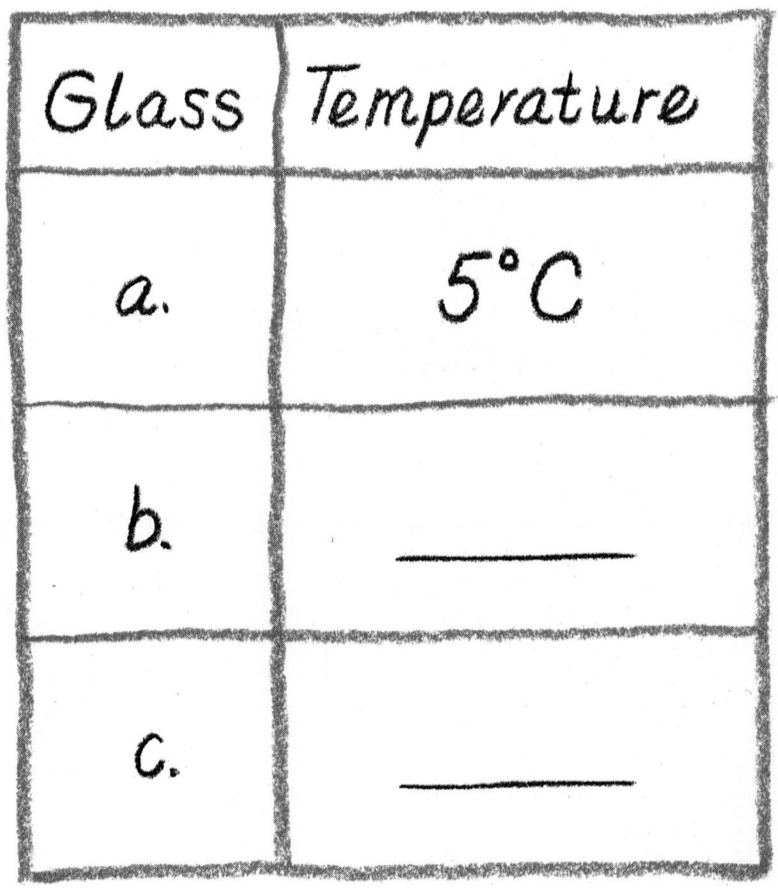

Glass	Temperature
a.	5°C
b.	______
c.	______

3. Which glass has the warmest water? Which has the coolest water?

Chapter 5 Review

Review Chapter Ideas

1. Tell where heat comes from.
2. Tell where light comes from.
3. Explain how light moves.
4. Look at the child in the picture.
   Tell how he uses light safely.
5. Tell what makes all sounds you hear.
6. Tell four ways sounds can change.
7. Tell how sound is helpful.

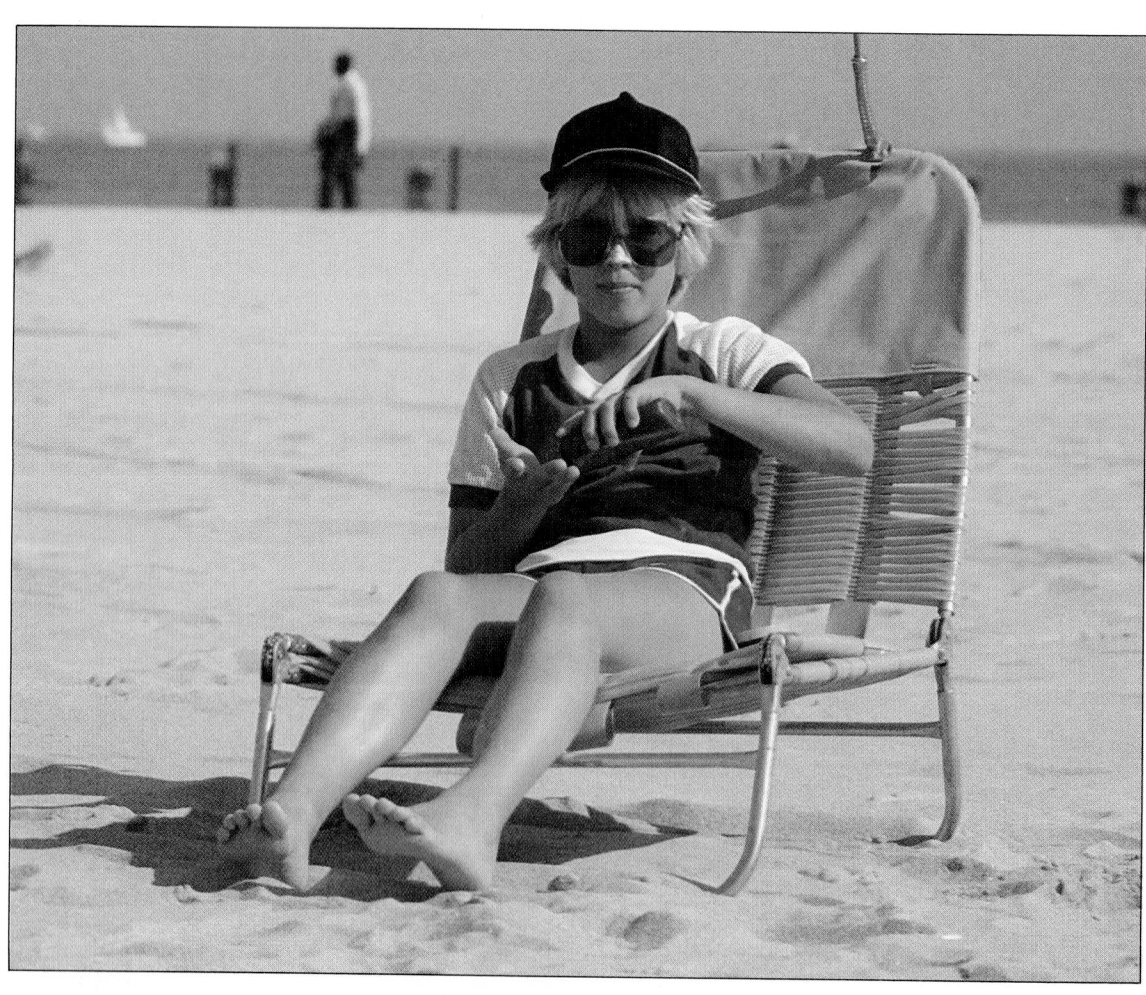

Review Science Words

Match the words and the pictures.

1. heat
2. light
3. thermometer

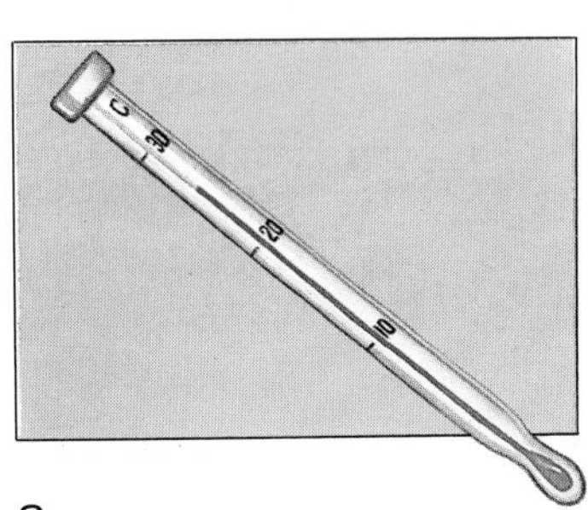

a.

b.

c.

Tell what the words mean.

4. energy
5. sound
6. temperature
7. vibrate
8. eardrum

Use Science Ideas

Tell how you hear the sounds from a television.

Chapter 6

Machines and Electricity

Machines are many shapes and sizes. Large machines are made up of smaller machines.

Starting the Chapter

Tools are machines. You can put together objects to make a tool that makes work easier. Then read on to learn more about machines.

TRY THIS

Lifting a Book

Stack some books on a desk. Tie a string around a book. Use the string to lift the book onto the stack of books. Now put the cardboard against the books the way you see here. Use the string to pull the book up the cardboard. What was different about how you lifted the book each time?

Lesson 1 What Can Machines Do?

Machines are different in many ways. They work differently. They are different sizes. They have different parts. However, machines make work seem easier for people.

Look at the pictures of tools. These tools are machines that help people cut, dig, and pull. What machine helps people cut paper? Which machines like these do you use?

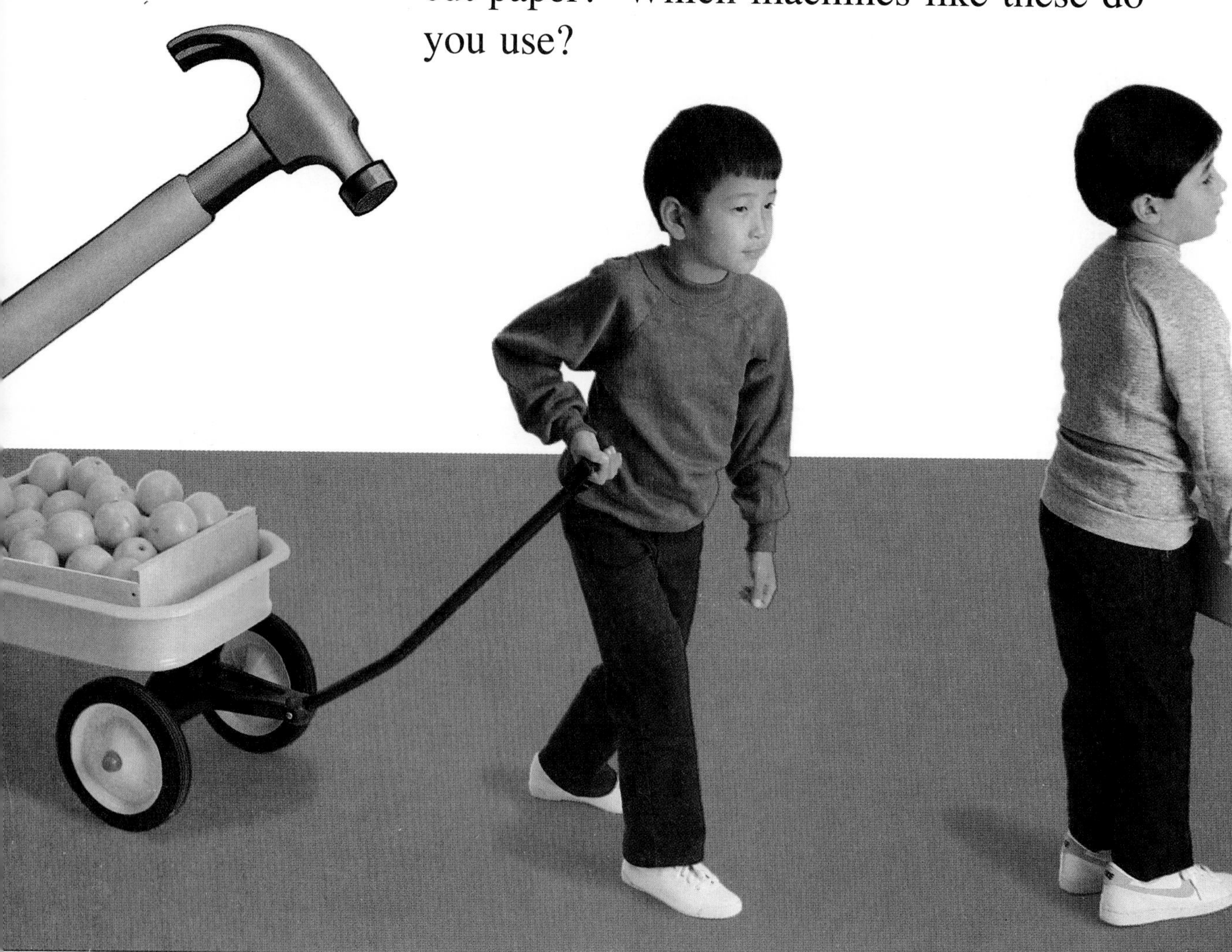

Objects do not start moving by themselves. You must use **force** to move objects. A force is a push or a pull. A little force will move light objects. You need more force to move heavy objects. Which child uses more force here? What machine helps move the box?

Lesson Review

1. How do machines help people?
2. What is force?

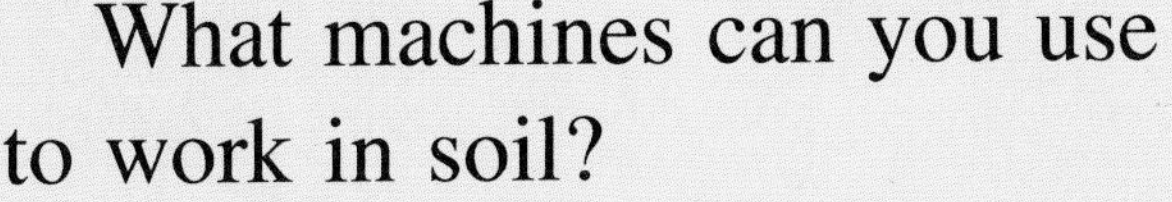

What machines can you use to work in soil?

EARTH SCIENCE
Find Out
CONNECTION

Lesson 2 What Can Magnets Do?

This child uses a **magnet** to pick up paper clips. Most magnets are metal. Magnets can push or pull some metal objects.

Magnets have different sizes and shapes. What different kinds of magnets do you see here?

Magnets have **poles.** The poles are the parts of the magnets that push or pull hardest. Some magnets have poles at each end, like the ones in the picture. Find the **S** and the **N** on the ends of the magnets. The **S** is for south pole. The **N** is for north pole.

Different poles pull toward each other. Like poles will push apart. What poles pull together here?

People use magnets in many ways. Some tools and machines have magnets. Some games and toys use magnets. How are magnets used here? When have you used a magnet?

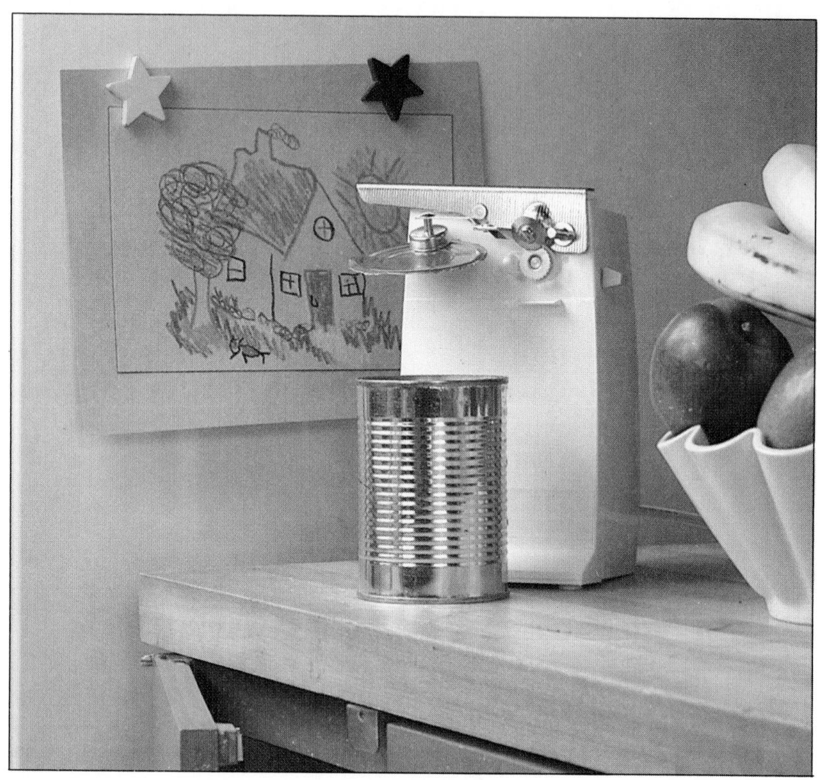

Lesson Review

1. What is a magnet?
2. How are magnets used?

PHYSICAL SCIENCE

Find Out

Collect different objects. Find out which ones you can pick up with a magnet.

Finding the Poles of Magnets

Follow the Directions

1. Put a bar magnet on your desk.
2. Carefully drop paper clips on the magnet the way you see here.
3. Observe that more paper clips collect over the magnet poles.
4. Move the magnet and try again.

Tell What You Learned

Tell how you knew where the poles of the magnets were. Tell what other objects you could use to find the poles of a magnet.

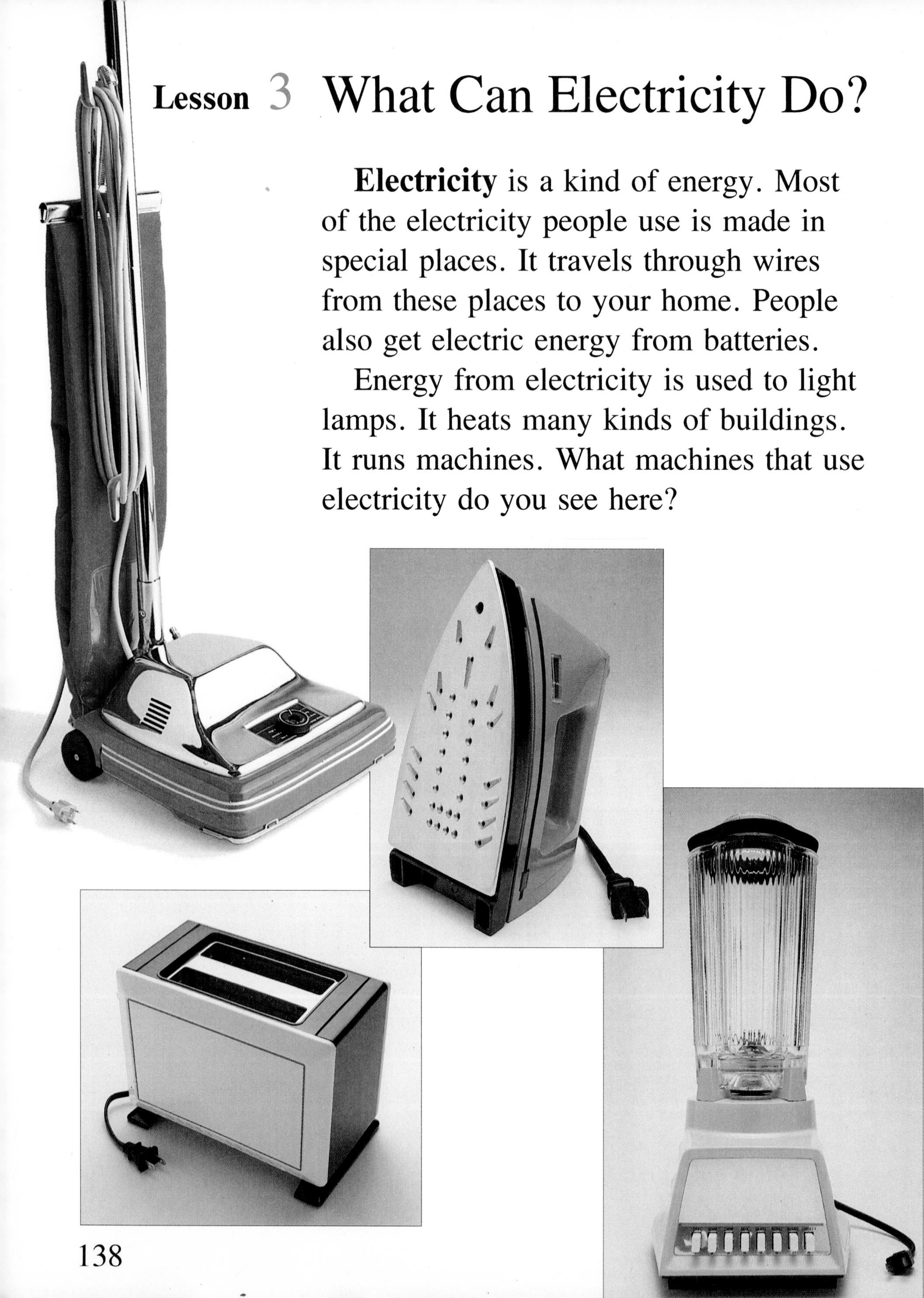

Lesson 3 What Can Electricity Do?

Electricity is a kind of energy. Most of the electricity people use is made in special places. It travels through wires from these places to your home. People also get electric energy from batteries.

Energy from electricity is used to light lamps. It heats many kinds of buildings. It runs machines. What machines that use electricity do you see here?

Suppose someone plugs in a lamp. Then the person turns it on. The lamp wire carries electricity. It makes the light go on.

People use electric energy from batteries in many ways. The electricity moves to toys, radios, and flashlights.

Lesson Review

1. What is electricity?
2. What is electricity used for?

EARTH SCIENCE
Find Out
CONNECTION

Some electricity travels through wires in the ground. What kinds of weather are the wires safe from?

ACTIVITY

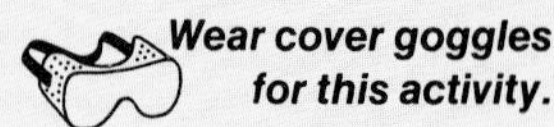
Wear cover goggles
for this activity.

Lighting a Bulb

Follow the Directions

1. Bend one end of a wire around the metal part of a light bulb.
2. Tape the other end of the wire to the bottom of a battery.
3. Touch the bulb to the top of the battery.
4. Observe the bulb light up.

Tell What You Learned

Tell one way to light a bulb. Tell how people use batteries with bulbs.

Making Machines Better

Sometimes people change machines. They find ways to make the machines better. The engine is one kind of machine that has had many changes.

In 1885, Paul Daimler drove a machine with an engine. It looked like a bicycle. It went very slow. Now most cars have engines that make them go very fast.

What Do You Think?

Why do people want to make machines better?

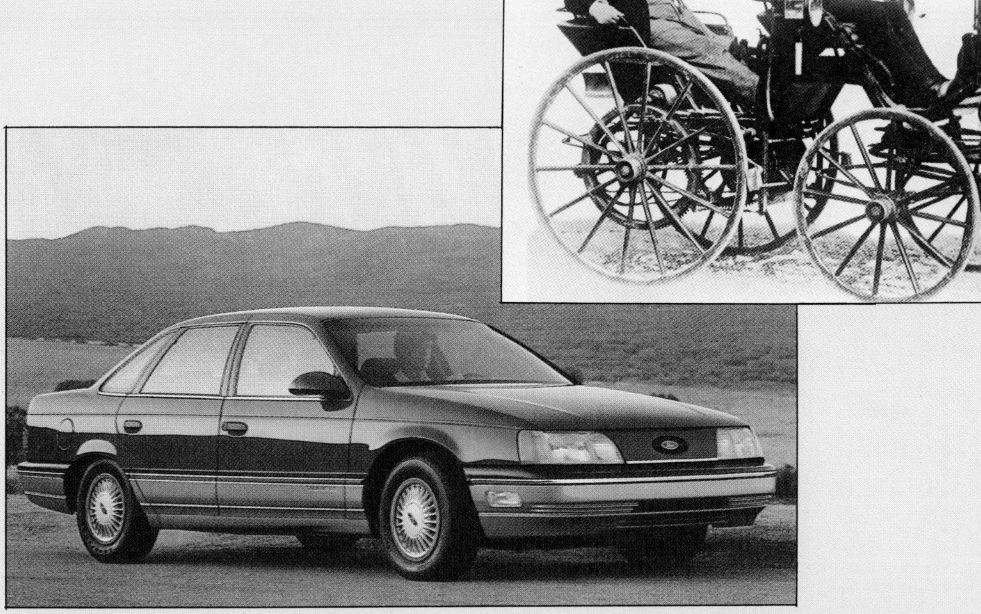

Lesson 4 How Can Machines and Electricity Be Used Safely?

People often work with machines. They need to keep their hair and clothes away from the machines. Why is that a safe thing to do?

All of these tools and machines belong in special places. The children ask for help before using any of the tools. How are the people working safely?

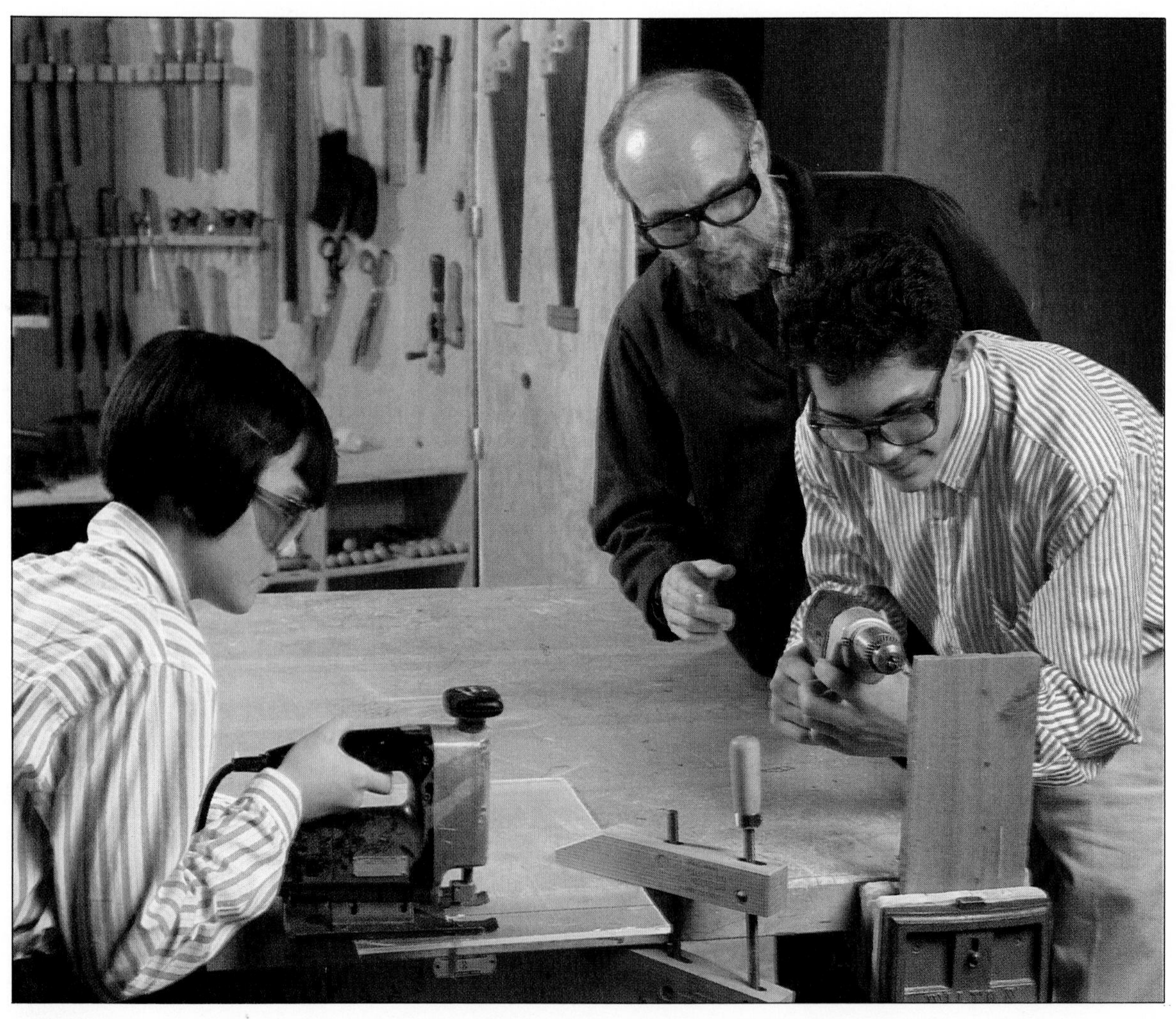

Ask an adult for help when using an **electric appliance.** Do not use an appliance that has a broken cord.

Electricity moves through water. Only use electric appliances if your hands are dry and you are in a dry place. How is electricity used safely here?

Lesson Review

1. How can people use machines safely?
2. How can people use electricity safely?

PHYSICAL SCIENCE

Find Out

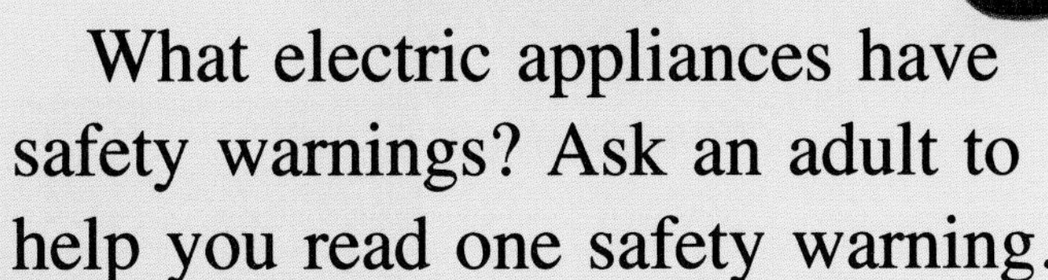

What electric appliances have safety warnings? Ask an adult to help you read one safety warning.

Reading a Timer and Making a Chart

Which machine moves the fastest?

1. Pretend you are going on a trip. You want to go from Lake City to Park City. You could ride in an airplane, a car, or a train. Look at the timers below each machine. A train trip would take 80 minutes or 1 hour and 20 minutes. How long would a car trip and an airplane trip take?

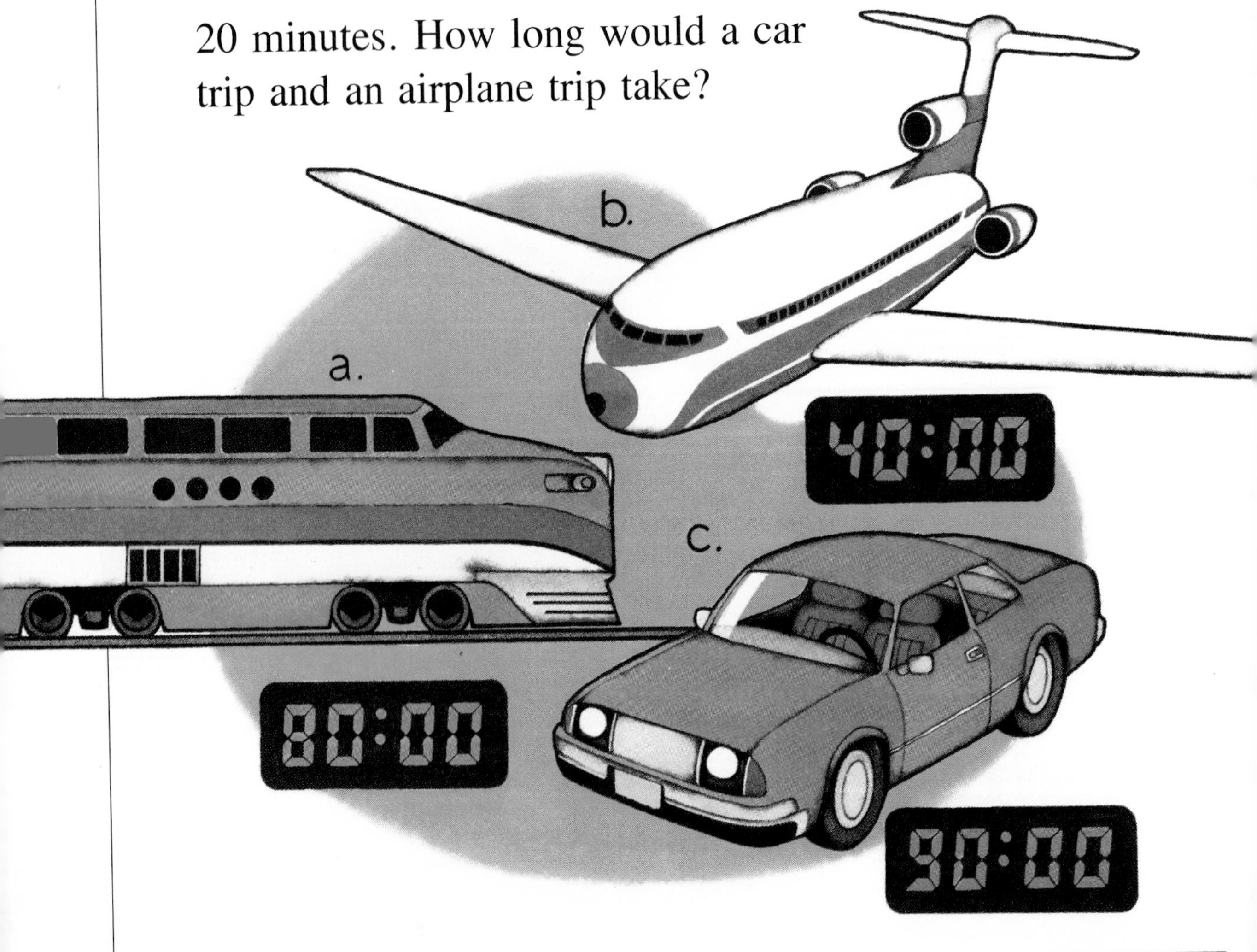

b.

a.

40:00

c.

80:00

90:00

2. Make a chart like this one. Write in the trip time for each machine. Then tell if the trip took more or less than 1 hour.

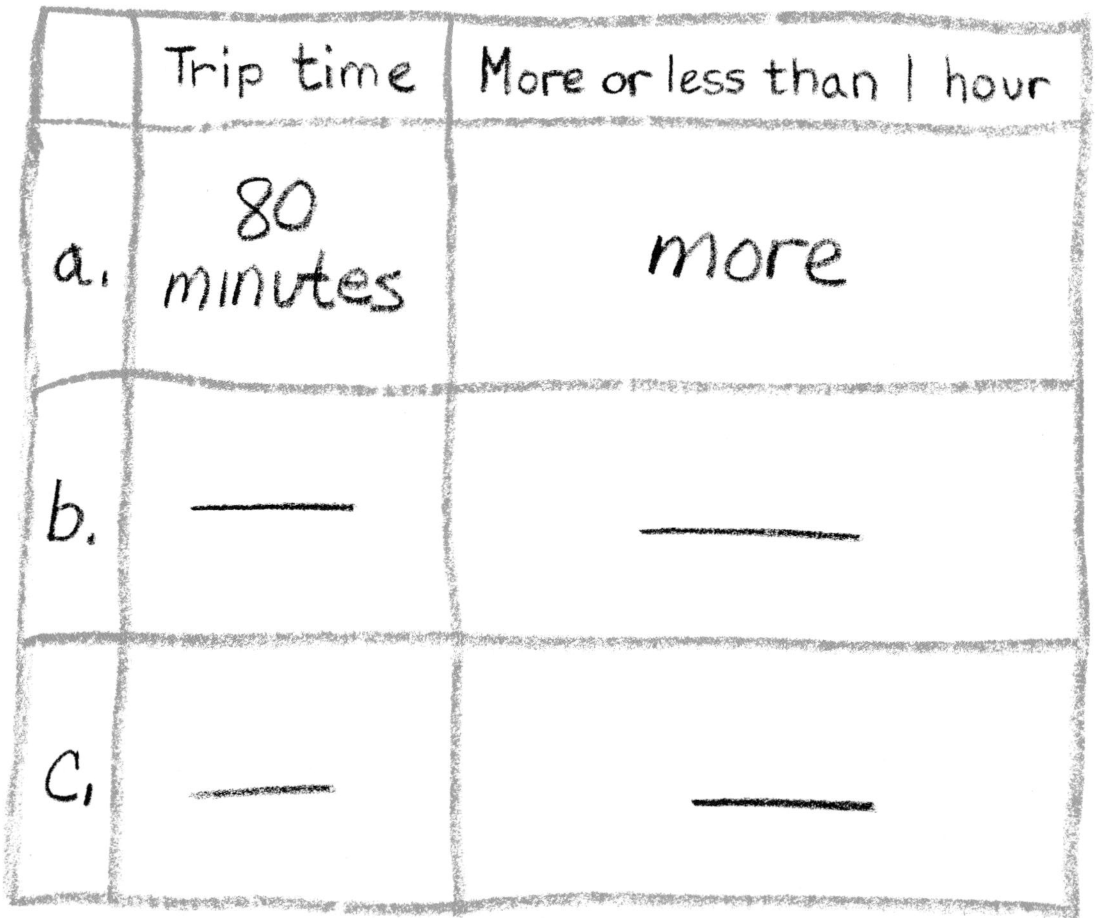

	Trip time	More or less than 1 hour
a.	80 minutes	more
b.	———	———
c.	———	———

3. Which machine took the longest time? Which machine took the shortest time?

Chapter 6 Review

Review Chapter Ideas

1. Look at the picture. Tell how the machines make work easier.
2. Tell what a magnet is.
3. Explain how magnets are used.
4. Tell how electricity is used.
5. Tell how people use machines safely.
6. Tell how people use electricity safely.

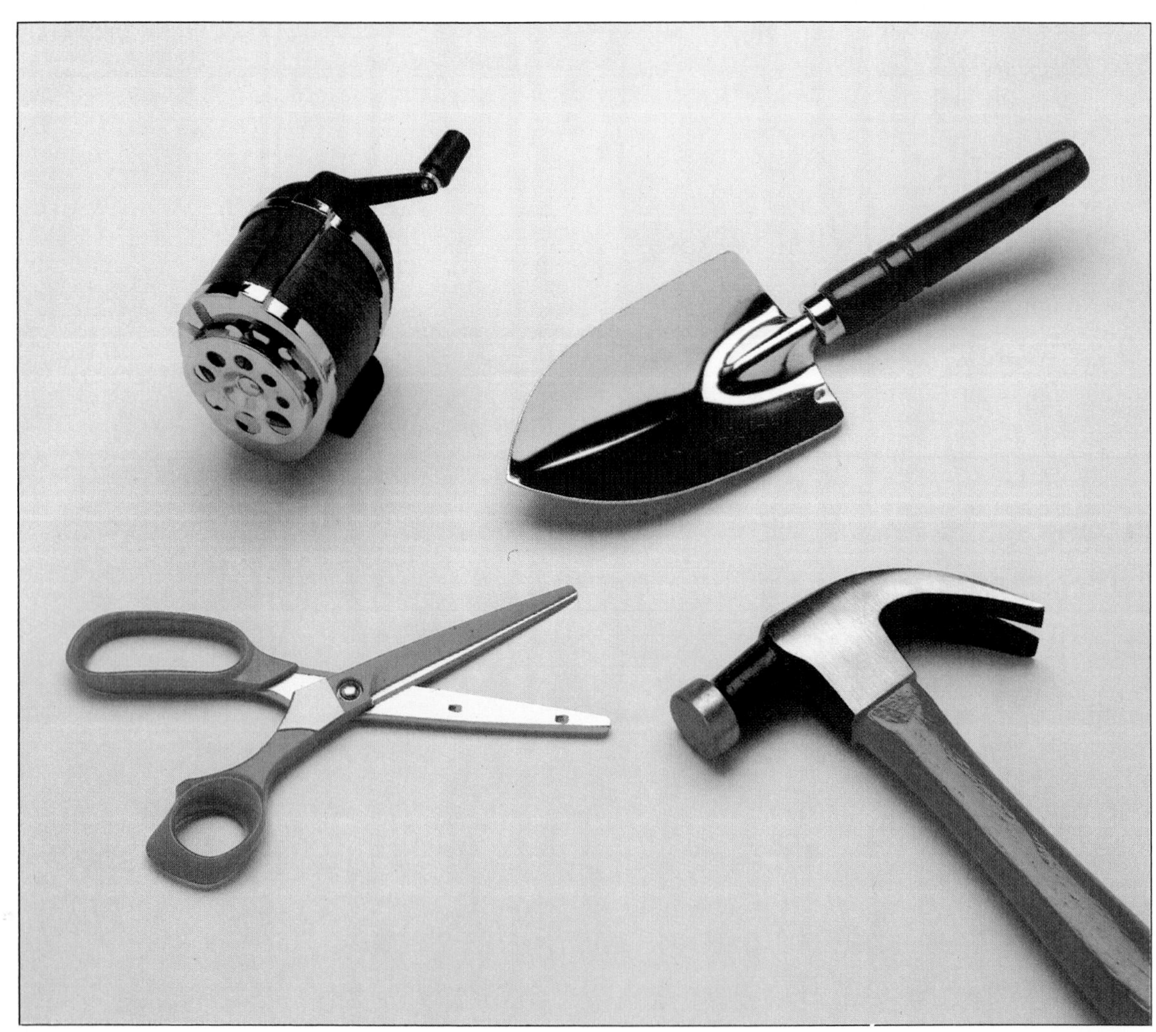

Review Science Words

Match the words and the pictures.

1. magnet
2. poles
3. electric appliance

a.

b.

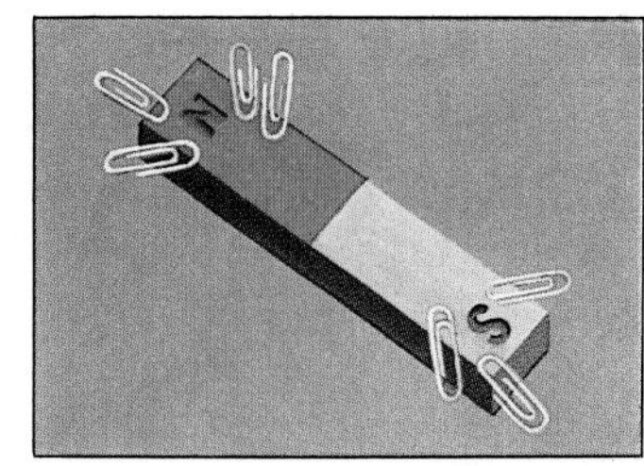

c.

Tell what the words mean.

4. force
5. electricity

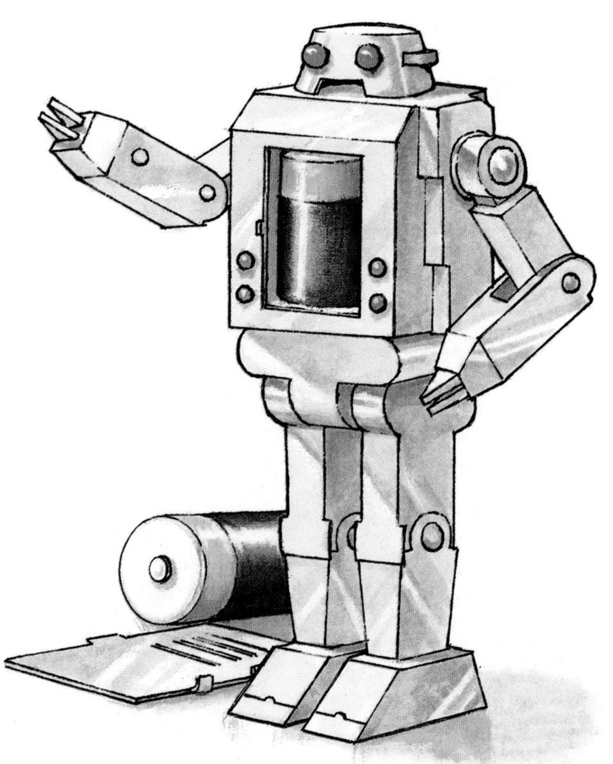

Use Science Ideas

What will happen when electricity from a battery reaches the object?

Heating Technician

Heating technicians put heating machines in buildings. They check parts of the machines and fix them. They make sure all rooms in a building get enough heat.

Large pipes sometimes carry heat through buildings. The technician checks the air temperature in the pipes. If the air is too cool or too warm, the worker fixes the problem.

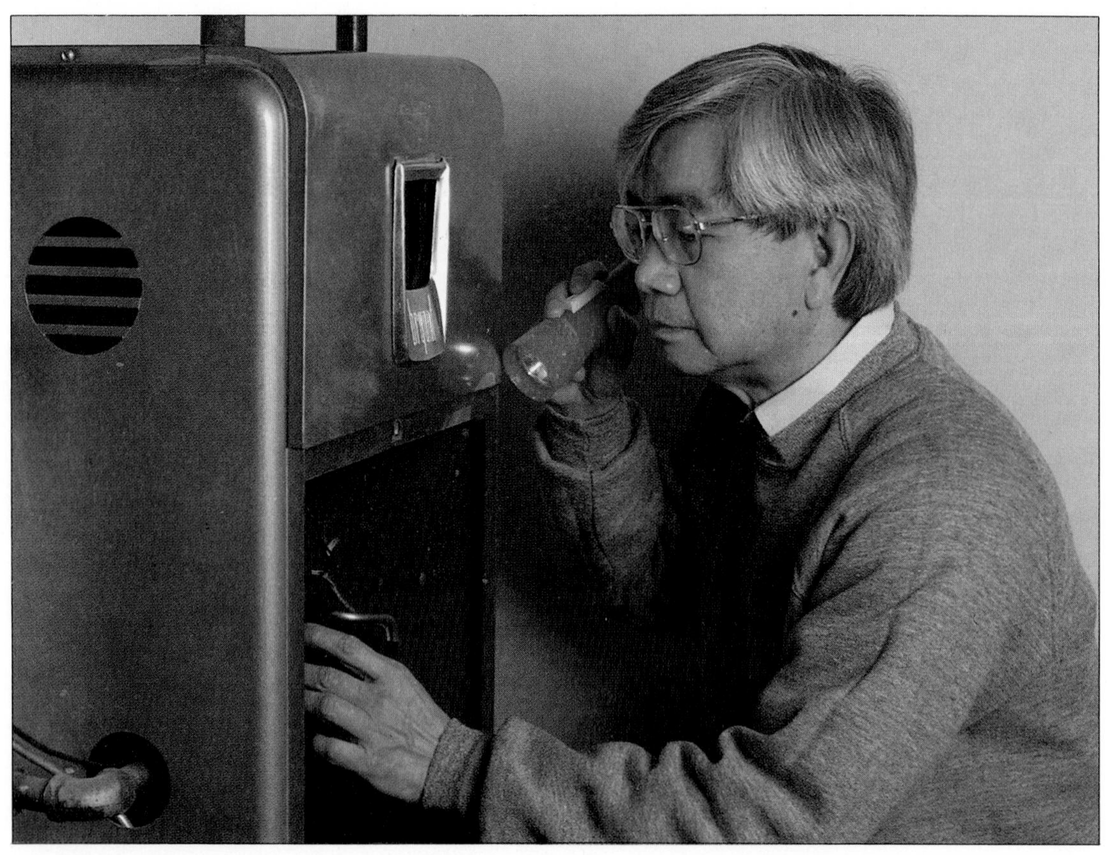

A Mirror

How does a mirror show what is in front of it?

glass surface

shiny silver coating

A mirror is a flat, glass surface. Behind the glass is a thin layer of shiny, silver coating. When you stand in front of a mirror, light moves from you, through the glass, to the shiny layer. As light hits the shiny layer behind the glass, it bounces straight back to you.
Then you see yourself!

Unit 2 Review

Answer the Questions

1. What are three kinds of matter?
2. How does each machine make work easier?

3. What gives off heat?
4. How does light move?
5. How do machines help people?
6. What is a magnet?

Study the Picture

What happened to the liquid matter in the picture?

What to Do

1. Make a collection of solid objects. Group the objects in three different ways. Draw a picture of your collection. Tell your class about it.
2. Collect objects that make different sounds. Make up a story using the sounds. Tell the story to your family and use the objects to make the sounds.
3. Make up a new machine. Draw a picture of it. Tell how your machine could help make work easier.

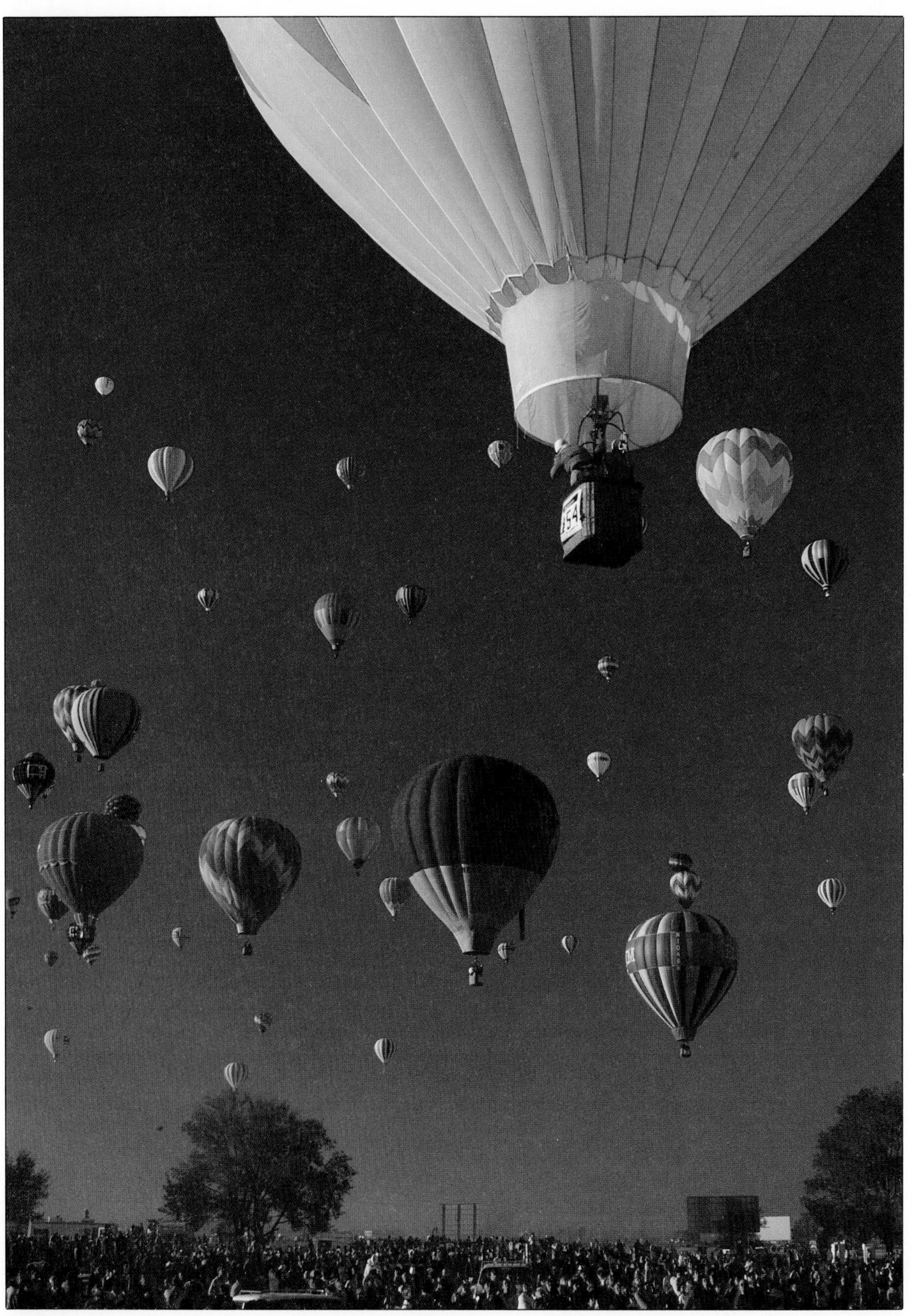

Unit 3

Earth Science

Have you ever seen balloons like these? The picture shows hot-air balloons. The balloons float because the hot air inside the balloons is lighter than the air around the balloons. Scientists use hot-air balloons to carry machines that measure weather. Draw a picture of a colorful hot-air balloon.

Chapter 7 Water and Air
Chapter 8 Changes in Weather
Chapter 9 The Sun and Other Stars

Chapter 7

Water and Air

Air and water are all around you. What might the air and water feel like here?

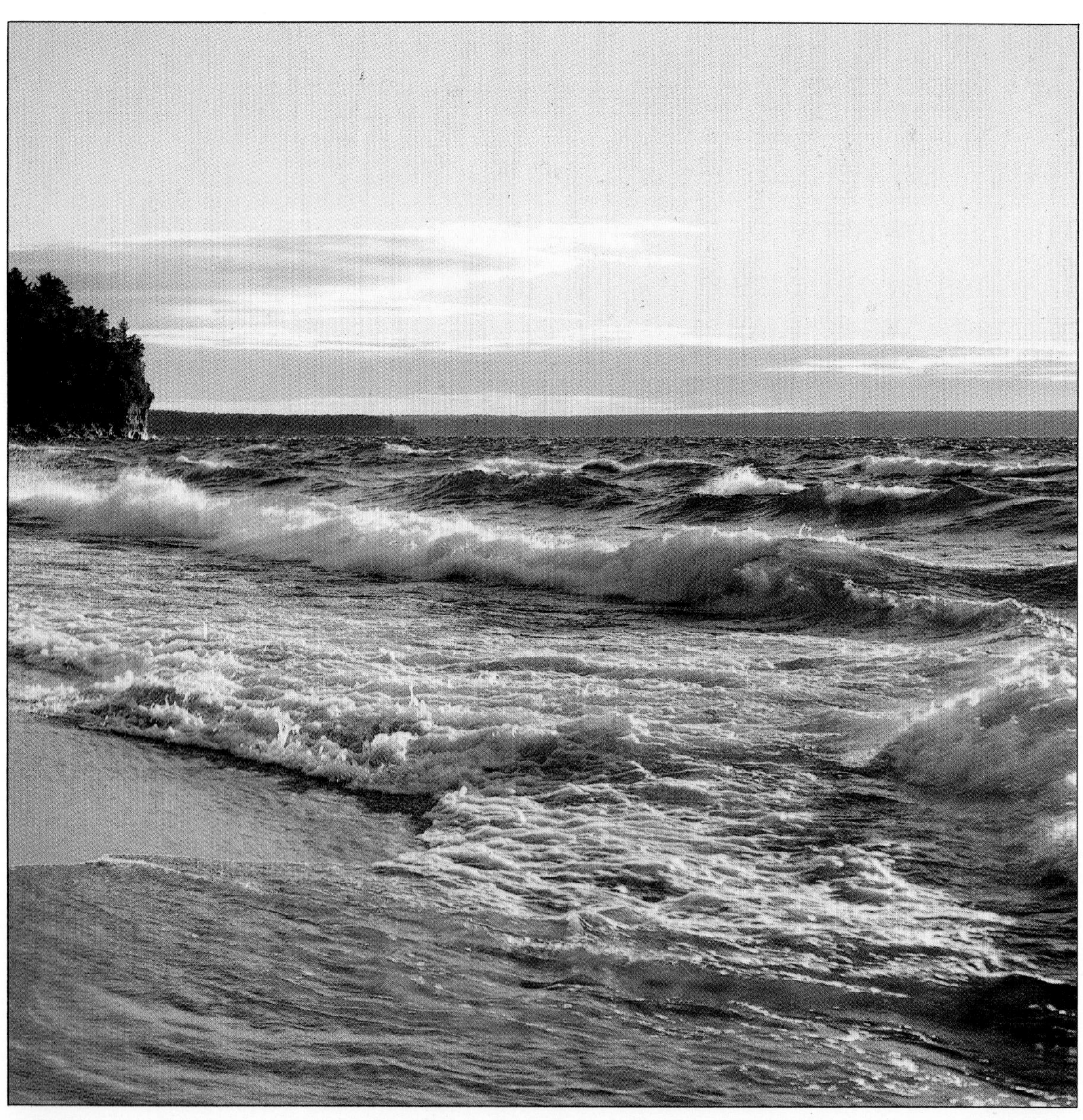

Starting the Chapter

Did you know that you can sometimes see air in water? Find out how. Then read on to learn more about water and air.

Observing the Air in Water

Look at the small cup of water your teacher will give you. Observe it for a few minutes. Watch bubbles come to the top of the water. Where do the bubbles come from? What is inside the bubbles? Where do the bubbles go?

Lesson 1 Where Do You Find Fresh Water?

Water that has very little salt is called fresh water. People drink fresh water. You find fresh water in ponds, streams, and rivers. Most lakes have fresh water. You can also find fresh water under the ground.

Most fresh water comes from rain and melting snow and ice. What will happen to the snow in this river?

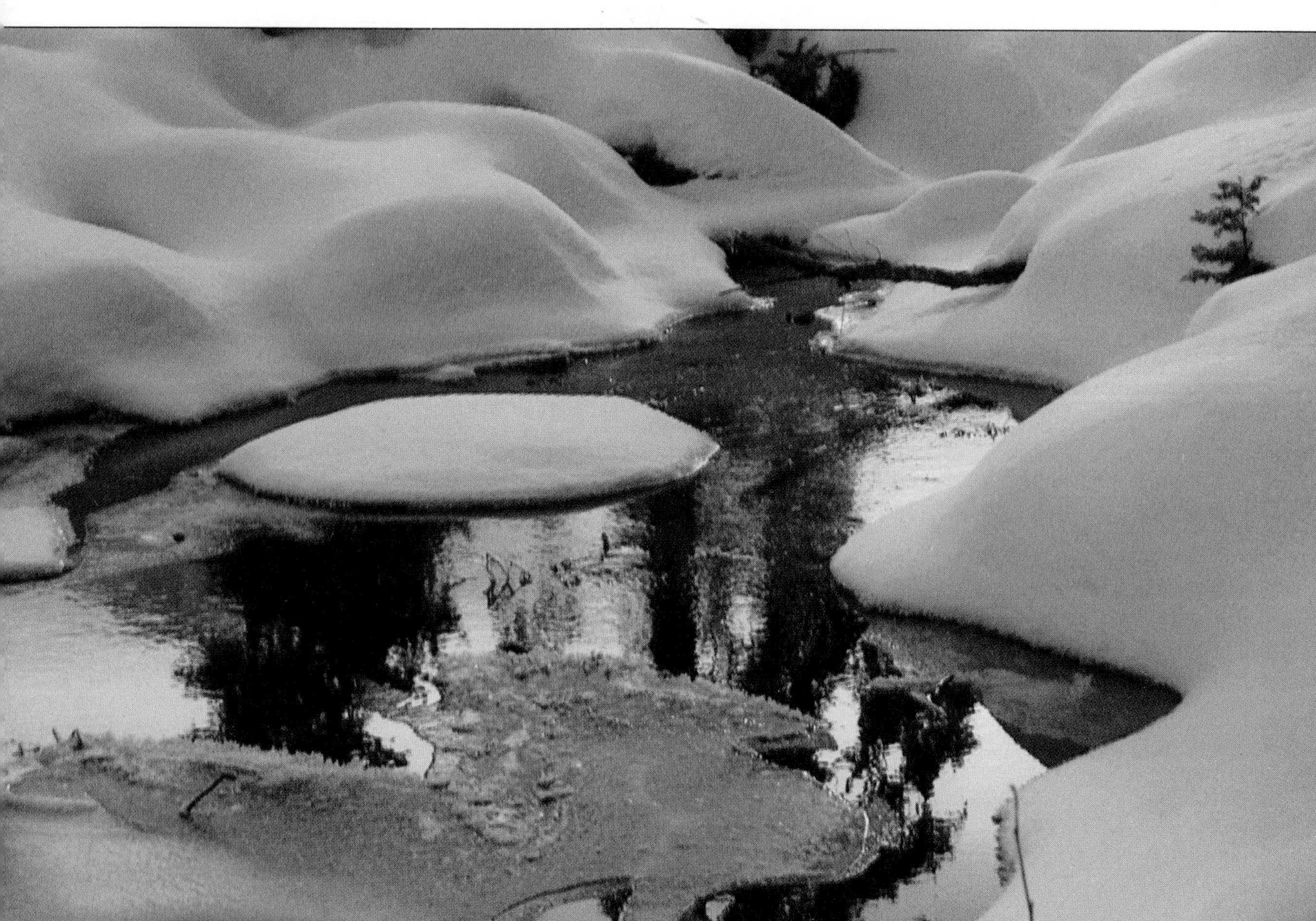

Some water soaks into the ground. It comes from rain, snow, rivers, and lakes. The water fills tiny spaces in rocks and soil in the ground. The water is called **groundwater.**

Most groundwater goes into rivers and oceans. People also build wells to use groundwater. How will the children use the water from this well?

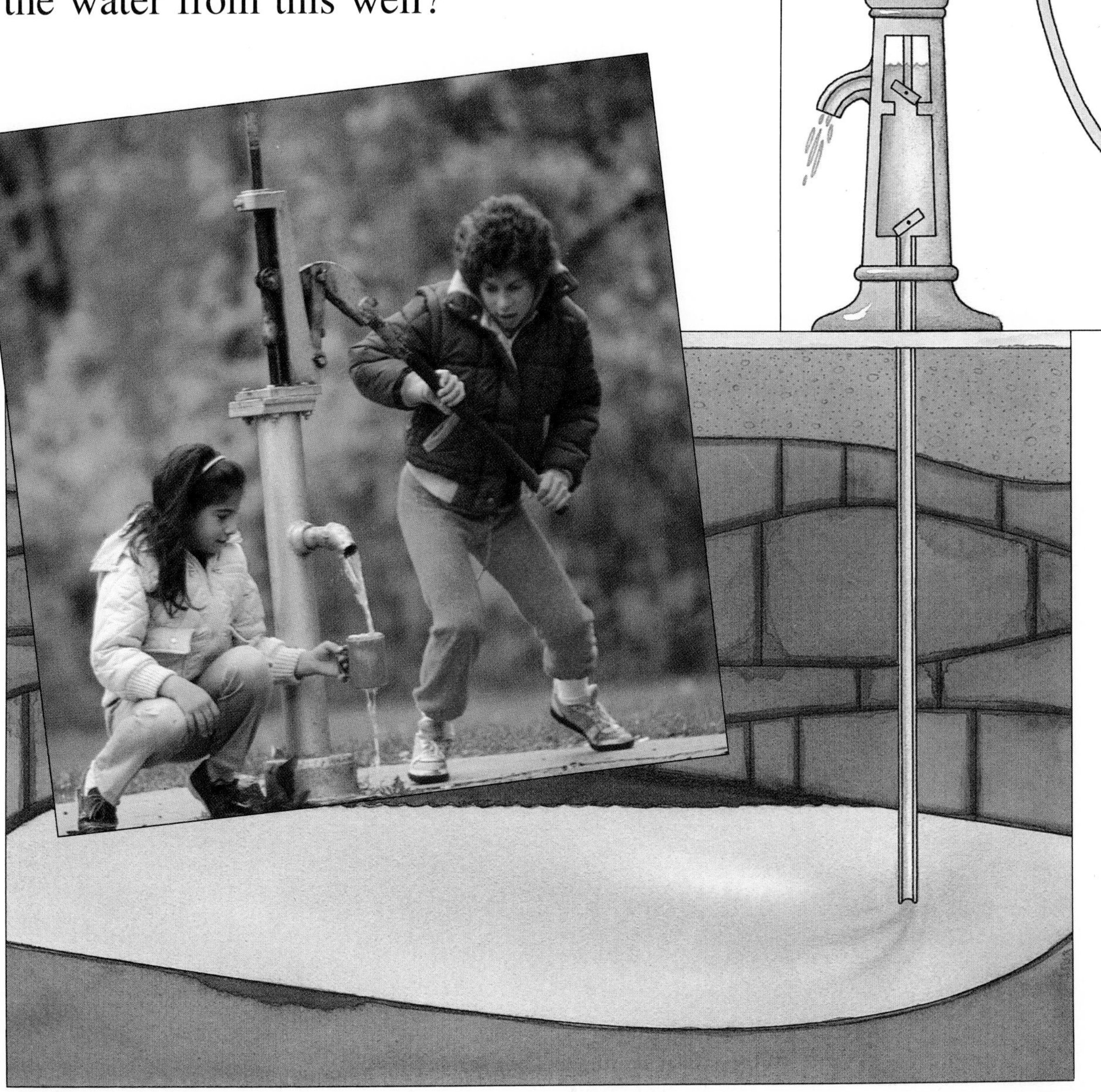

Sometimes people change parts of a river. They build a **dam** across a river. The dam stops the river from moving. The dam keeps water behind it. The water makes a lake. Find the dam in the picture. Where is the lake?

Lesson Review

1. Where can fresh water be found?
2. What is groundwater?

EARTH SCIENCE

Find Out

Where can you find fresh water near where you live?

Observing a Groundwater Well Model

Follow the Directions

1. Make a model of a groundwater well.
2. Place a paper tube in a can.
2. Pour gravel around the tube the way the picture shows.
3. Pour sand on top of the gravel.
4. Pour in water to cover the gravel and the sand.
5. Observe what happens inside the tube.

Tell What You Learned

Tell what happened to the water inside the tube. Tell what happens to groundwater when there is no rainfall.

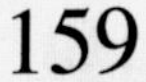

Lesson 2 What Are Oceans Like?

Oceans cover most of the earth. People cannot drink ocean water because it is salty. Ocean water is called **salt water.**

Ocean water is very, very deep in some places. The deep parts of oceans have cold water. Ocean water is not very deep in other places. The sun warms the ocean water near the top.

Some places at the bottom of oceans are flat. Some places have mountains. Find the land in the picture. The land is the tops of mountains.

Wind can make the water in oceans move. Wind blows across oceans and makes waves. Strong winds make big waves. When the wind does not blow as much, waves are smaller.

What is another way ocean water can move? It can move high up on the land. In the same day, the water near the land can be very low.

Look at the two pictures. One shows the ocean in the morning. The second picture shows the same place later in the day. How are the two pictures different?

Many kinds of fish and other living things live in oceans. You can often see colorful fish in oceans. What ocean life do you see in the picture?

Lesson Review

1. What is the bottom of the ocean like?
2. What different ways can ocean water move?

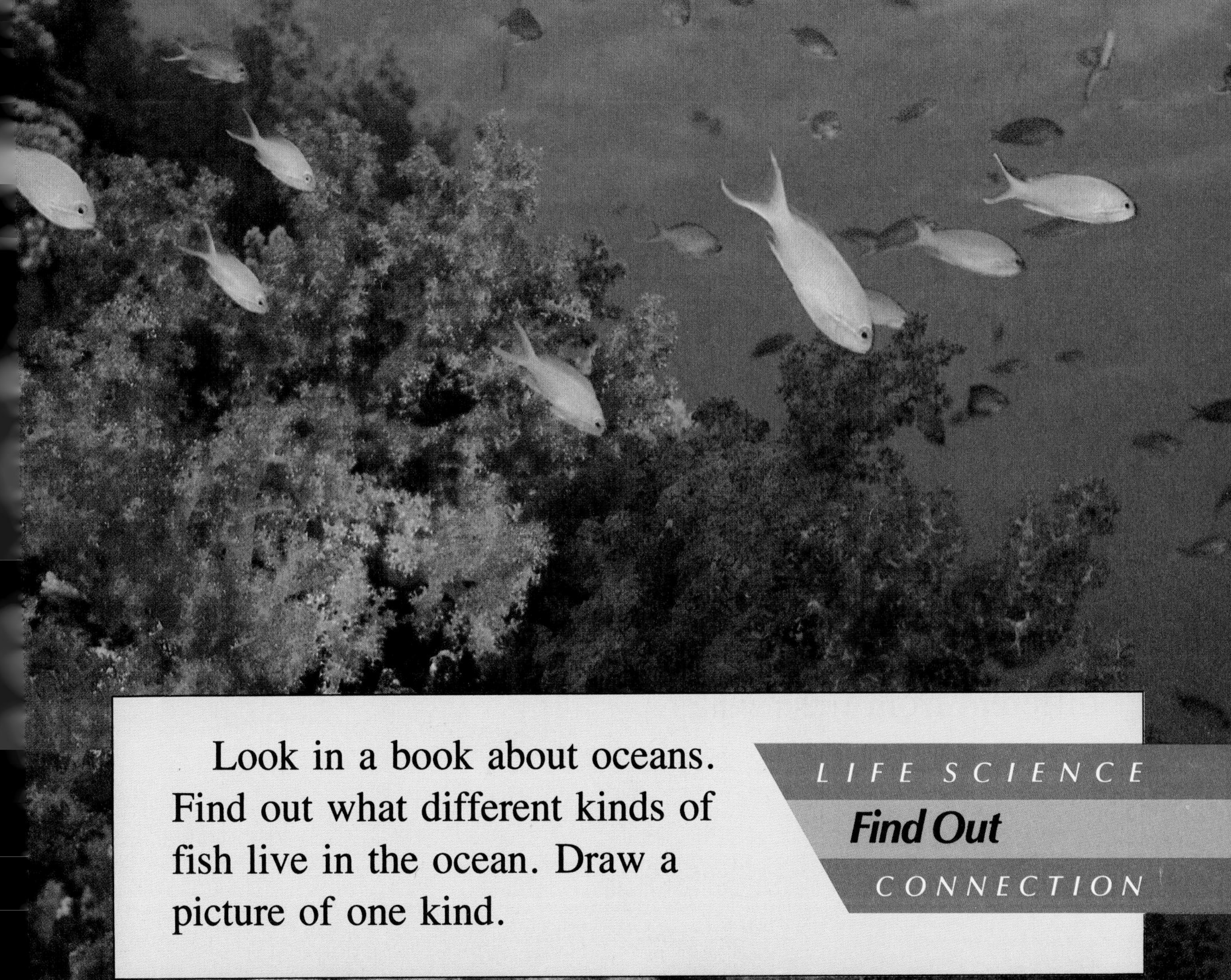

Look in a book about oceans. Find out what different kinds of fish live in the ocean. Draw a picture of one kind.

LIFE SCIENCE
Find Out
CONNECTION

Observing Differences in Water

Follow the Directions

1. Pour some bottled water into a dish.
2. Mix up some salt water. Use one spoonful of salt and one cup of warm water.
3. Pour some of the salt water into a dish.
4. Leave the dishes in a warm place for a few days.
5. Observe and feel the bottom of each dish.

Tell What You Learned

Tell what you observed and felt on the bottom of each dish. Tell how ocean water tastes different from fresh water.

Studying Oceans

Jacques Cousteau studies oceans and living things in oceans. He writes books and makes movies that teach people about oceans.

Jacques Cousteau found ways for people to stay under water for a long time to study the ocean. He helped invent an underwater air tank, a diving station, and an oceancraft.

What Do You Think?

How can staying underwater for a long time help people study the ocean?

Lesson 3 Why Is Clean Water Important?

Living things need clean water to stay alive and healthy. Fish and plants that live in water can die if the water is very dirty, or **polluted.**

People need clean water. People use water for cooking and drinking. They use water for taking baths and for washing clothes. How do these people use water for fun?

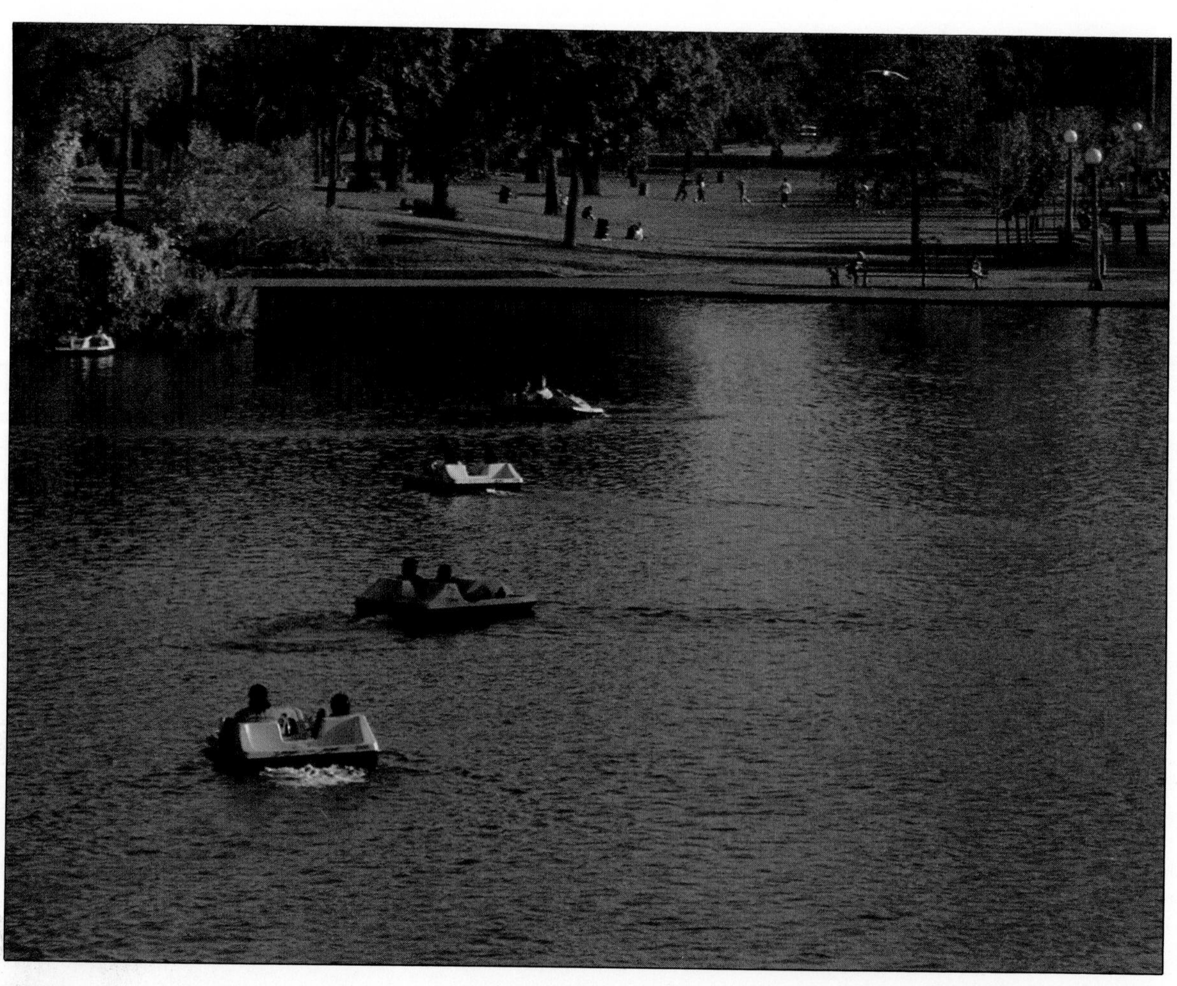

Some people have jobs using boats on water. They use the boats for fishing. They use the boats to take people and things from place to place.

Some of the food people eat comes from oceans, lakes, and rivers. What foods from water do you like to eat?

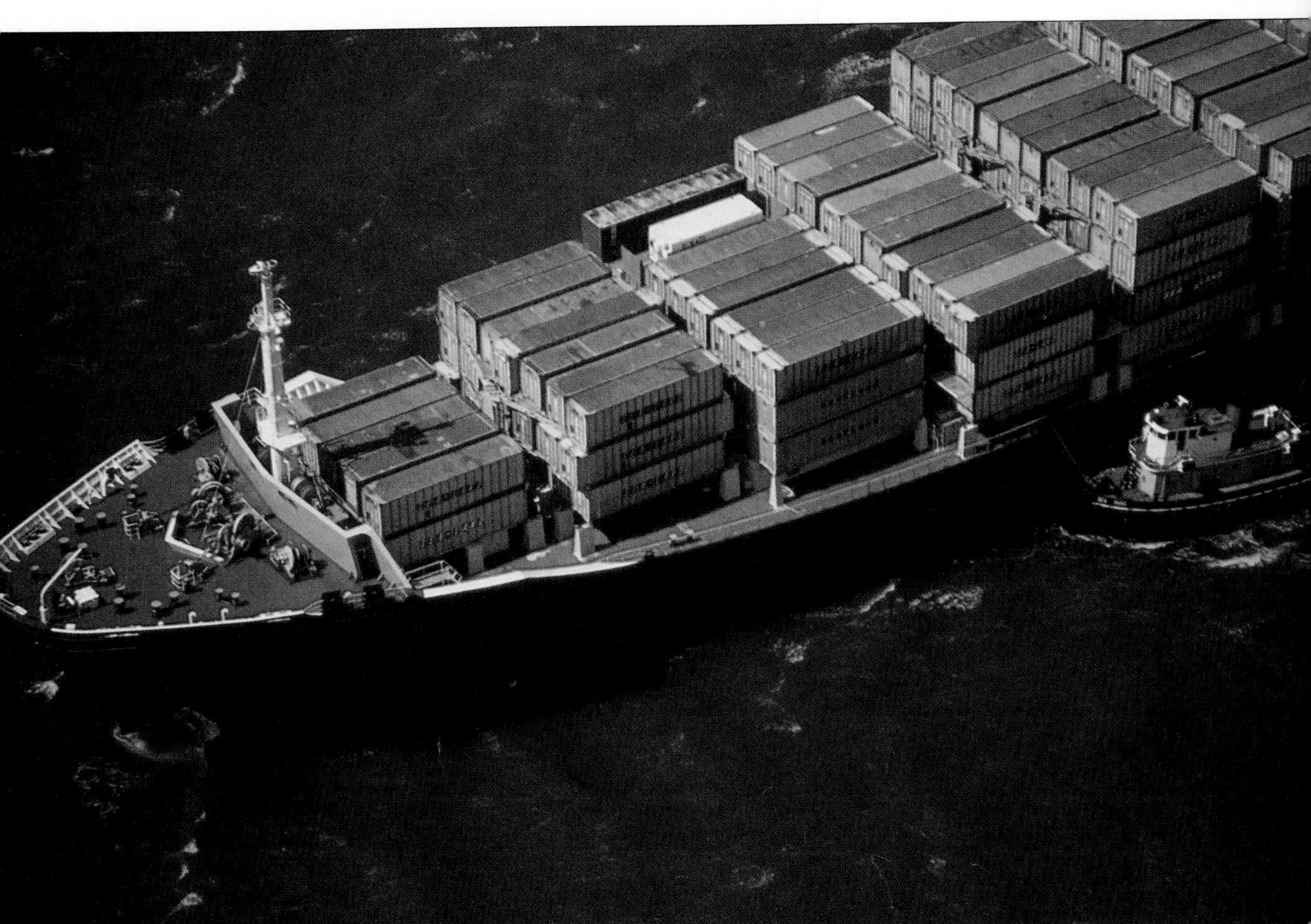

Polluted water can harm people. It has germs that make people and animals sick. It might have harmful wastes from a **factory.** Oil spilled from a ship might pollute the water.

People should not use polluted water. They should not swim or fish in it. People should not eat fish from polluted water.

People can help keep rivers and lakes clean. Trash and garbage must not be thrown into water. People can also try not to use more clean water than they need. How is this boy helping keep water clean?

Lesson Review

1. What do people need clean water for?
2. How can polluted water harm living things?

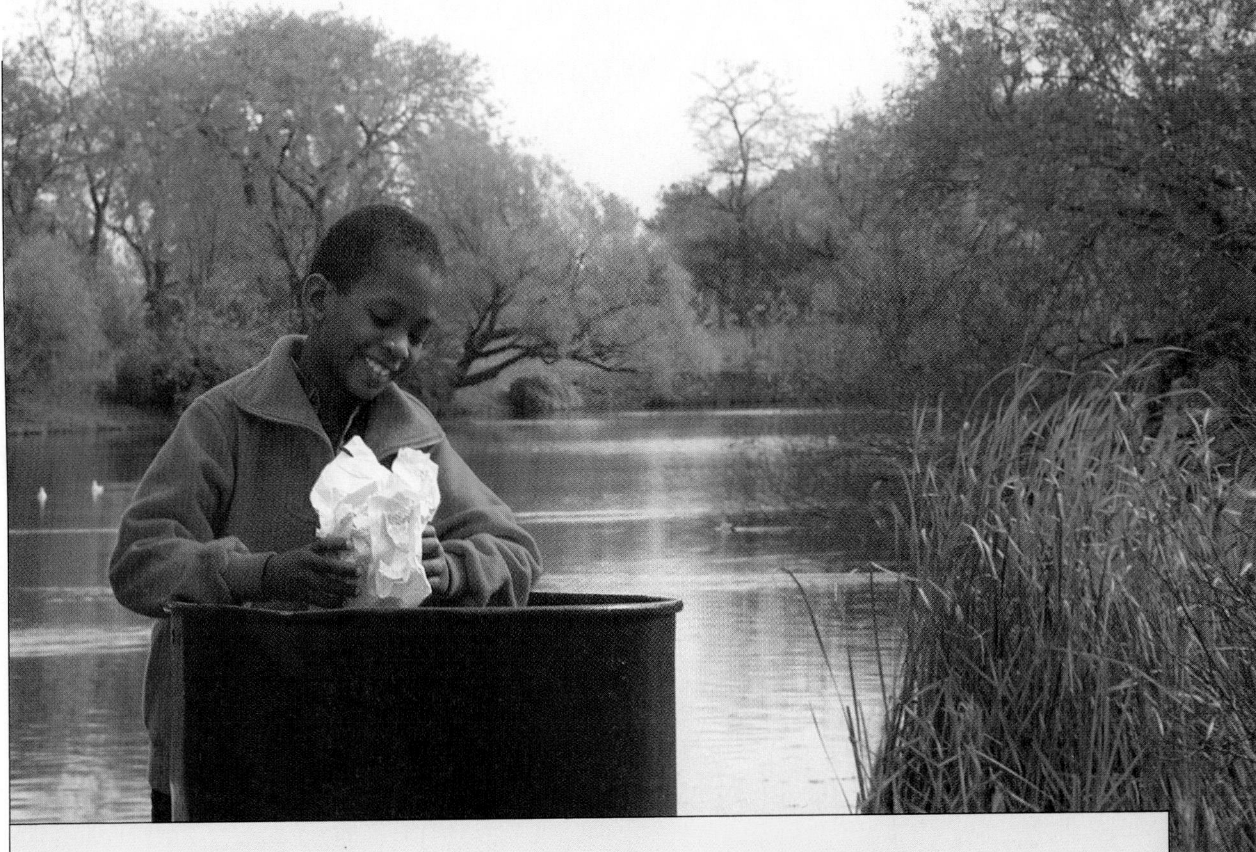

EARTH SCIENCE

Find Out

Draw a picture to show how you help keep water clean.

Lesson 4 What Is Air Like?

Air is all around you and all around the earth. Air is made of gases you cannot see. Air has water vapor in it. Air can also have dust, smoke, and tiny bits of dirt. The temperature of air can change. It can feel cold, warm, or hot.

Sometimes you can feel air moving. Hold your hand close to your mouth and blow. You can feel air moving from your mouth. What shows that air is moving here?

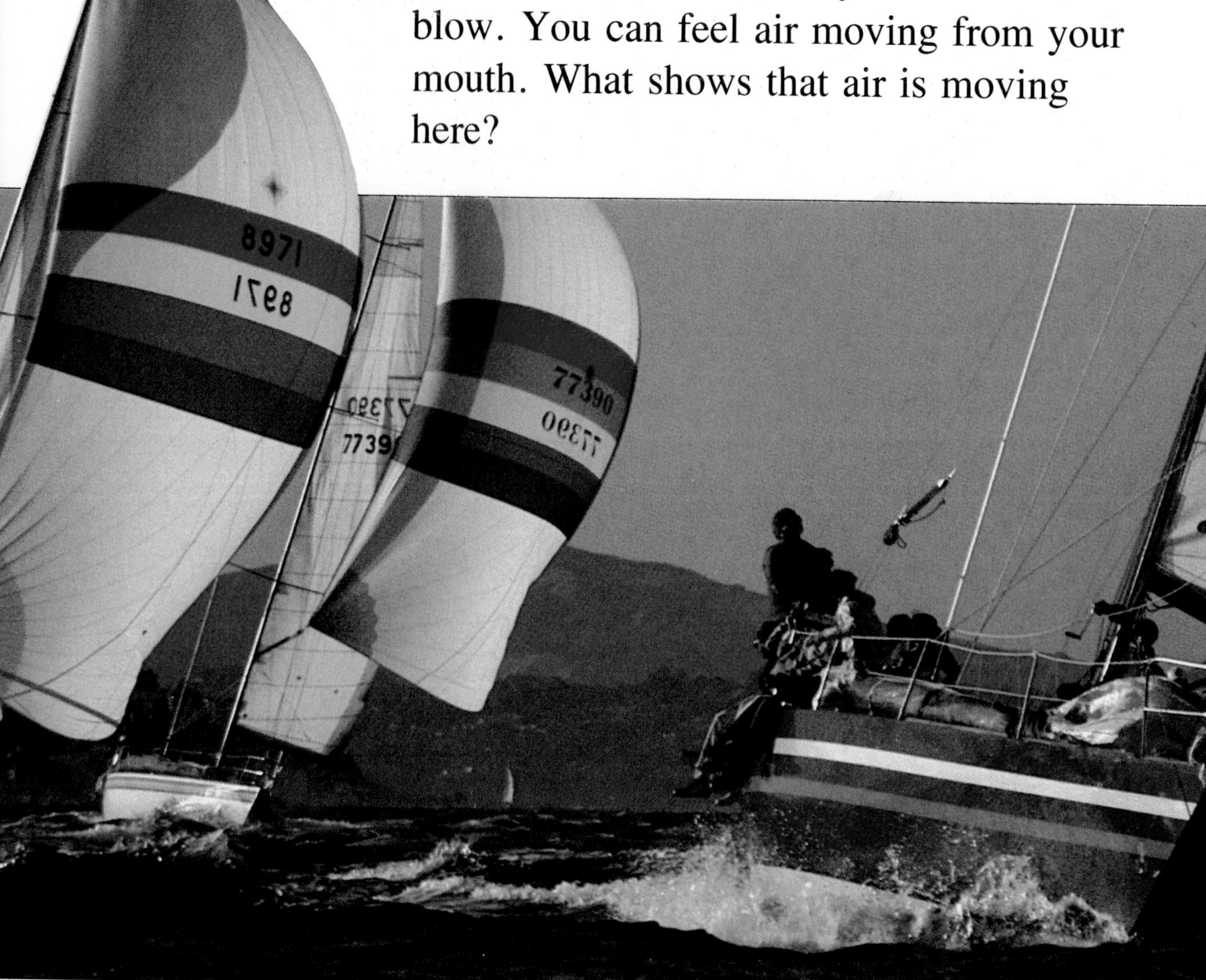

Wind is moving air. Sailboats need wind to move. Kites need wind to fly. You can feel air move. What other things does wind move?

Lesson Review

1. What can air have in it?
2. What is wind?

PHYSICAL SCIENCE

Find Out

What sounds can you hear when air is moving? Write a story about the sounds.

Lesson 5 Why Is Clean Air Important?

Living things need air to stay alive. Plants need clean air to grow. People need clean air to breathe.

The polluted air in the picture is very dirty. The air has dust, dirt, and smoke from cars and factories.

Polluted air can make people sick. It can harm eyes and lungs. It can harm plants and animals.

People can help keep air clean. Factories can keep some dirt out of smoke. People can make cars, trucks, and buses that make less smoke and harmful gases. People can use cars less. How are these children keeping the air clean?

Lesson Review

1. Why do living things need clean air?
2. How can people help keep air clean?

EARTH SCIENCE

Find Out

How can you tell when the air is polluted?

Measuring Rainfall and Making a Pie Graph

How much rain fell on each day?

1. Look at the pictures of the three rain gauges. Notice that 4 centimeters of rain fell on Tuesday. Write down how much rain fell on Wednesday and Thursday. Add the numbers to find out how much rain fell in three days.

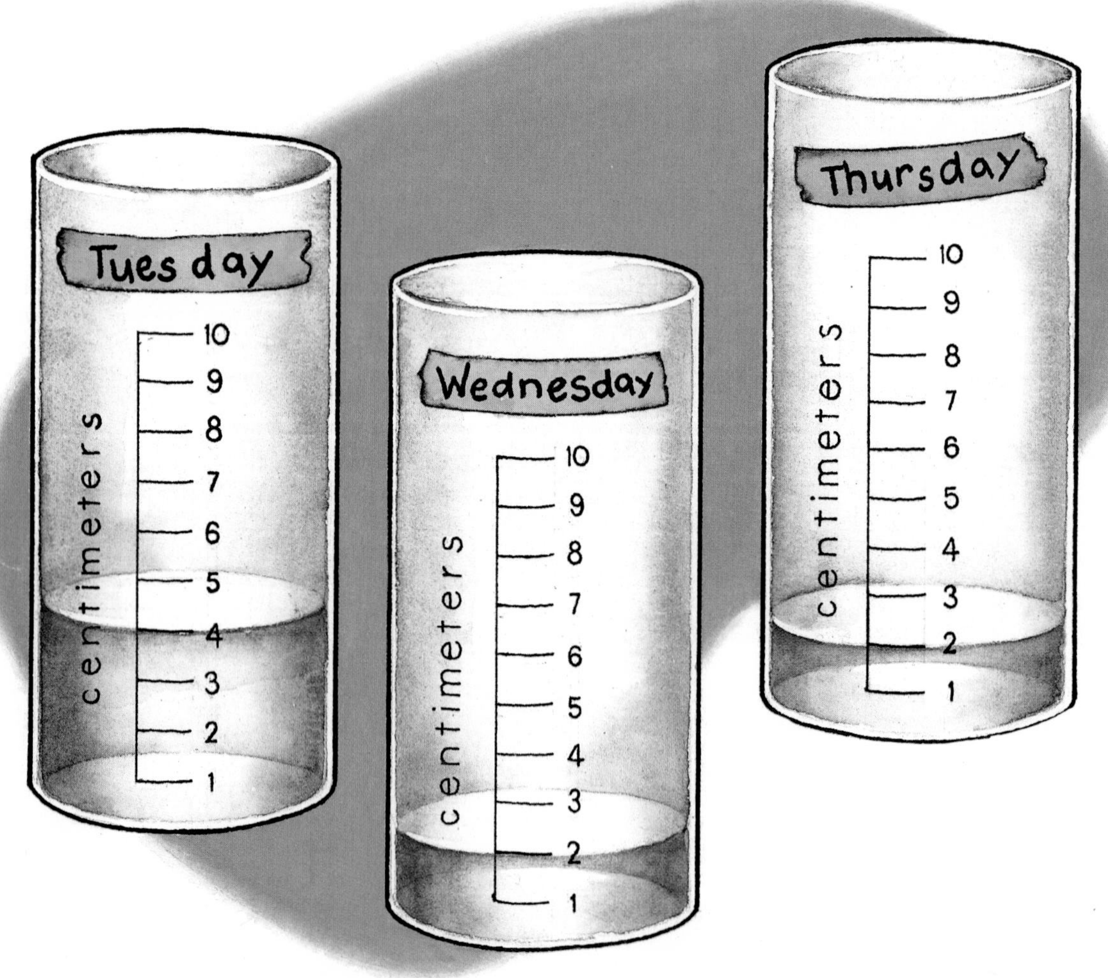

2. Draw a graph like this one. The circle stands for the amount of rain that fell in three days. Write the missing numbers on your graph.

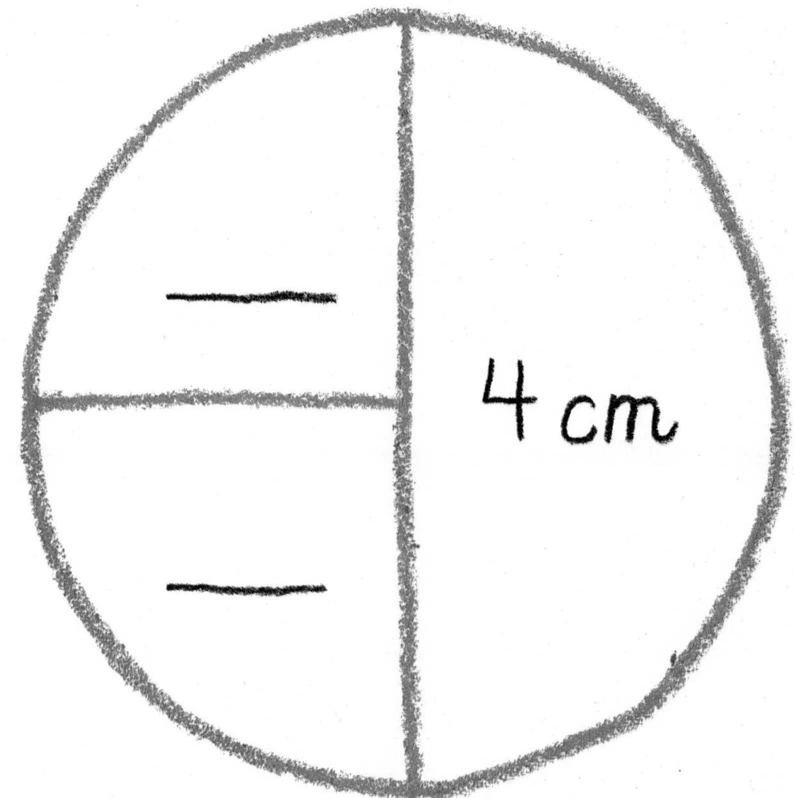

3. How much rain fell on Tuesday? How much rain fell in the three days?

Chapter 7 Review

Review Chapter Ideas

1. Look at the picture. Tell where the fresh water comes from.
2. Tell three things about an ocean.
3. Tell ways people use water.
4. Explain what polluted water can do to living things.
5. Tell three things about the air around you.
6. Explain how polluted air can be harmful.

Review Science Words

Match the words and the pictures.

1. groundwater
2. dam
3. polluted

a.

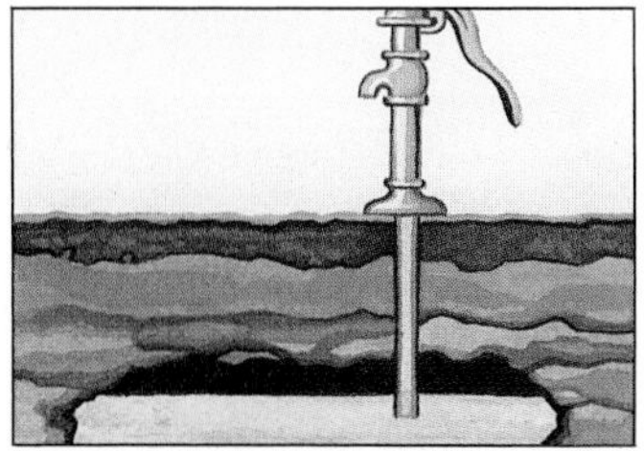

b.

c.

Tell what the words mean.

4. factory
5. salt water

Use Science Ideas

Look at the picture. Tell whether a person can breathe when under water. Explain your answer.

Chapter 8

Changes in Weather

Perhaps you have seen weather like this.
What might you see flash in the sky?
What might you hear?

Starting the Chapter

Suppose you want to play outside, but it is raining. You might wonder if it will rain all day. You can find out about the weather from a weather map. Then read more about ways weather can change.

TRY THIS

Observing a Weather Map

Look at this weather map. Notice the signs for different kinds of weather. Which signs mean clouds and rain? Which sign shows sunny weather?

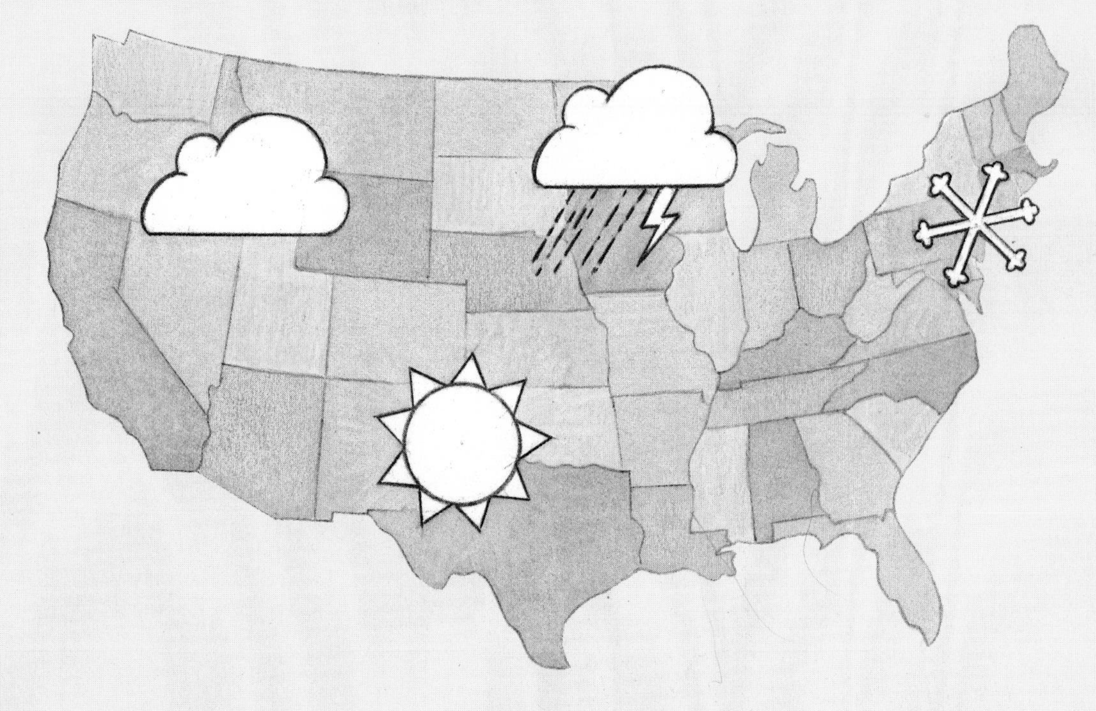

Lesson 1 How Can Weather Change?

What did the air feel like when you left your home this morning? Do you think the weather has changed since then? Weather can change all through the day. It can change from hot to cool and from sunny to cloudy.

Look at the weather in the pictures. First the day was sunny and dry. Then the wind came. The weather became windy and cool.

Air temperature can change. You use a thermometer to measure changes in air temperature. The temperature goes up as the air gets warmer. The temperature goes down as the air gets cooler. Is the temperature shown below warm or cool?

Wind can change. It can blow hard. It can blow gently. Wind can also change direction. This **wind vane** points in the direction the wind comes from.

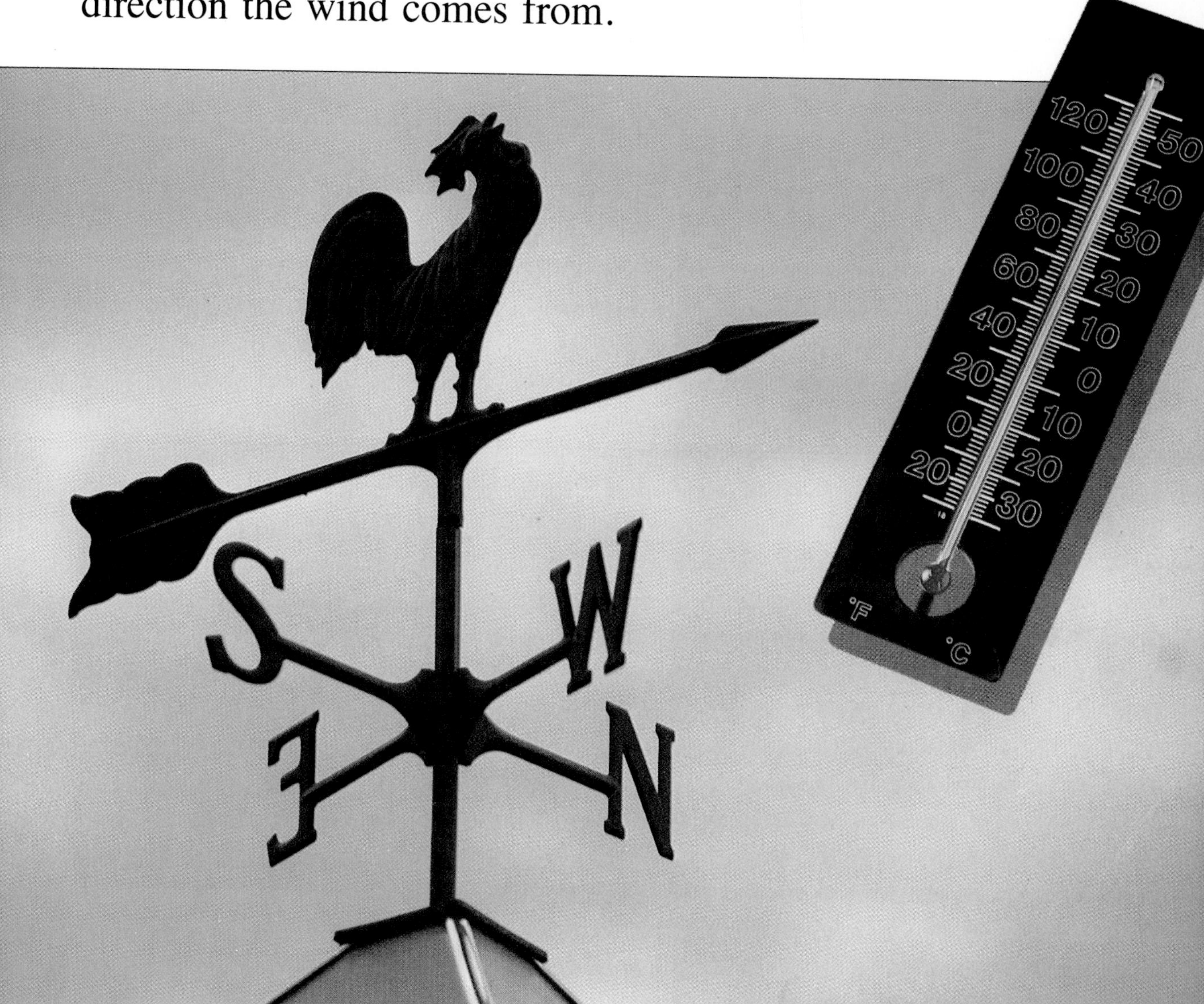

The weather changes through the year. In many places, the four **seasons** have different weather. Spring often has rain and warm temperatures. Summer can have very hot temperatures. The air can be wet or dry.

Fall usually has cool air. Rain might turn to snow in late fall. Winter often has cold and snowy weather. What season does each picture show?

In many places of the world, the weather does not change very much in different seasons. In many places, the air stays warm most of the year.

Many places stay cool most of the year. High on this mountain, the snow stays all through the year. What season does this weather remind you of?

How do living things change in different seasons? In spring, many plants get new leaves. Many animals have babies. What baby animals do you see here? Flowers and fruits often grow in summer and fall. In winter, many plants do not grow. Some animals hibernate.

Lesson Review

1. In what ways can weather change?
2. What measures air temperature and what shows wind direction?

LIFE SCIENCE
Find Out
CONNECTION

How do living things change during the seasons where you live?

Using a Wind Vane

Follow the Directions

1. Make a wind vane like this one.
2. Blow on it from one direction.
3. Blow on it from another direction.
4. Observe how the wind vane moves.

Tell What You Learned

Tell how your wind vane moved. Tell what a wind vane is used for.

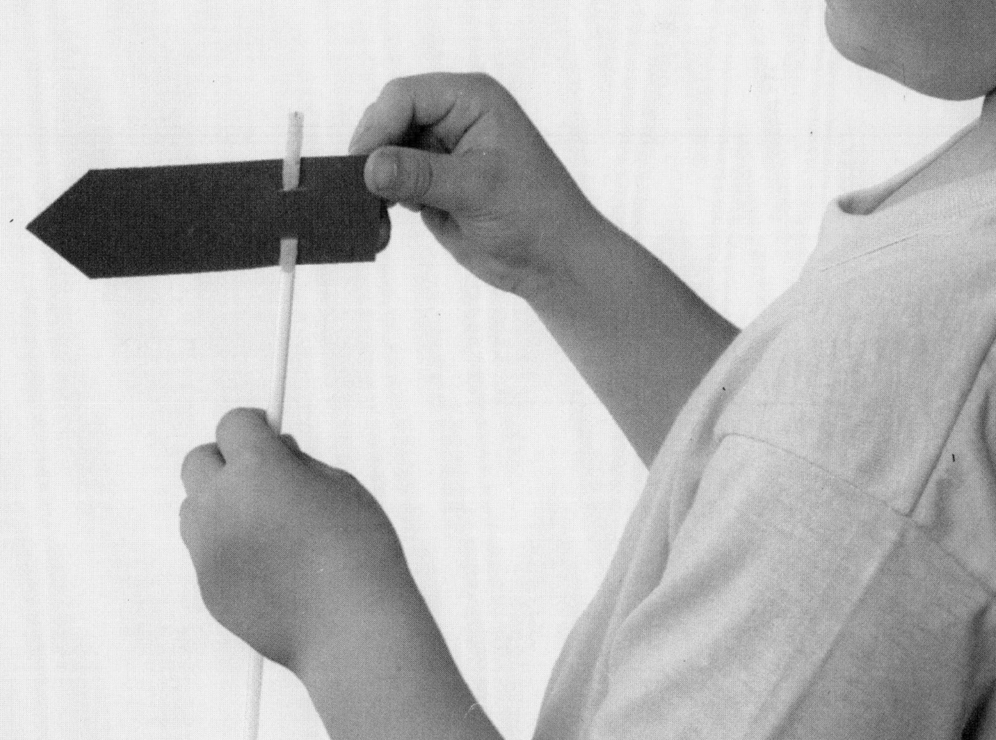

Lesson 2 What Makes Clouds, Rain, and Snow?

Close your eyes and try to picture a cloud. Which one of these clouds does your cloud look like? Some clouds are white and fluffy. Others are thick and dark. However, all clouds are made in the same way.

All clouds are made up of tiny drops of water. The sun heats the water from oceans, rivers, lakes, and ponds. Then the water evaporates.

Cirrus

Cumulus

The water that evaporates changes to water vapor. You cannot see water vapor. Water vapor moves high into the sky. The water vapor gets colder as it moves higher and higher. Very cold water vapor changes into tiny drops of water. The drops of water make clouds like these.

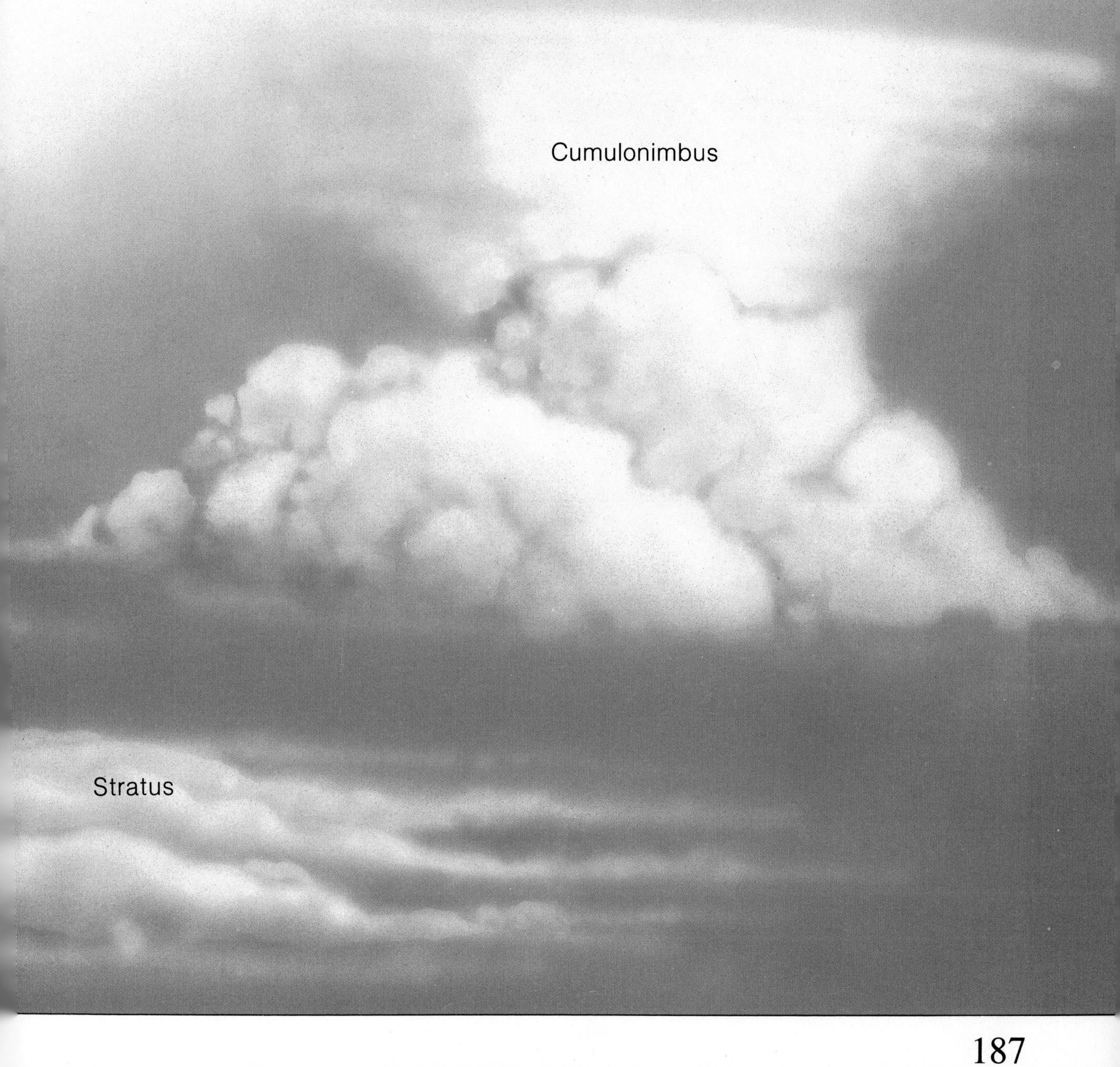

Cumulonimbus

Stratus

The picture shows what happens to some water in clouds. Drops of water in clouds can move and bump into each other. The drops of water join together to make bigger drops. These bigger drops get too heavy to stay in the clouds. They fall from the clouds as rain.

Some clouds are very high in the sky where the air is very cold. These clouds make snow. The clouds have tiny bits of ice and water drops. The bits of ice and water drops bump together and freeze.

The bits of ice get bigger and bigger. When the bits of ice get too heavy, they fall from the cloud as snow. If the air below the cloud is cold, the falling snow does not melt. The snow falls and covers the ground like this.

Lesson Review

1. What makes clouds?
2. How do clouds make rain and snow?

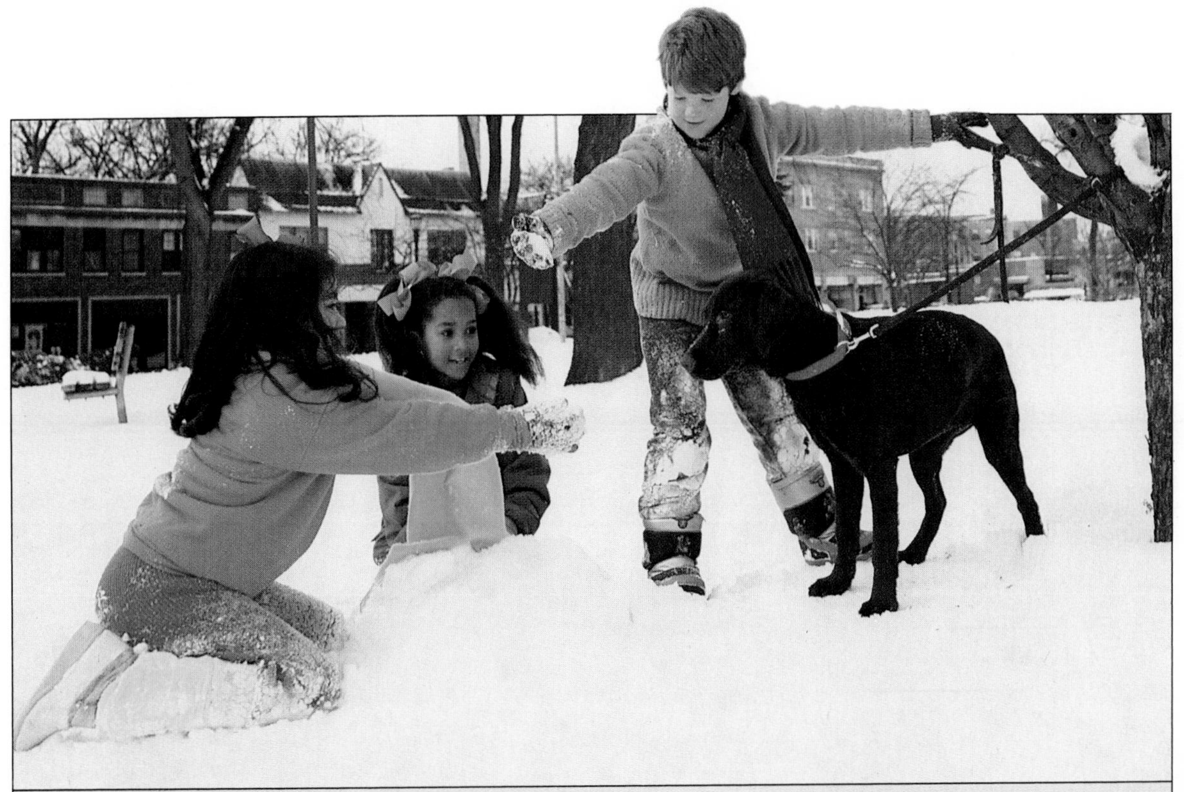

EARTH SCIENCE

Find Out

Look at a weather map in a newspaper. Where is it raining? Where is it snowing?

Finding Out About Water Vapor

Follow the Directions

1. Pour 1/4 cup of water into a plastic bag and close it part way.
2. Blow air into the bag and close it.
3. Put the bag in a sunny place. Look for water drops in the bag.

Tell What You Learned

Tell what part of the bag has water vapor. Explain how water vapor helps make rain.

Reporting Dangerous Weather

Stormy weather is often dangerous weather. Storms with high winds and heavy rain can damage buildings and cause floods. This picture shows what a storm on the earth looks like from far away.

People at the National Weather Service use special machines to study weather. When they find out where a storm is they can warn people.

People can hear storm warnings on the radio and TV. People can prepare for a storm if they know it is coming.

What Do You Think?

How might a weather report help you?

Lesson 3 What Is Weather Like Around the World?

Look at the globe. Find the **North Pole** and the **South Pole** on the globe. These two places have the coldest weather in the world. The line in the middle of the globe shows where the **Equator** is. The weather at the Equator is the warmest weather in the world.

Rain falls almost every day in some places. Very little rain falls in other places.

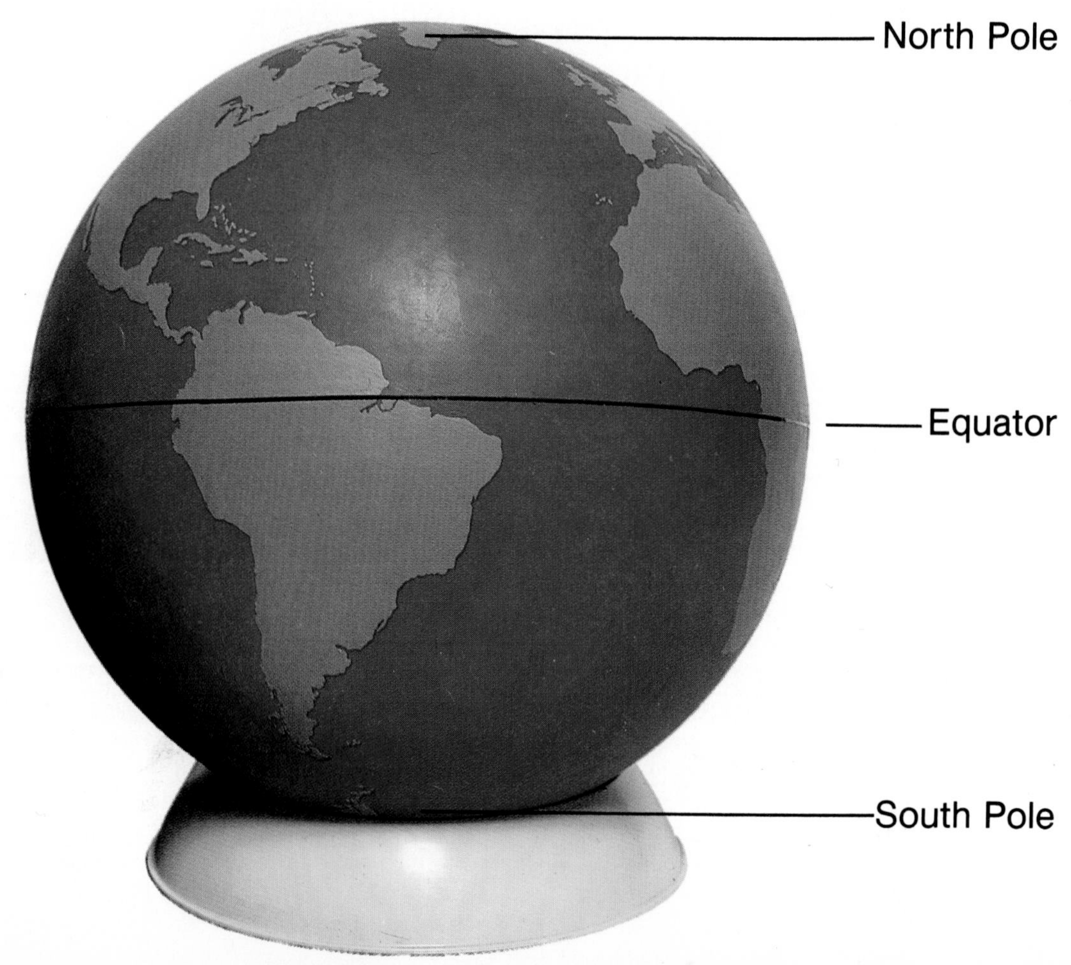

These friends live in towns a long way from each other. Sometimes one town has rain or snow. The other town stays dry. The temperature in each town also might be different. How is the weather different in each picture?

Lesson Review

1. Where is the world's weather coldest and hottest?
2. How might the weather be different in two places?

EARTH SCIENCE

Find Out

Listen to a weather report. Find out where the temperature was the coldest and the hottest in this country.

Measuring Snow and Drawing a Map

What can a map show about snow?

1. The containers show how much snow fell in three different cities. Measure how high the snow comes in each container. Use a metric ruler. Write down how much snow fell in each city.

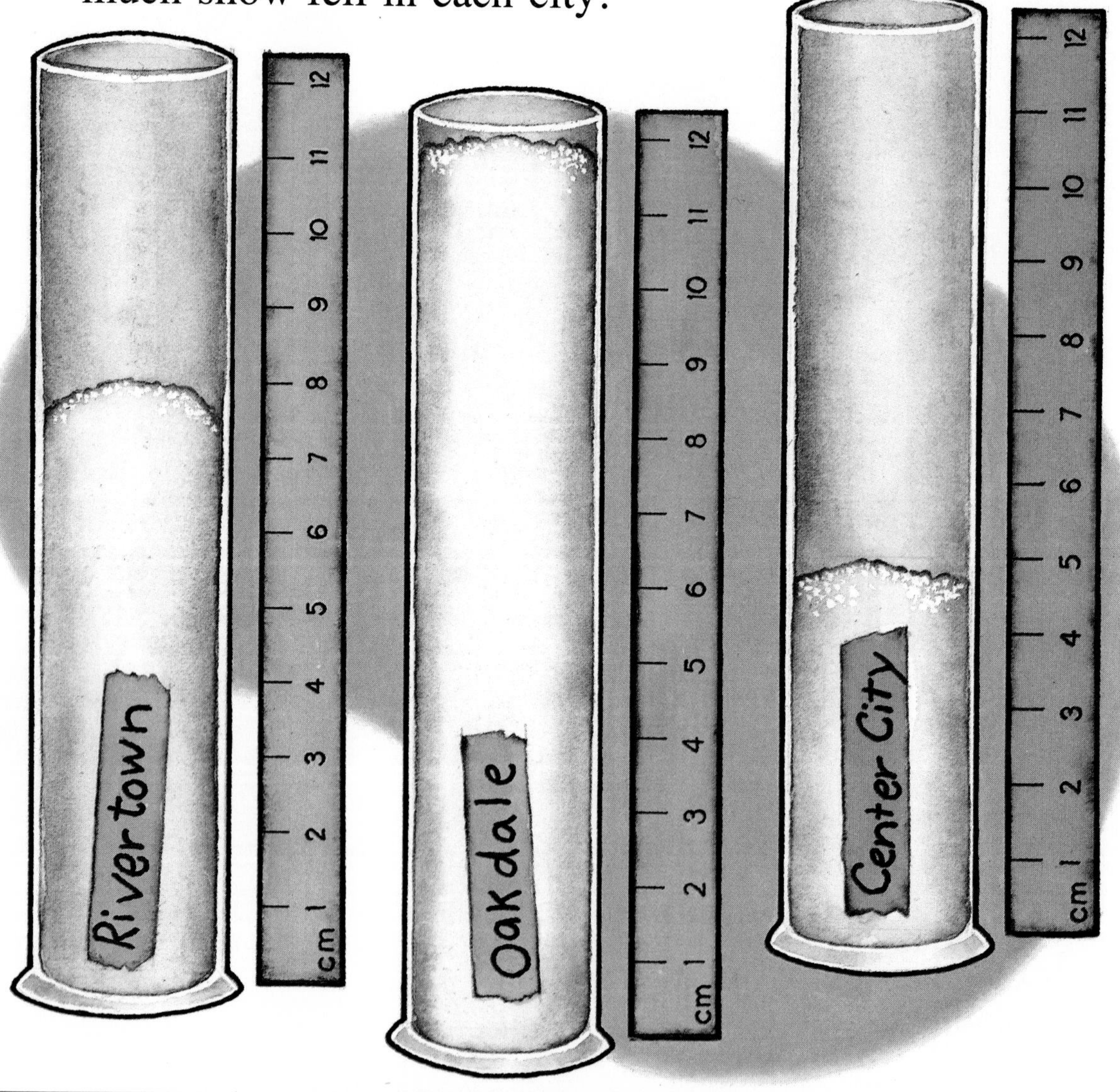

2. Draw a weather map for the three cities. Your map might look something like this one. Show each city on your map. Write on the map how much snow fell on each city.

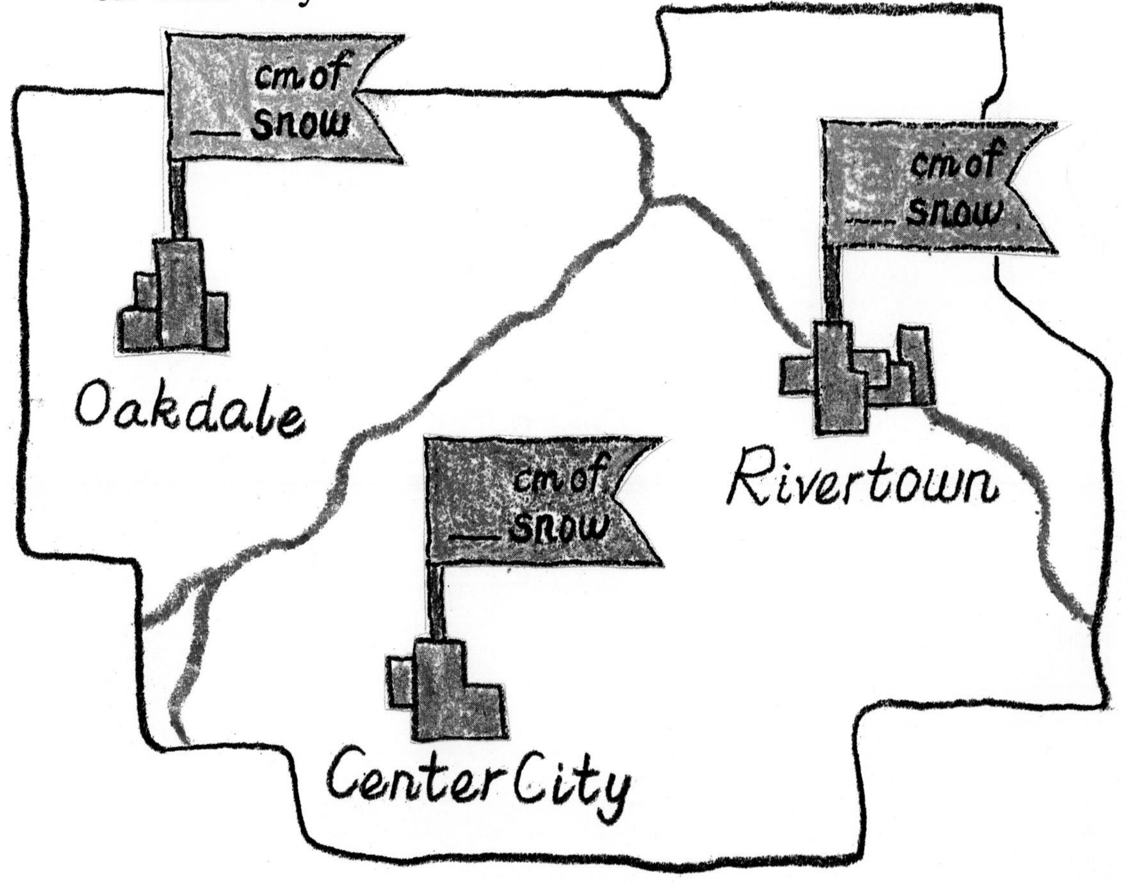

3. Which city had more snow than Rivertown?

Chapter 8 Review

Review Chapter Ideas

1. Explain how weather can change.
2. Tell how to measure temperature and how to find wind direction.
3. Explain what makes clouds.
4. Tell what makes rain fall.
5. Look at the picture. Tell what season will come next.

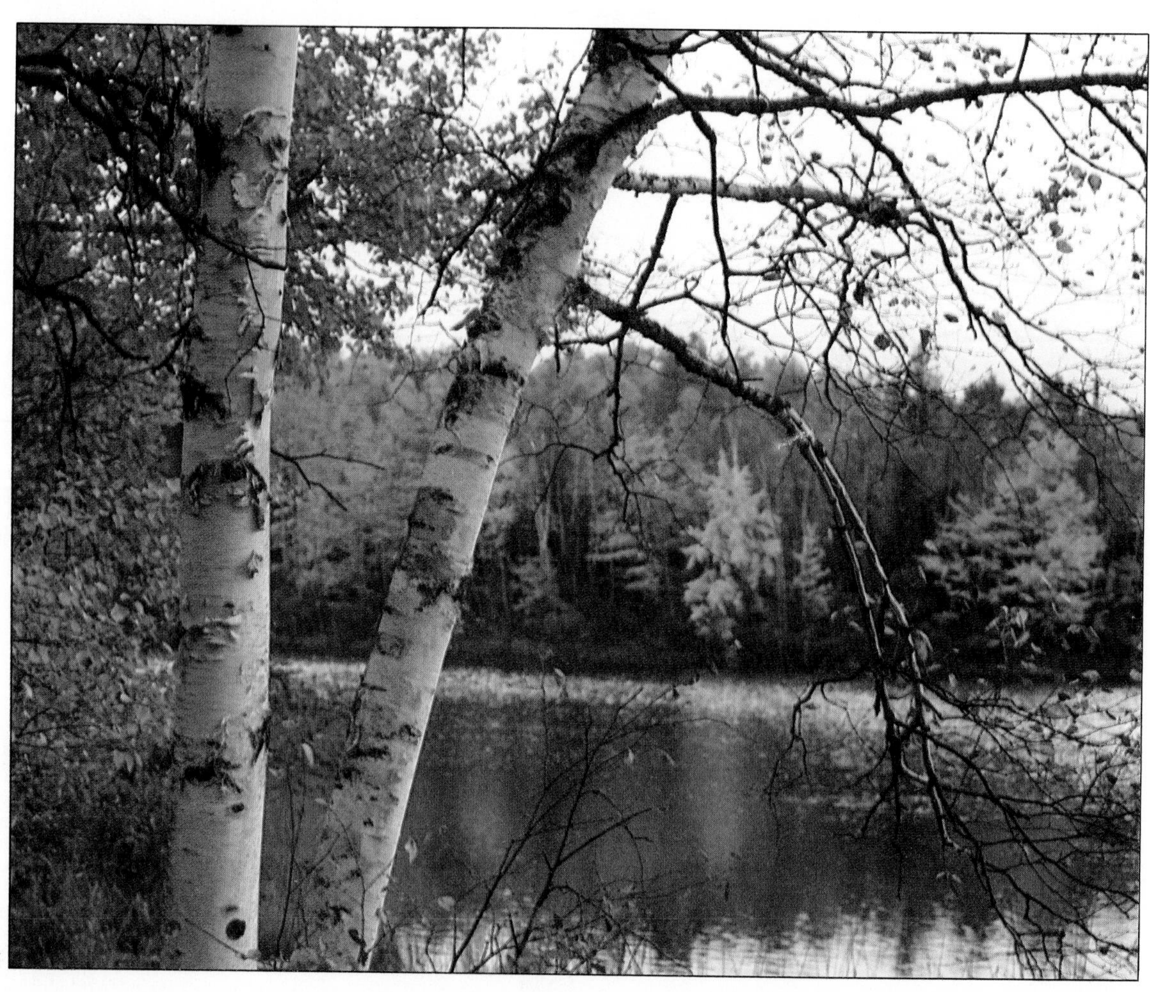

Review Science Words

Match the words and the pictures.

1. wind vane
2. South Pole
3. Equator

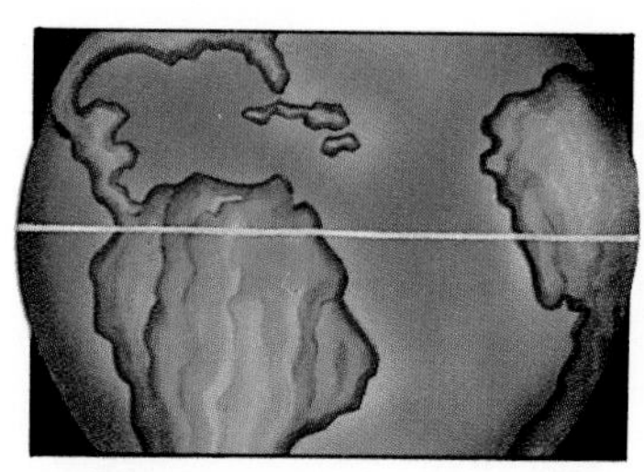

a.

b.

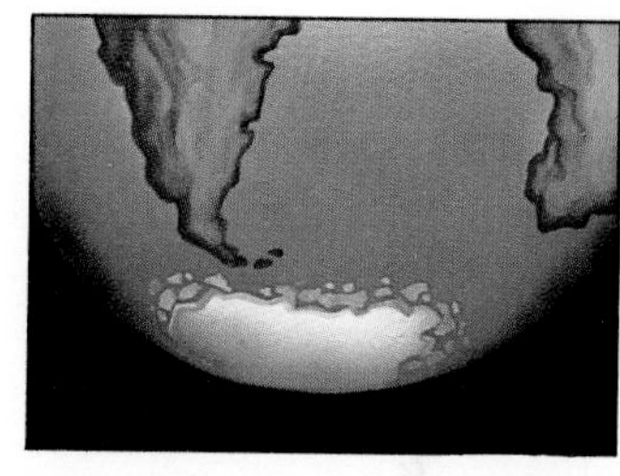

c.

Tell what the words mean.

4. seasons
5. North Pole

Use Science Ideas

Tell how you would dress for this weather.

Chapter 9

The Sun and Other Stars

The sun gives off light. So do the stars. Have you ever seen the sun look like this?

Starting The Chapter

The sun is very big. It is much bigger than the earth. Read below to find out how the sun seems to move. Then read on to learn more about the sun.

TRY THIS

Observing the Sun

Find the sun when you get to school in the morning. On which side of your school is the sun? Find the sun when you leave school in the afternoon. On which side of your school is the sun? Draw two pictures to show how the sun seems to move.

Lesson 1 What Is the Sun?

The **sun** is a star. It is the closest star to the earth. Look at the picture and notice the shape of the sun.

The sun is shaped like a ball. It is not a solid ball. The sun is a ball of glowing gases. What does the sun look like?

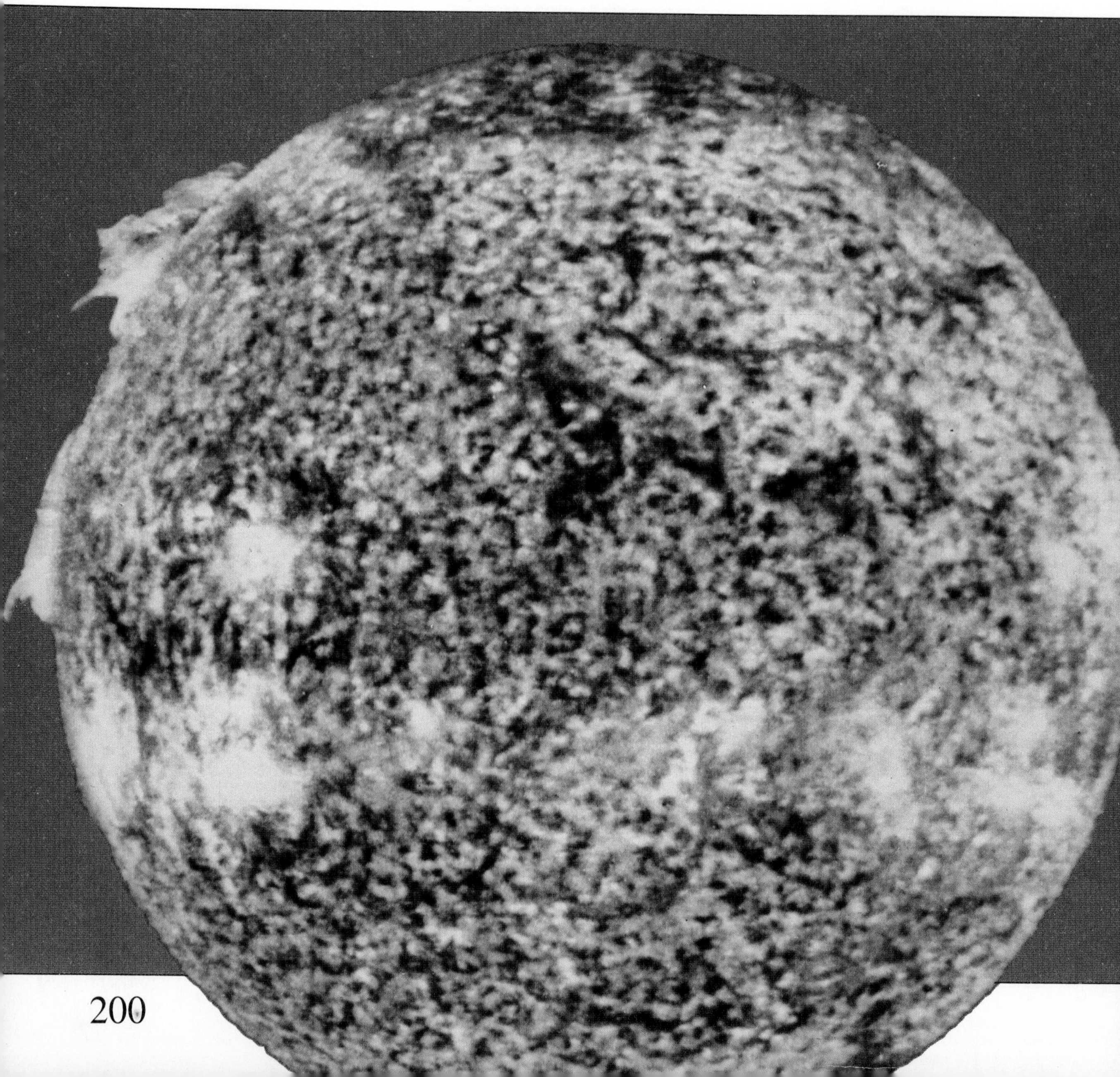

Here you can see the **earth.** Notice how much bigger the sun is than the earth.

How far from the earth is the sun? Imagine you could drive from the earth to the sun. You would drive all day and night. It would take about 193 years to get to the sun.

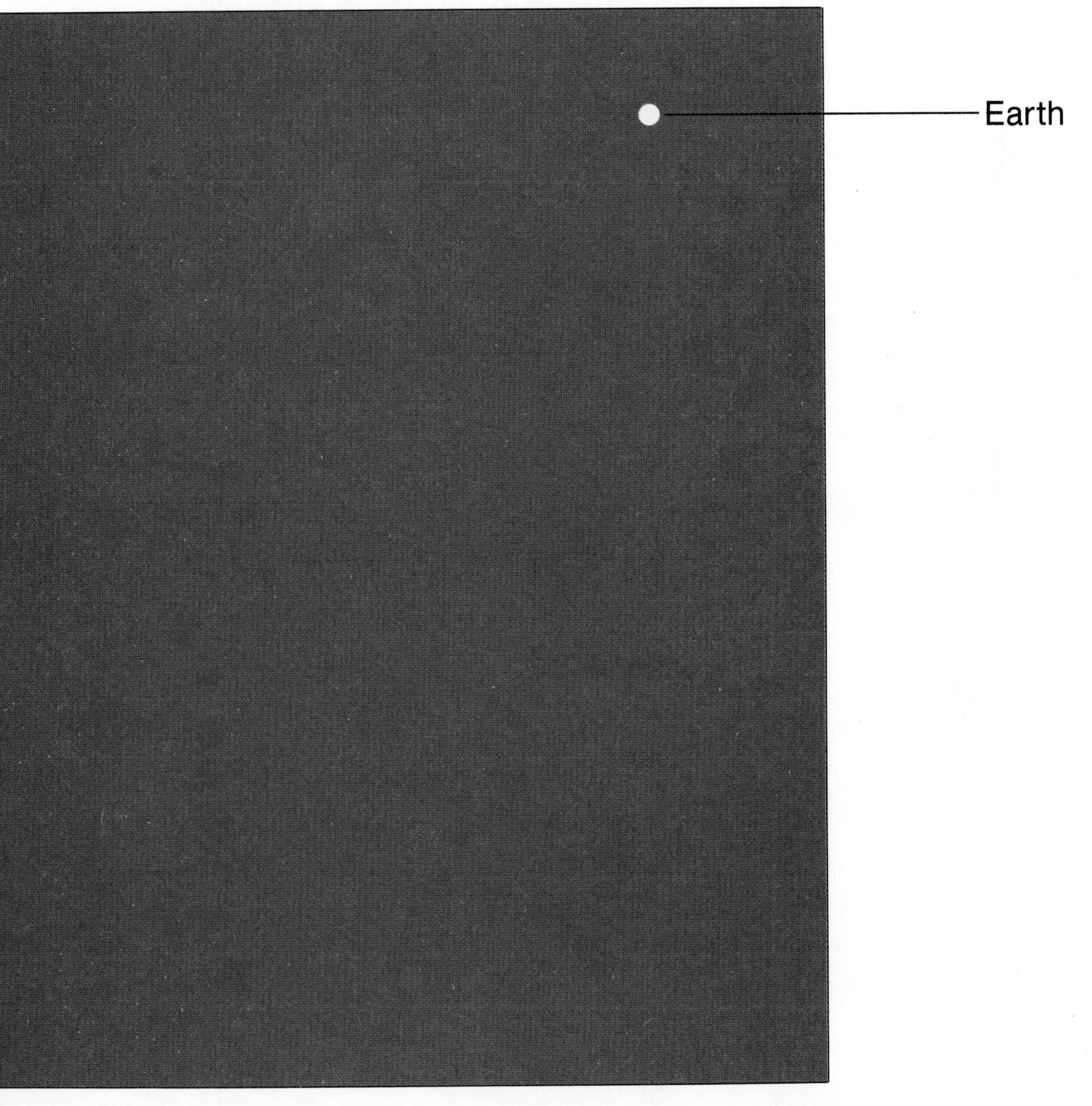

The sun gives light and warmth to the earth. Living things on earth need light and warmth from the sun.

Light from the sun makes day on the earth. Which part of the earth does the sun shine on here? That part has day. The sun is not shining on the other part. The other part has night. Day and night happen because the earth is always turning. As it turns, different parts have day and night.

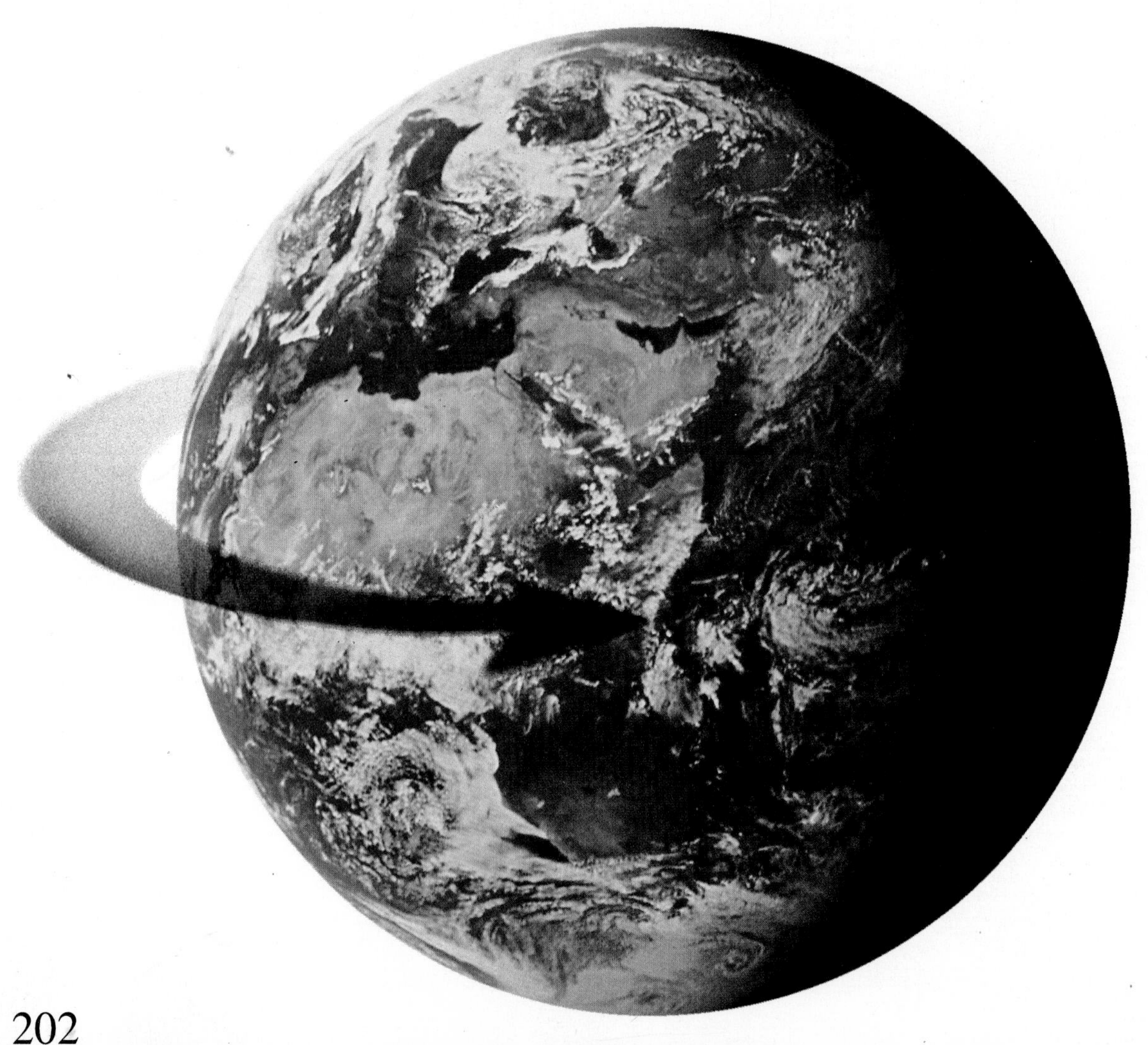

While the earth turns, it also moves around the sun. The trip around the sun takes one whole year. This path around the sun is called an **orbit.**

A **globe** is a model of the earth. It can be used to show how the earth turns. Use a classroom globe to find where you live.

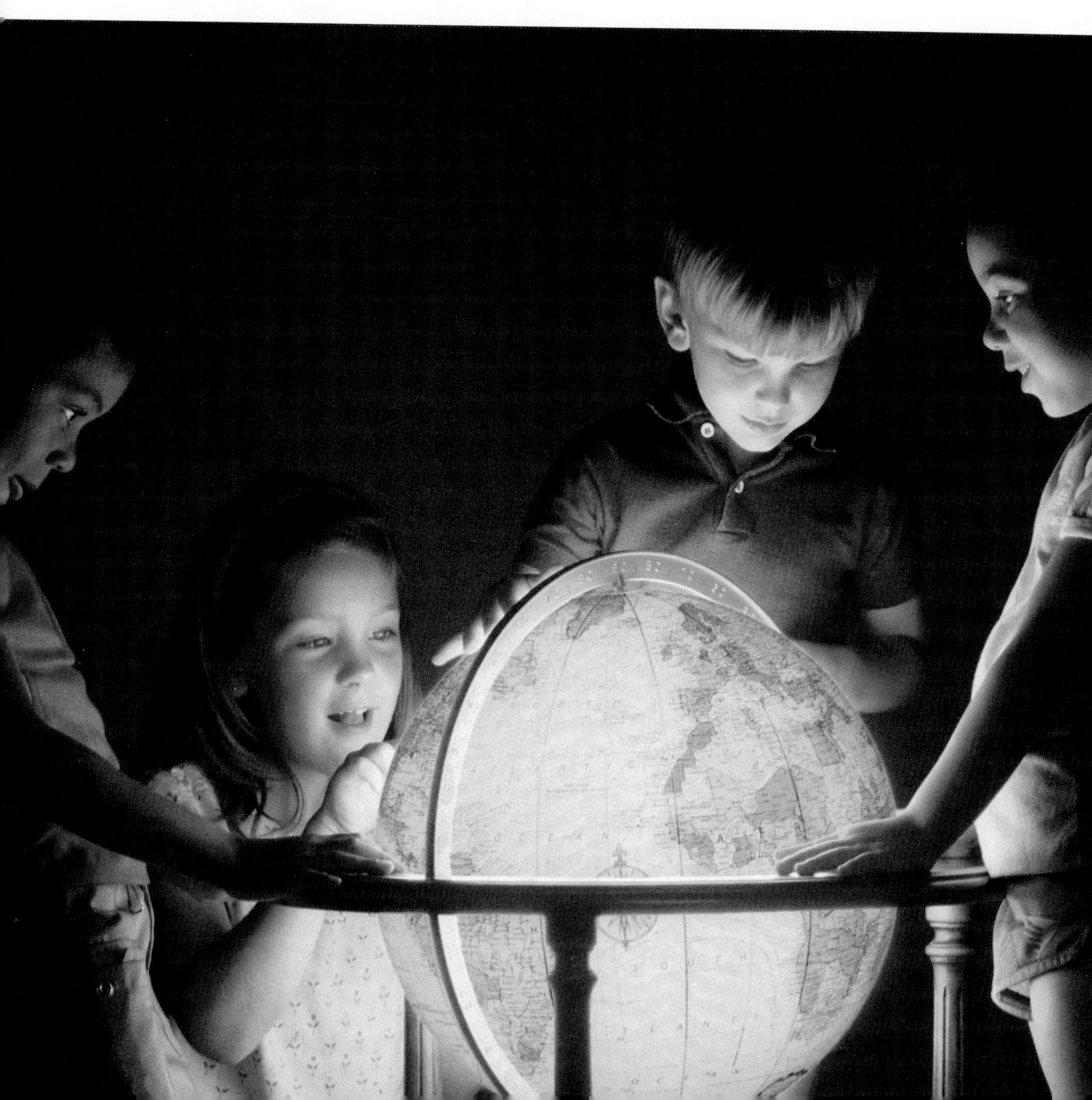

The Equator gets direct sunlight all year. That part of the earth stays warm. The North Pole and the South Pole do not get direct sunlight. Would you feel hot or cold here?

Lesson Review

1. Is the sun larger or smaller than the earth?
2. What makes day and night?

EARTH SCIENCE

Find Out

Look in a newspaper. Find out the times of sunrise and sunset for 3 days. Chart your findings.

ACTIVITY

Observing How the Earth Moves

Follow the Directions

1. Look at a globe.
2. Put a small ball of clay on the globe where you live.
3. Observe the globe in a dark room.
4. Step away from the globe and shine a flashlight on it. Pretend the light is the sun.
5. Turn the globe to show day and night for the place where you live.

Tell What You Learned

Tell where the mark is when the earth has day and night.

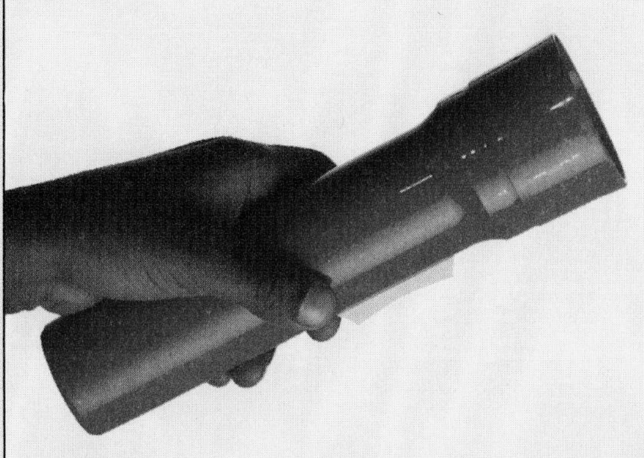

Lesson 2 What Moves Around the Sun?

Earth is a **planet.** The earth takes about 365 days, or one year, to move in an orbit around the sun. Look at the other planets that move around the sun. Count them. How many planets do you count?

Each planet is a different size. Each is a different distance from the sun. Mercury is closest to the sun. What planets have you heard of before?

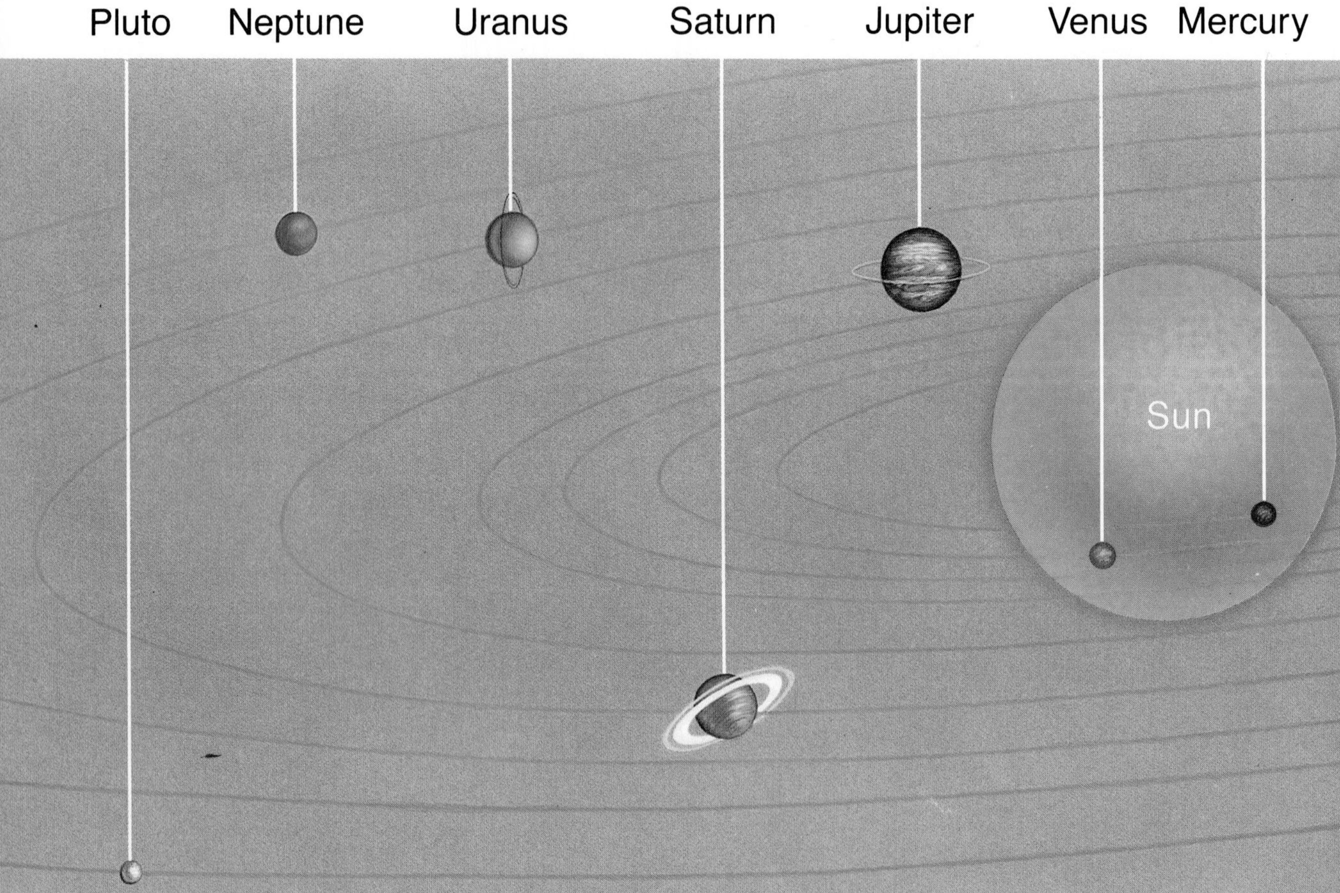

The **moon** orbits the earth. While the moon orbits the earth, the earth is moving around the sun. The earth and moon orbit the sun together.

Moonlight comes from the sun. The sun shines on the moon, just as it shines on the earth. We can see this light in the night sky.

Lesson Review

1. How many planets orbit around the Sun?
2. What moves in an orbit around earth?

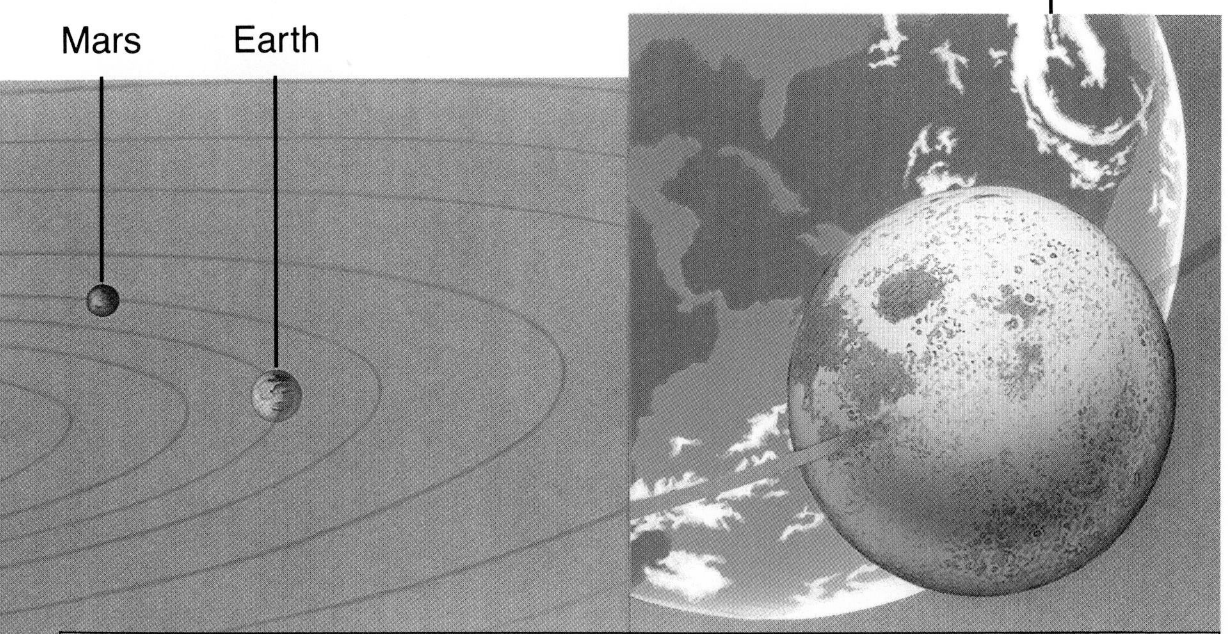

EARTH SCIENCE

Find Out

Look in a book about the moon. Find out how the shape of the moon seems to change. Draw a picture of each shape.

Making Models of Planets

Follow the Directions

1. Cut out paper circles for all nine planets.
2. Write the name of the planet on each circle.
3. Tape the circles to pieces of string. Tie the strings to a hanger.
4. Keep the planets in their order from the sun.

Tell What You Learned

Tell which two planets are the largest and which two planets are the smallest. Tell the order of the planets from the sun.

Studying a Moon

Linda Morabito studies pictures of planets taken from spacecraft. One picture showed a moon of Jupiter. The moon had a cloud that no one had ever seen clearly before.

Linda Morabito studied the picture carefully for days. She found that the cloud came from a volcano. She was the first to discover an active volcano on a moon.

What Do You Think?

Why do you think Linda Morabito studied the picture for days?

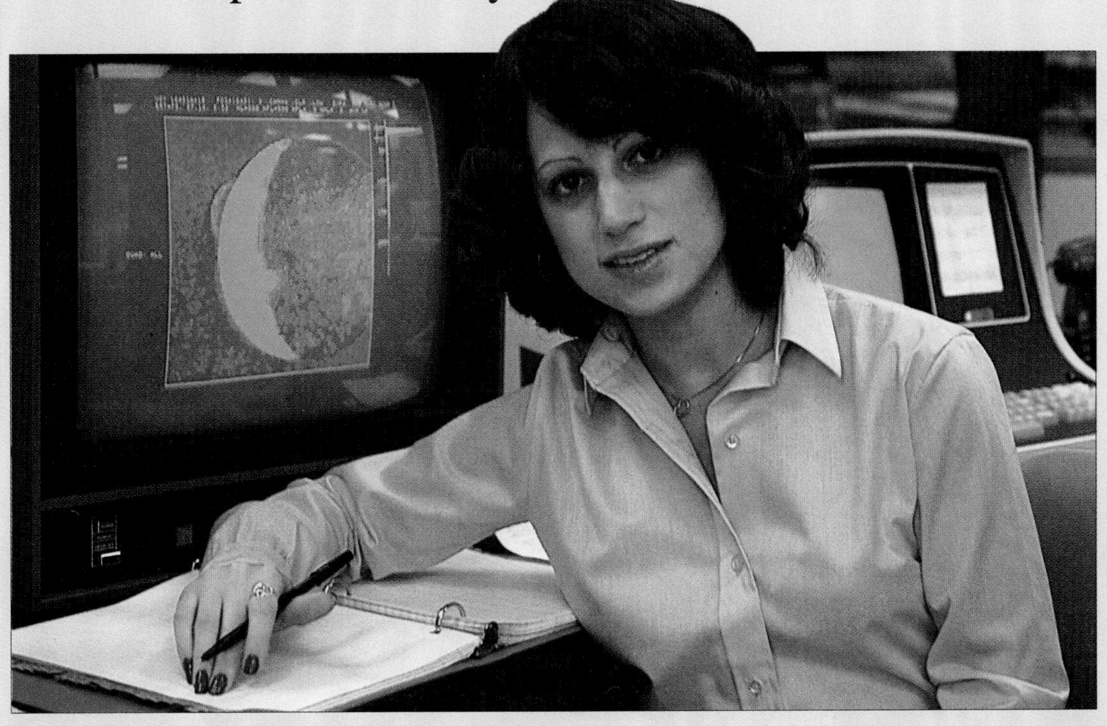

Lesson 3 Why Do Most Stars Look Small?

Many stars shine in the sky. Some stars are larger than the sun. Stars look tiny because they are very far away from the earth.

You know a jet airplane is very large. Yet it looks small when you see it far away in the sky. The stars you see here look small because they are far away. The sun looks larger and brighter than other stars. The sun is much closer to the earth than other stars.

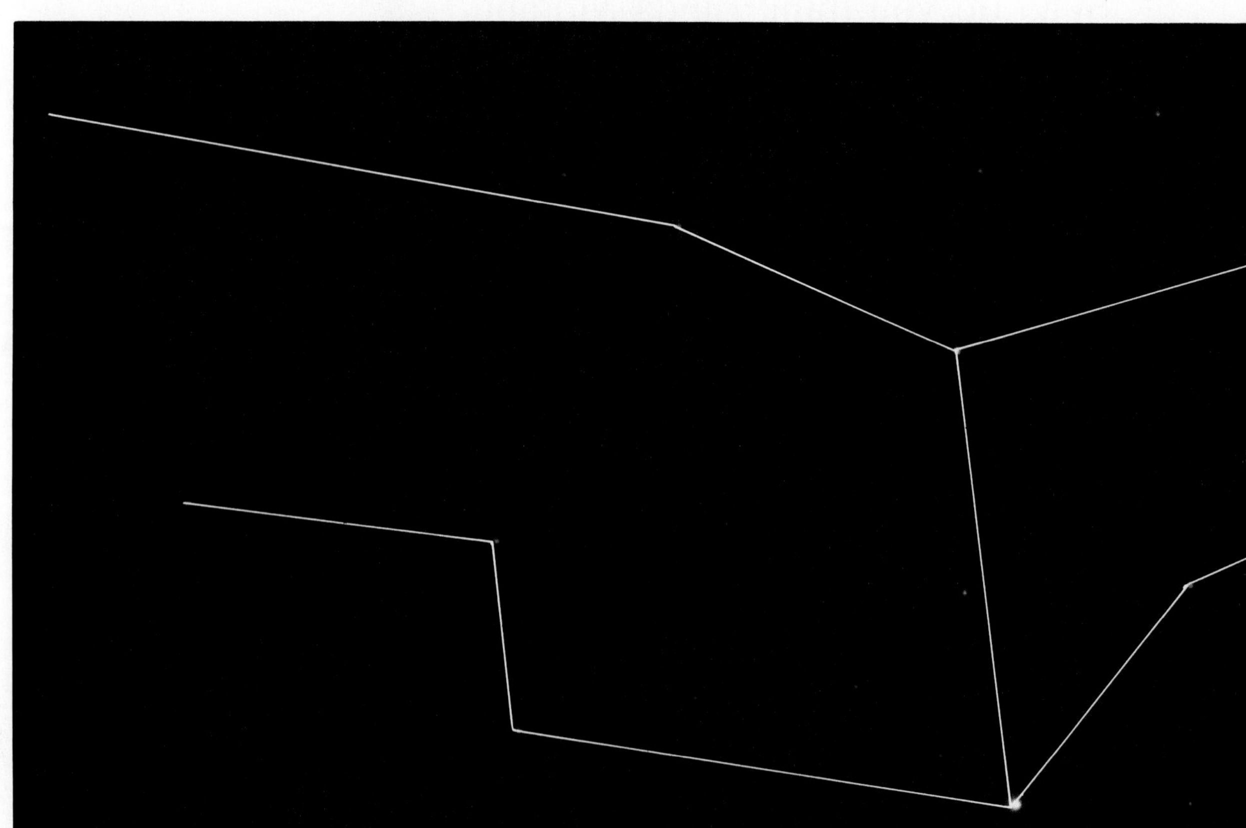

Some groups of stars seem to make pictures in the sky. These groups of stars are named for objects, animals, or people. What does the group of stars on this page look like? This group has the name Virgo, for a woman.

Lesson Review

1. Why do stars seem so small?
2. What do groups of stars seem to make in the sky?

LIFE SCIENCE **Find Out** CONNECTION

Look at pictures of groups of stars in a book on stars. Find out some animals the groups were named for.

Reading a Diagram and Making a Chart

How can you use a diagram to tell when it is day and when it is night?

1. Look at each diagram of the earth orbiting the sun. Pretend that the **X** on each earth is where you live. Notice how the **X** in diagram **a** is away from the sun. Is the **X** in day or night? Look at the other diagrams. Decide if the **X** is in day or night.

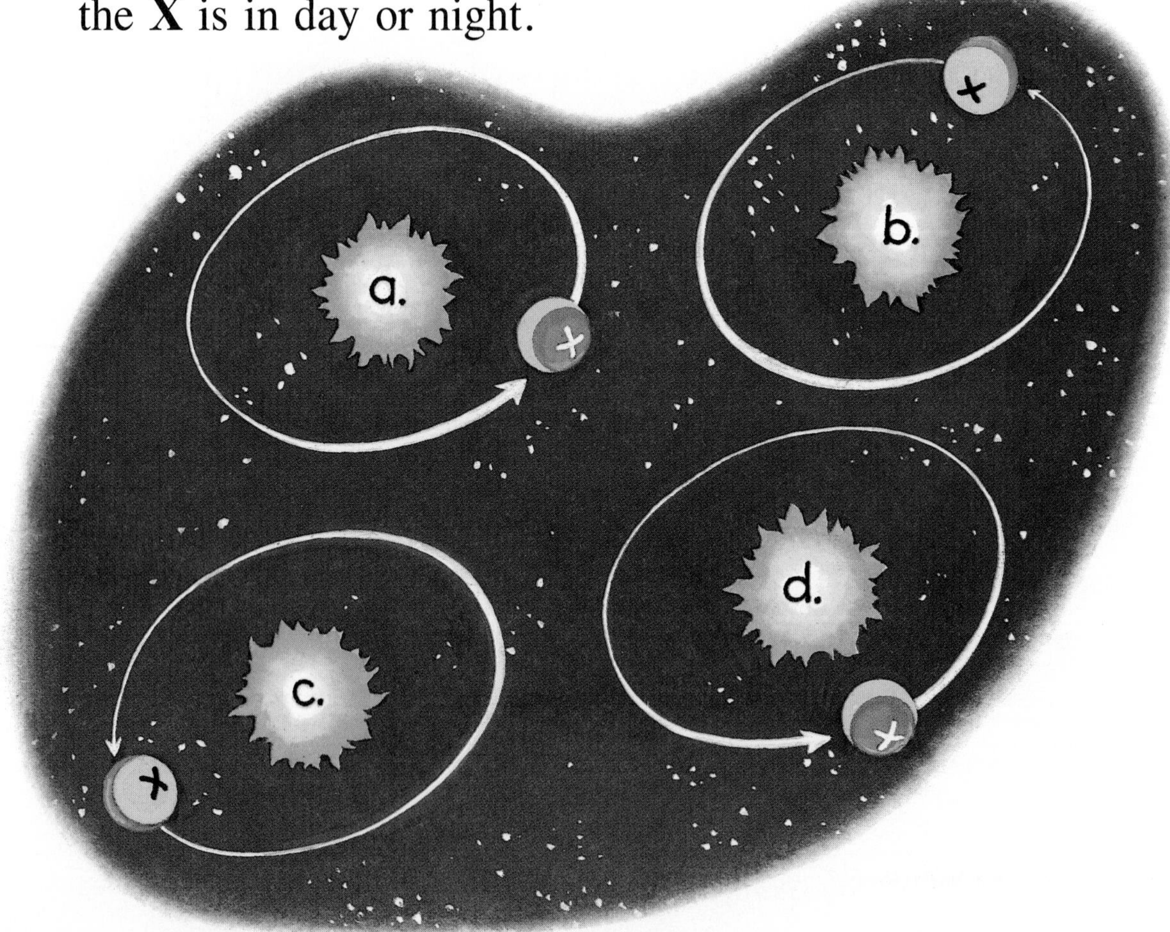

2. Make a chart like this one. Write day or night to show if each **X** is in day or night.

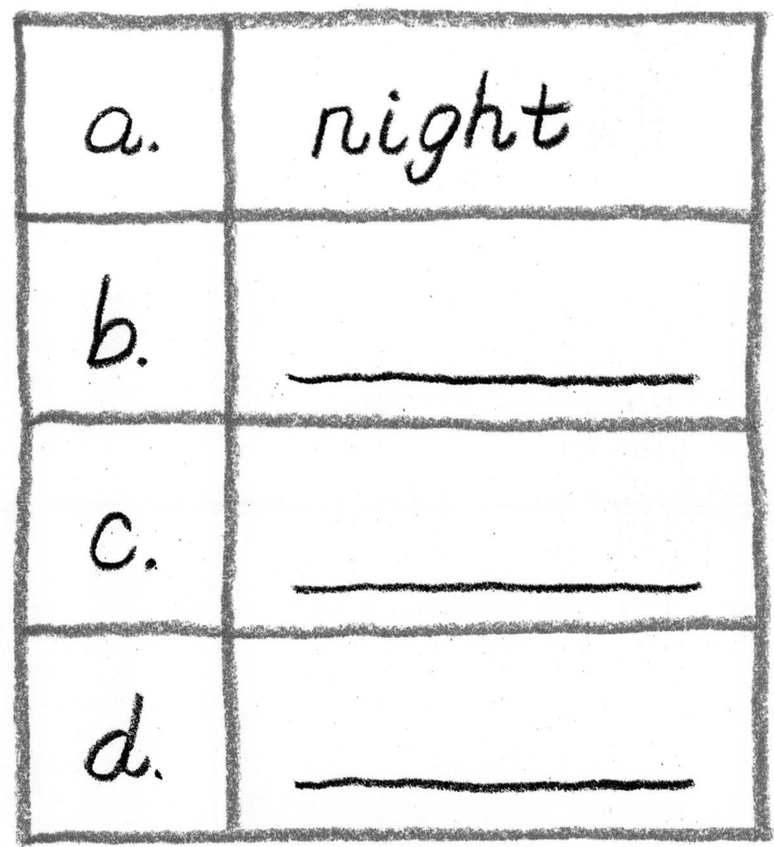

3. Look at your chart. When was the **X** in daytime? When was it in night?

Chapter 9 Review

Review Chapter Ideas

1. Tell what the sun is made of.
2. Explain what living things on earth need from the sun.
3. Explain how the moving earth and light from the sun make day and night.
4. Tell how many planets move around the sun.
5. Look at the picture. Identify the sun, the earth, and the moon.
6. Tell why stars look so small.

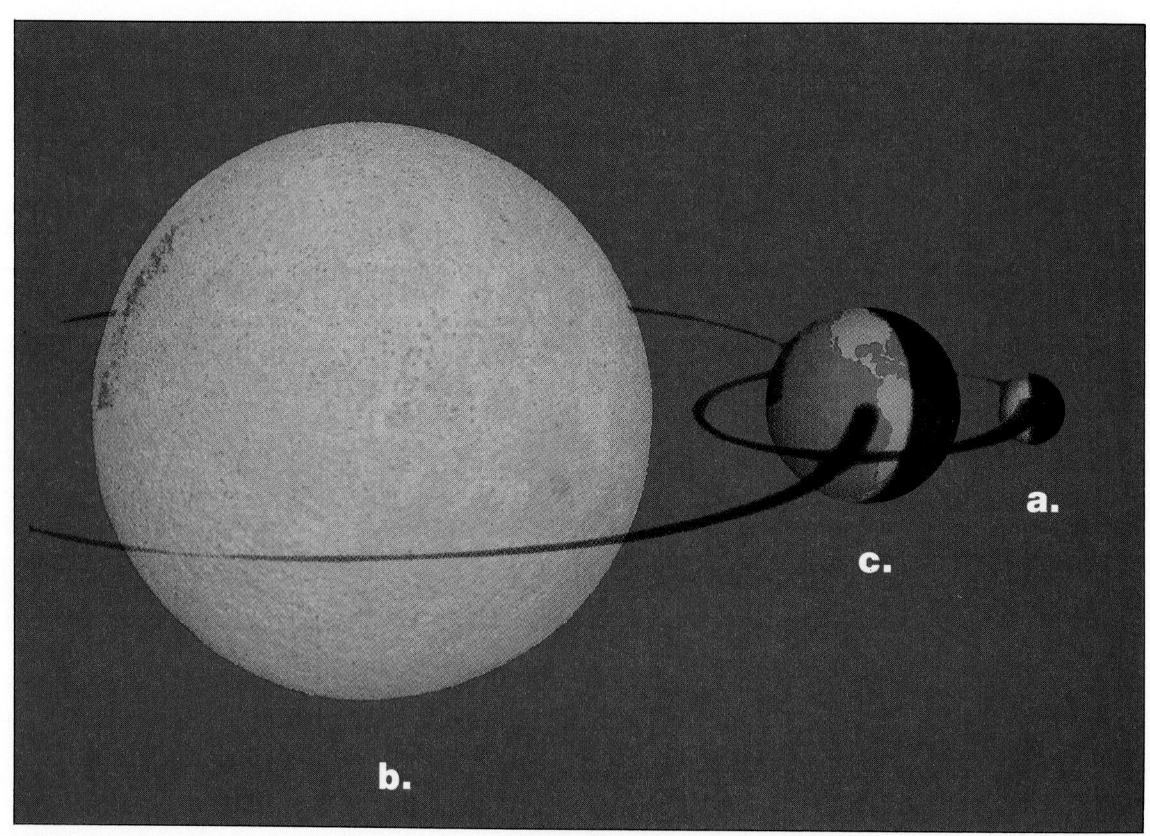

Review Science Words

Match the words and the pictures.

1. sun
2. earth
3. moon

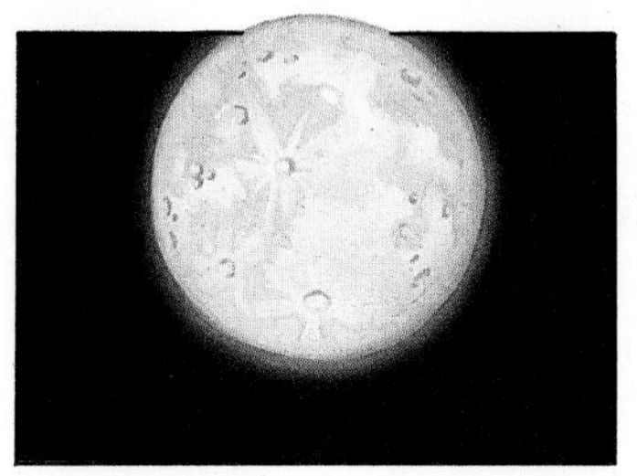

a.

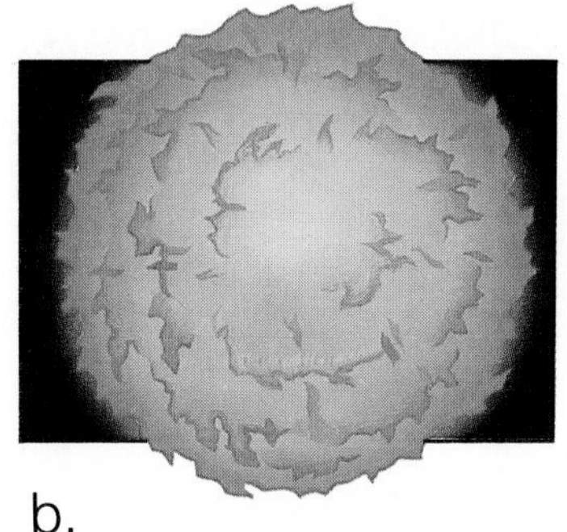

b.

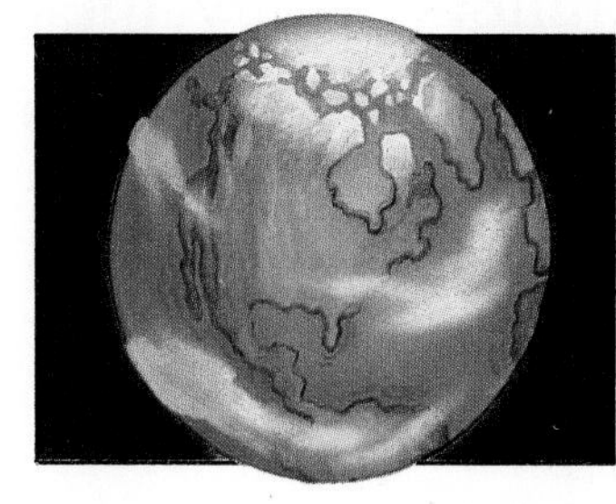

c.

Tell what the words mean.

4. globe
5. orbit
6. planet

Use Science Ideas

The place you live is marked with an **X** in the picture. Is it day or night where you live?

Astronomer

Astronomers study the moon, the sun, other stars, and the planets. Astronomers measure and draw maps as they do their work. They measure the size of stars and planets. They measure how far away stars and planets are from the earth. They draw maps of the stars in the sky. They also study pictures taken from space.

How It Works

A Thermometer

A thermometer is a glass tube that holds a liquid. When the temperature gets warmer, the liquid expands, or gets bigger. The liquid then takes up more space inside the tube and moves up the tube. The numbers and marks along the thermometer show degrees. You can read the temperature by looking at where the liquid is in the thermometer.

glass tube

liquid

Unit 3 Review

Answer the Questions

1. Where is fresh water found on earth?
2. How can people keep air clean?
3. In many parts of the world, how does the weather change in the four seasons?
4. Look at the pictures. How is the weather different in each picture?

5. How is the sun important to the earth?
6. How do the moving earth and light from the sun make day and night?

Study the Picture

Where does the water in the well come from?

What to Do

1. Think about how you use water in one day. Make a chart like this one.

How I Use Water			
Drink	Brush teeth	Wash	Other ways

2. Make up a booklet about weather. Draw a picture of what the weather is like each day for a week. Show what you do and wear in different kinds of weather.
3. Draw a group of stars on a piece of paper. Make your star group look like an object, person, or animal. Name your star group.

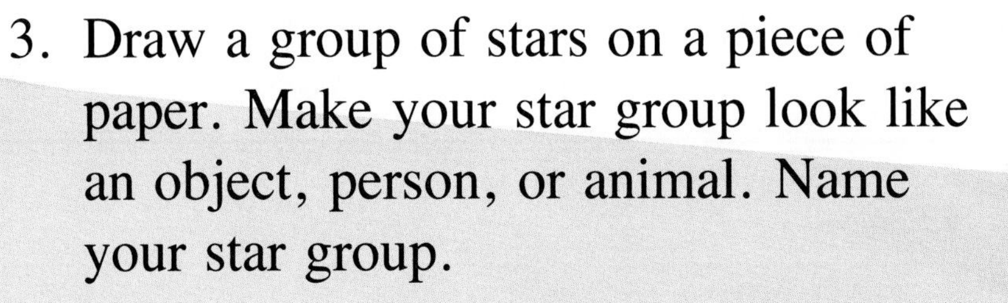

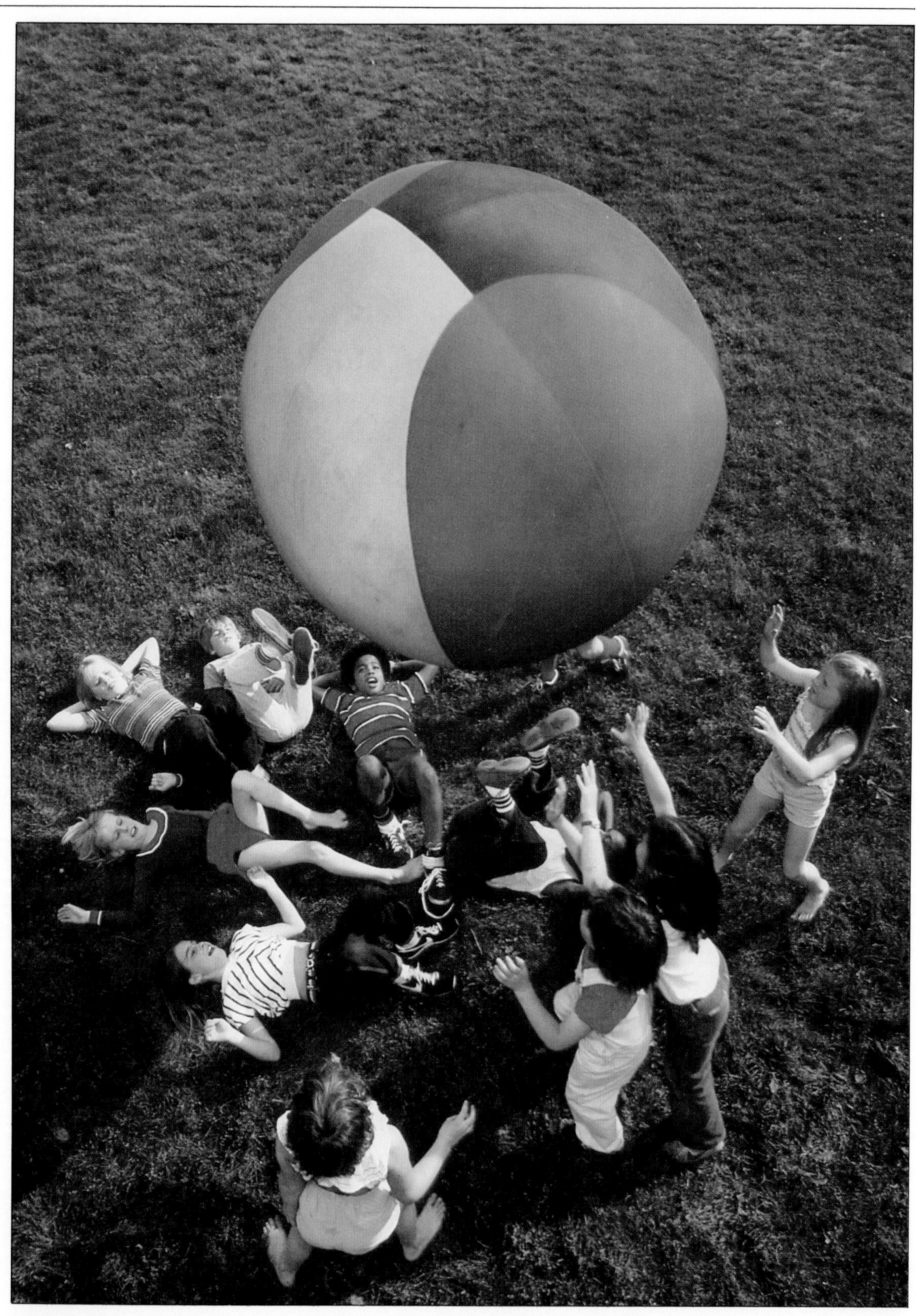

Unit 4

Human Body

These children are having fun and keeping healthy. They are playing outside in the fresh air. The children are also exercising as they play. How does exercise help people stay healthy? Which body parts are they using to lift the ball? Draw a picture of a fun way to keep healthy.

Chapter 10

How Your Body Works

These children are playing. How do you use your body when you play?

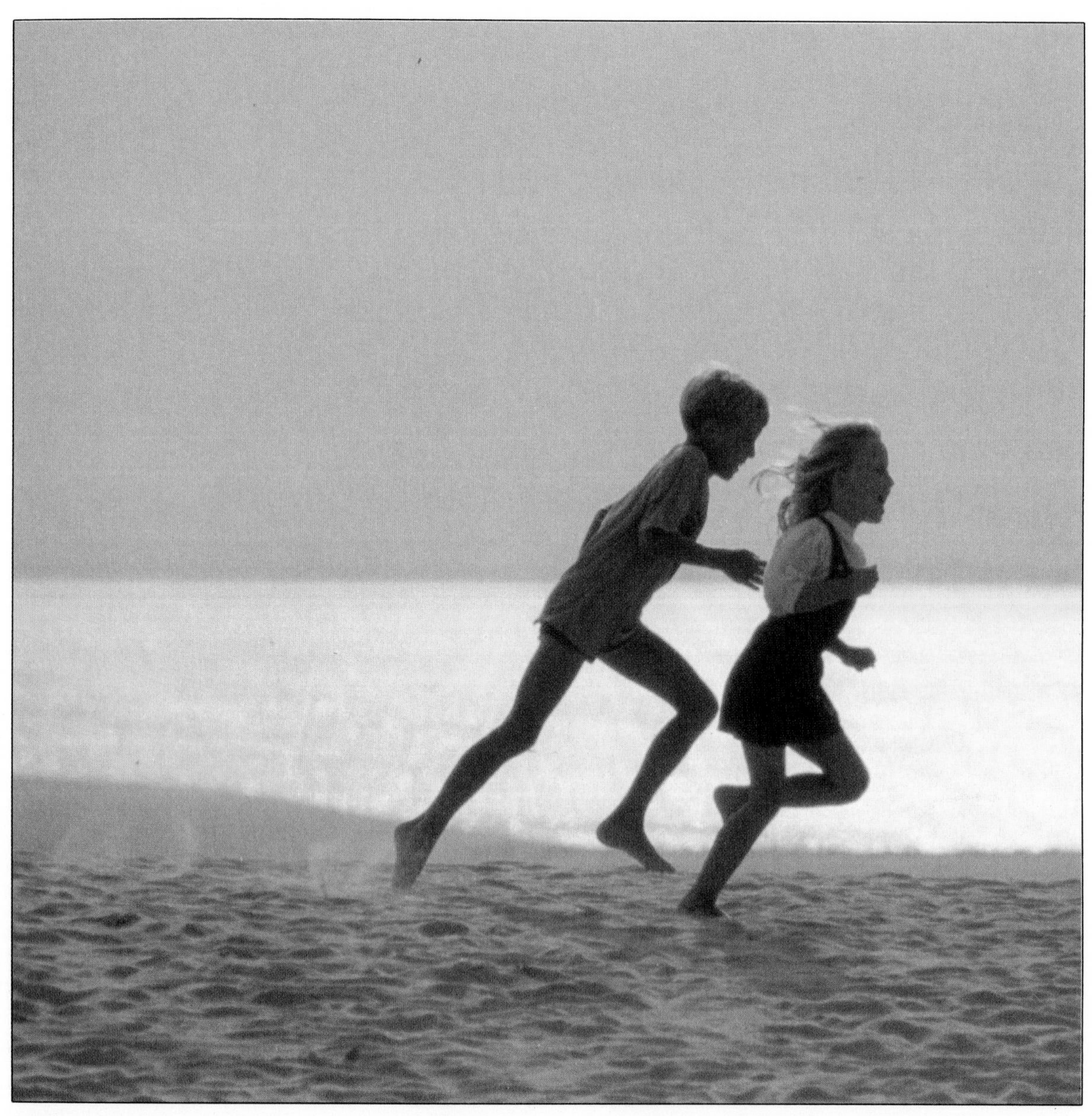

Starting the Chapter

What different bones can you feel in your body? You can find different bones on an X-ray picture. Then read more about bones and other parts of your body.

TRY THIS

Observing X rays of Bones

Look at this X-ray picture. Find bones in the hand, the wrist, and the arm. Try to feel these bones in your own body. How do the bones look different?

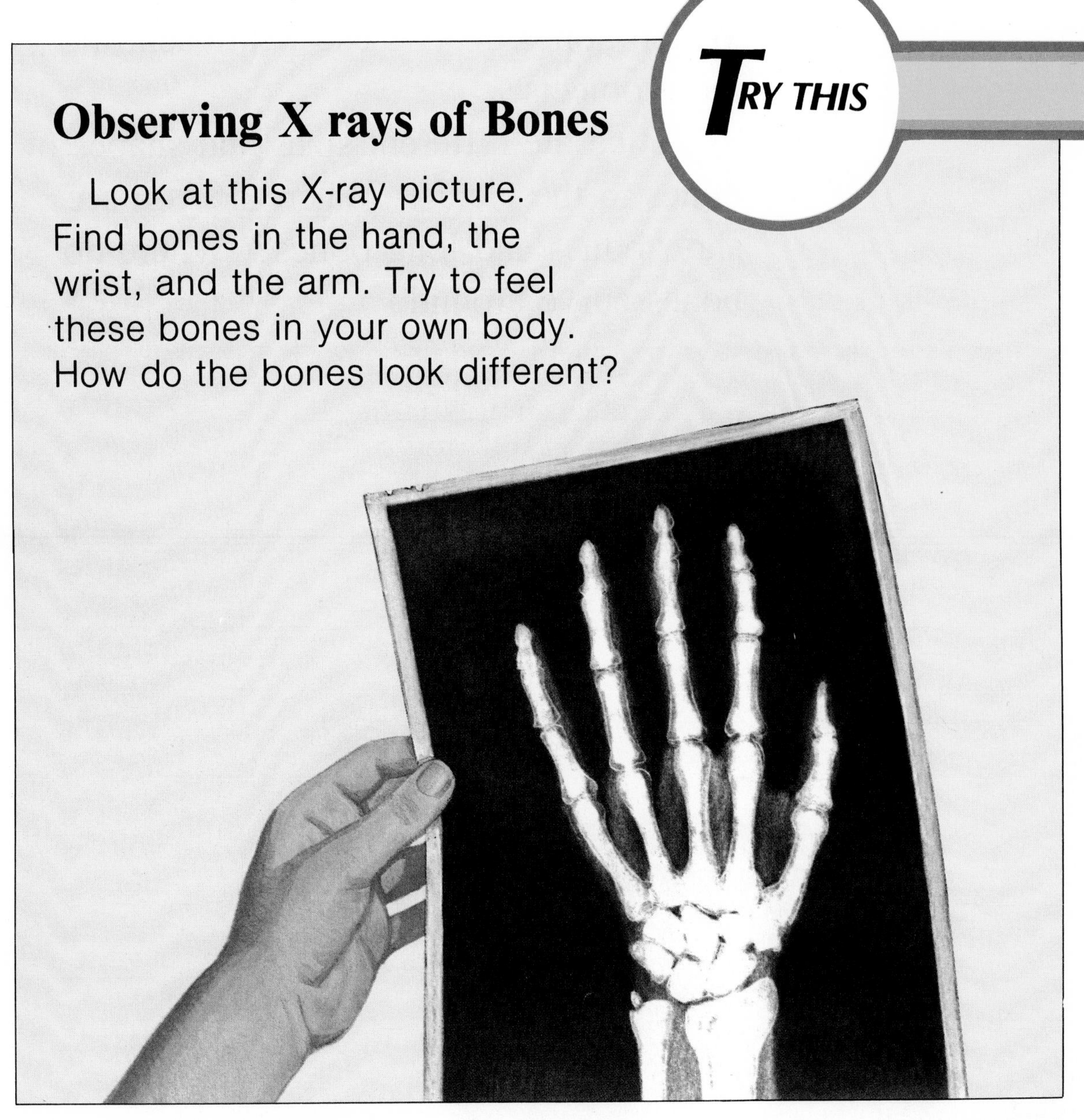

Lesson 1 How Do Your Bones and Muscles Work?

You have more than 200 **bones** in your body. Your bones help you move. Your bones also hold up your body and give it shape. Some bones protect inside parts of your body. Your bones grow as you grow. Which bones do you use with each of these objects?

Notice the different sizes and shapes of bones in the picture. Where do you see short bones and long bones? Where do bones curve around?

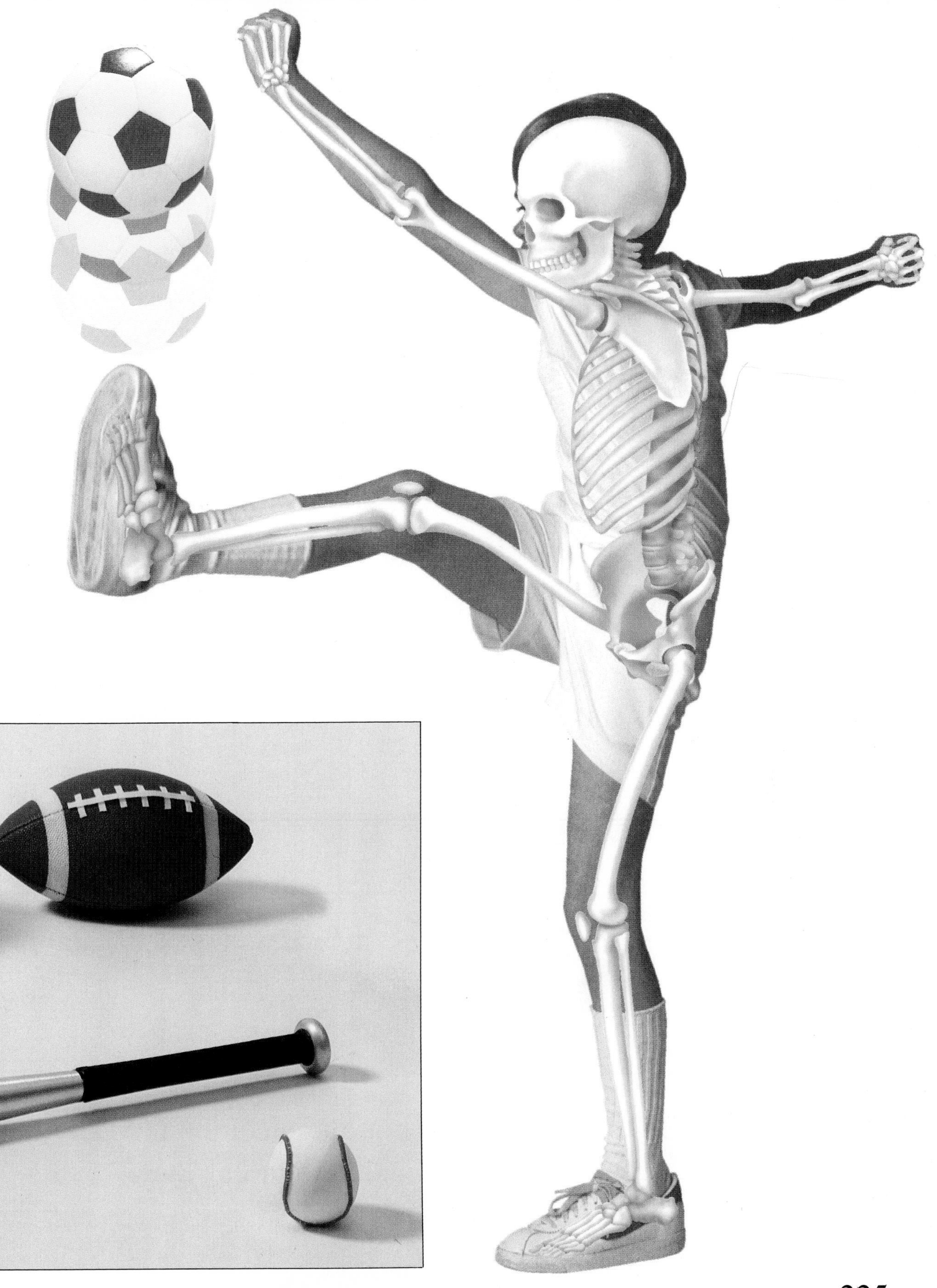

Your body has **muscles** of many different sizes and shapes. Muscles have some of the same jobs that bones do. Muscles give your body shape. Muscles help protect the inside parts of your body. Your bones and muscles work together to move your body.

Lesson Review

1. What are some jobs of the bones?
2. What are some jobs of the muscles?

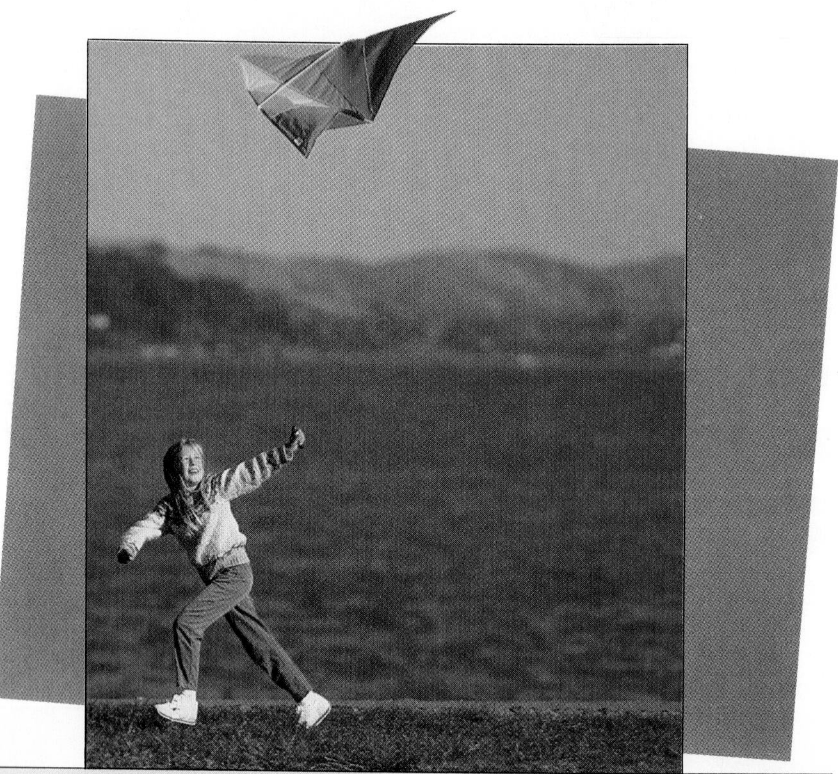

HUMAN BODY

Find Out

Look back at the picture on page 225. Find the places where your body can bend.

Lesson 2 What Can Your Brain Do?

You need your **brain** for everything you do. You use your brain when you think, feel, learn, and move. Your brain keeps your whole body working.

Nerves go from your brain to all parts of your body. Nerves carry messages from your body to your brain. Your brain figures out what the messages mean.

Then, nerves carry messages from the brain back to the body. You do what the messages tell you to do. Find the brain and nerves in the picture. How can you use your brain and nerves to play games?

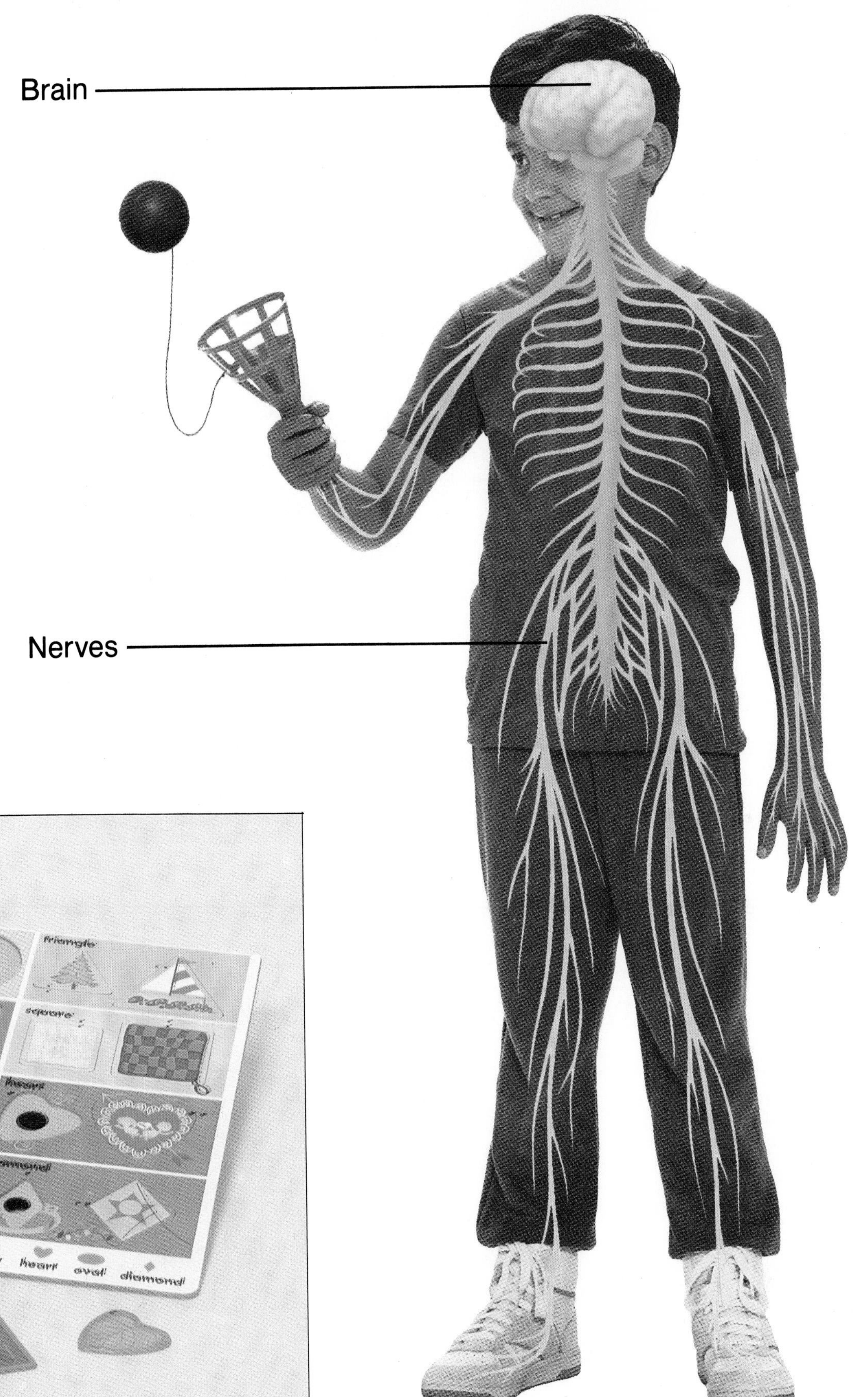
Brain
Nerves
triangle
square
heart
diamond
star
heart
oval
diamond

What happens when the girl sees the stop sign? Nerves carry a message from her eyes to her brain. Then nerves carry a message from her brain to her legs and feet. The girl pushes on the brakes and stops the bicycle.

Lesson Review

1. What do you use your brain for?
2. What carries messages to the brain?

LIFE SCIENCE
Find Out
CONNECTION

Most animals have brains and nerves in their bodies. Suppose you throw a ball to a cat. What messages go to and from the cat's brain?

ACTIVITY

Using Your Body

Follow the Directions

1. Use an index card.
2. Sit down.
3. Ask a classmate to stand in front of you and drop the index card.
4. Watch the index card as it drops and try to catch it with both hands.

Tell What You Learned

Tell what parts of the body you used when you tried to catch the index card.

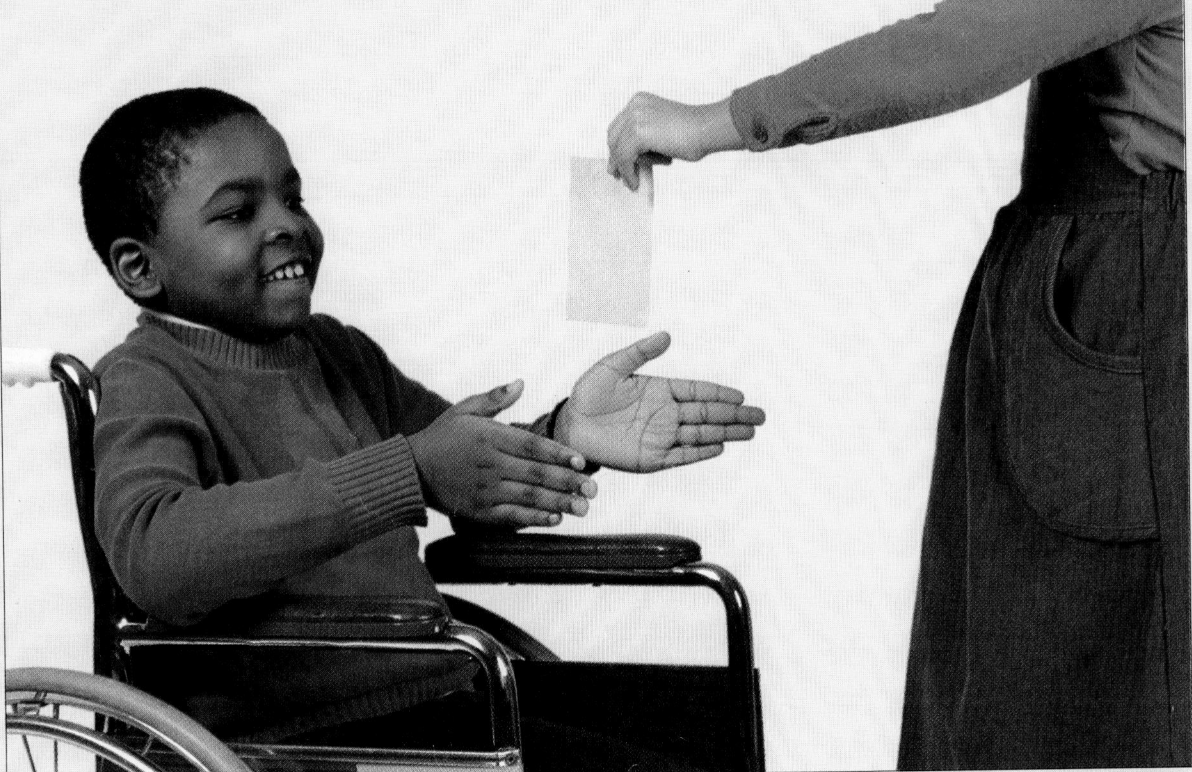

Lesson 3 How Do Your Heart and Lungs Work?

Your **heart** and **lungs** are in your chest. Find each one in the picture. Your heart pumps **blood** to every part of your body. Your lungs take air into your body. How can your lungs help you play music?

Oxygen is a special gas in the air. Your body needs oxygen. When you breathe in air, you bring oxygen to your lungs. Your heart pumps blood to your lungs. The blood picks up oxygen. The blood carries oxygen to all parts of your body.

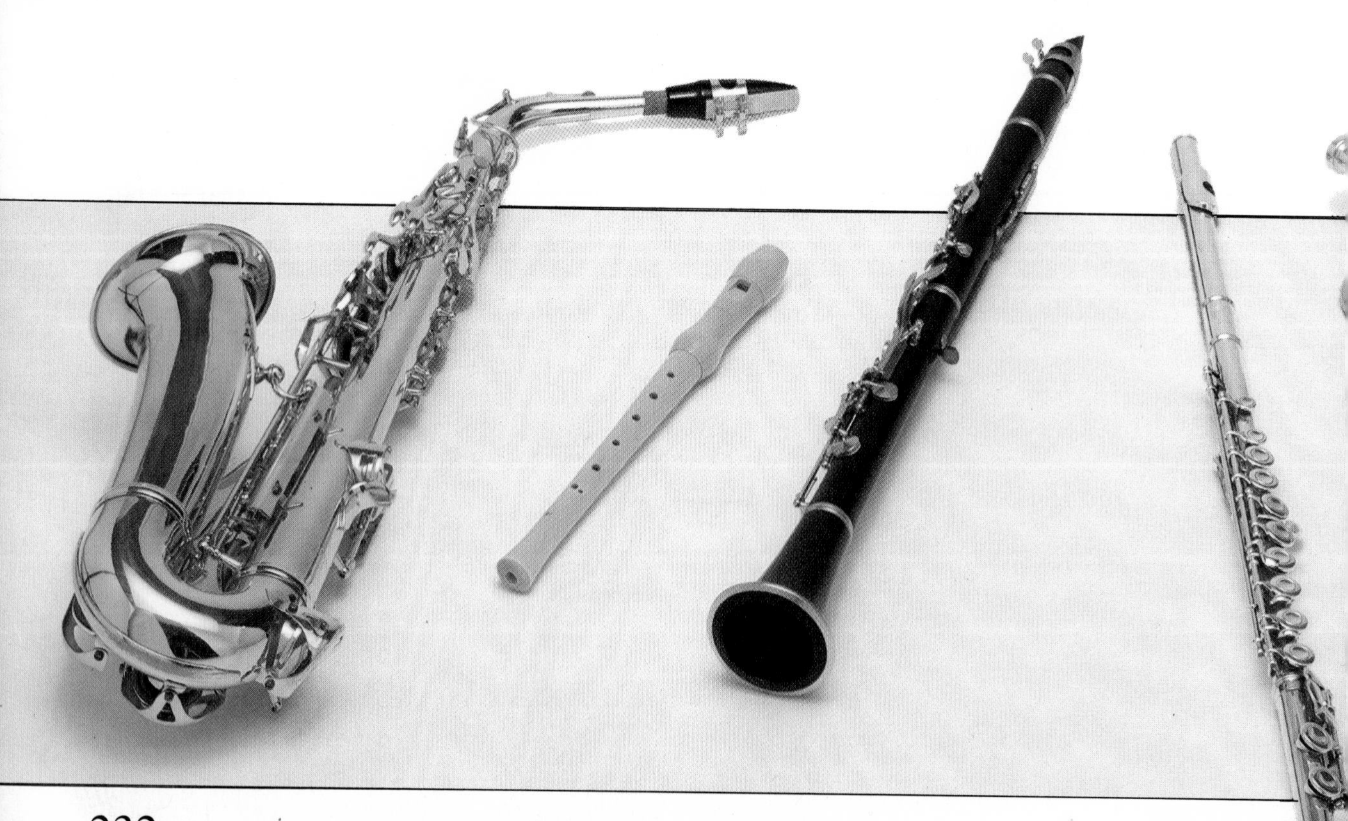

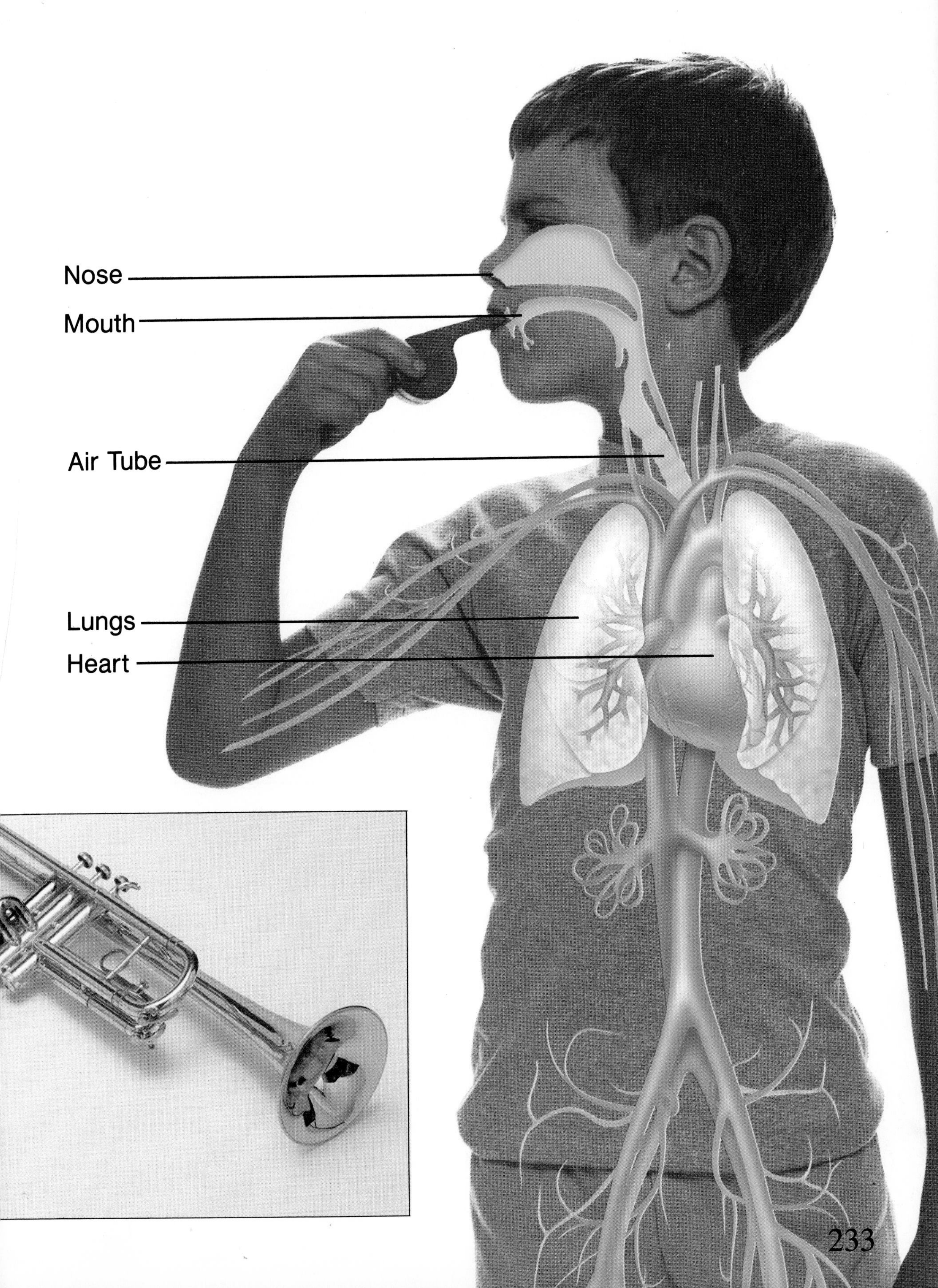
Nose
Mouth
Air Tube
Lungs
Heart

Try this. Put your hands on your chest the way the picture shows. Breathe in as much as you can. What happens to your chest? Now breathe out as much as you can. What happens to your chest?

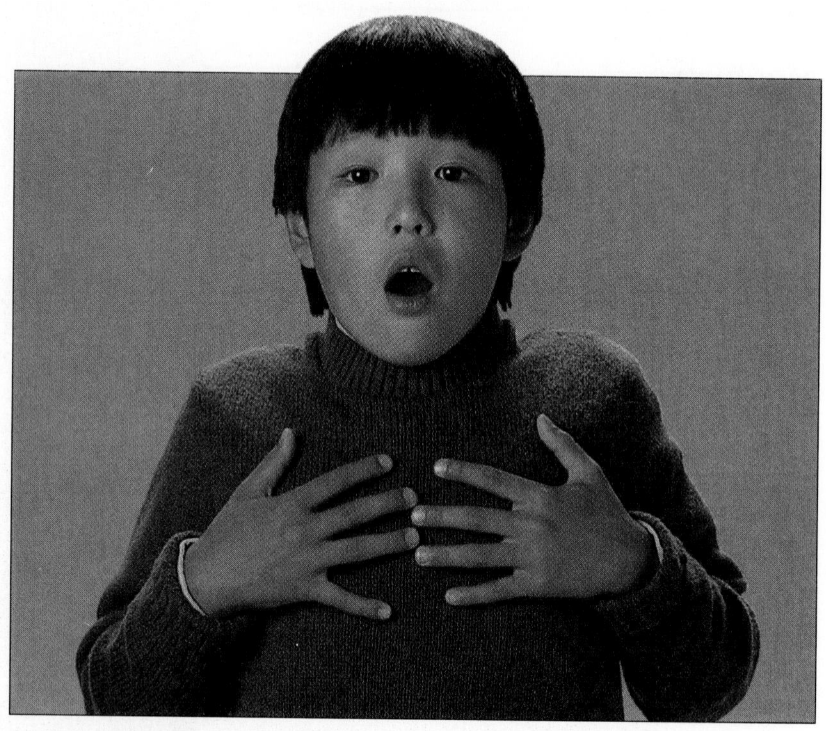

Lesson Review

1. What does the heart do?
2. What do your lungs take into your body?

HUMAN BODY
Find Out

Put your hand over your heart. Find out how many times it beats in one minute.

ACTIVITY

Listening to Your Heart

Follow the Directions

1. Choose a partner. Ask your partner to listen to your heart beat as you see here. Count slowly to thirty.
2. Jump in place twenty times.
3. Ask your partner to listen to your heart again. Count to thirty.
4. Next, listen to your partner's heart.

Tell What You Learned

Tell how the heart beats differently after jumping. Tell how your heart would beat after you ride a bike.

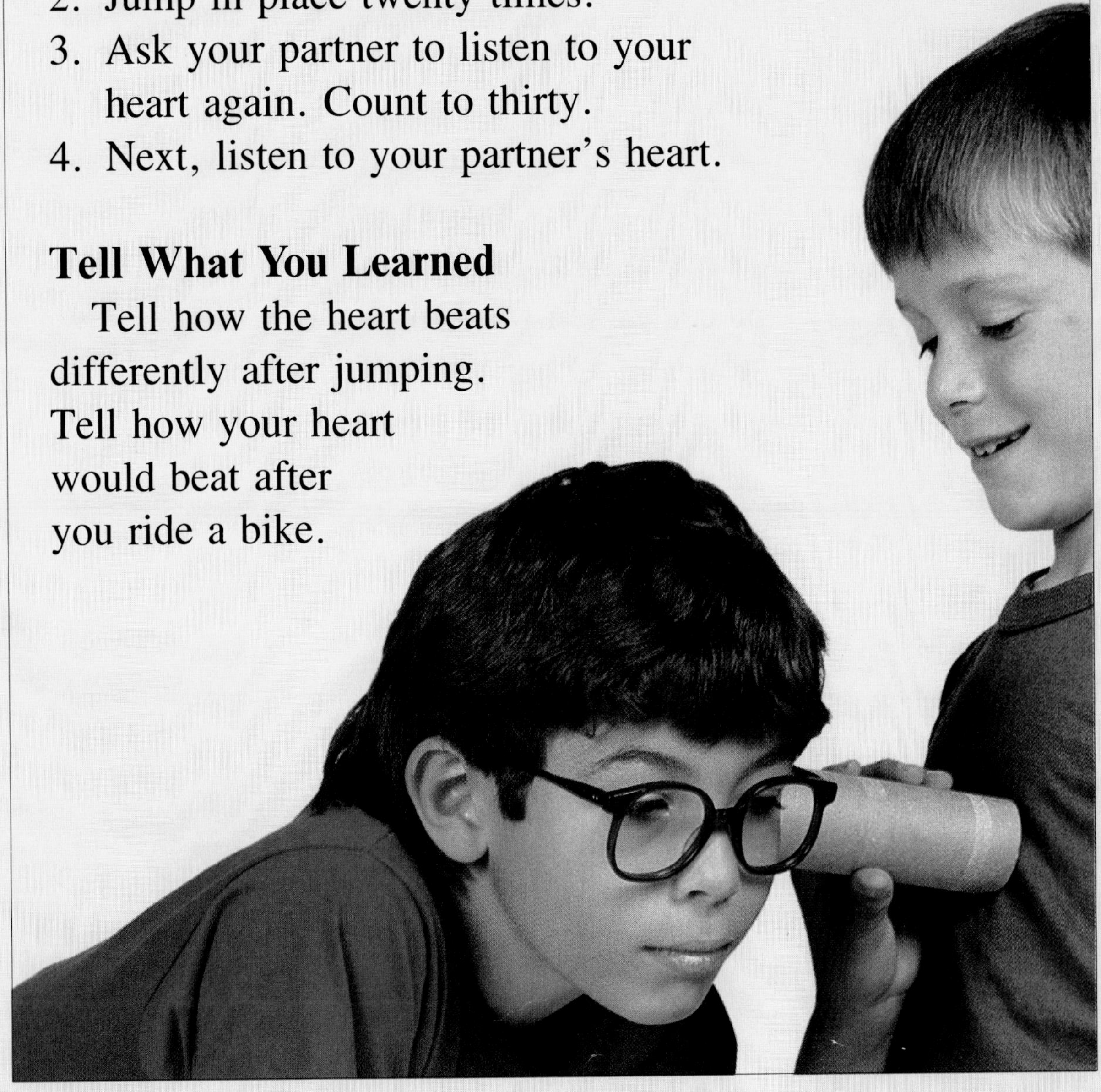

Lesson 4 What Happens to the Food You Eat?

The food you eat must change before your body can use it. Your teeth break food into small pieces when you chew it. Special juices in your mouth help make the food soft before you swallow it. The soft food moves down a tube to the **stomach**. Where is the stomach in the picture?

Muscles in your stomach move the food around. Special juices in the stomach help break food into very tiny pieces. Then food moves out of the stomach. Other parts of your body finish changing the food you eat.

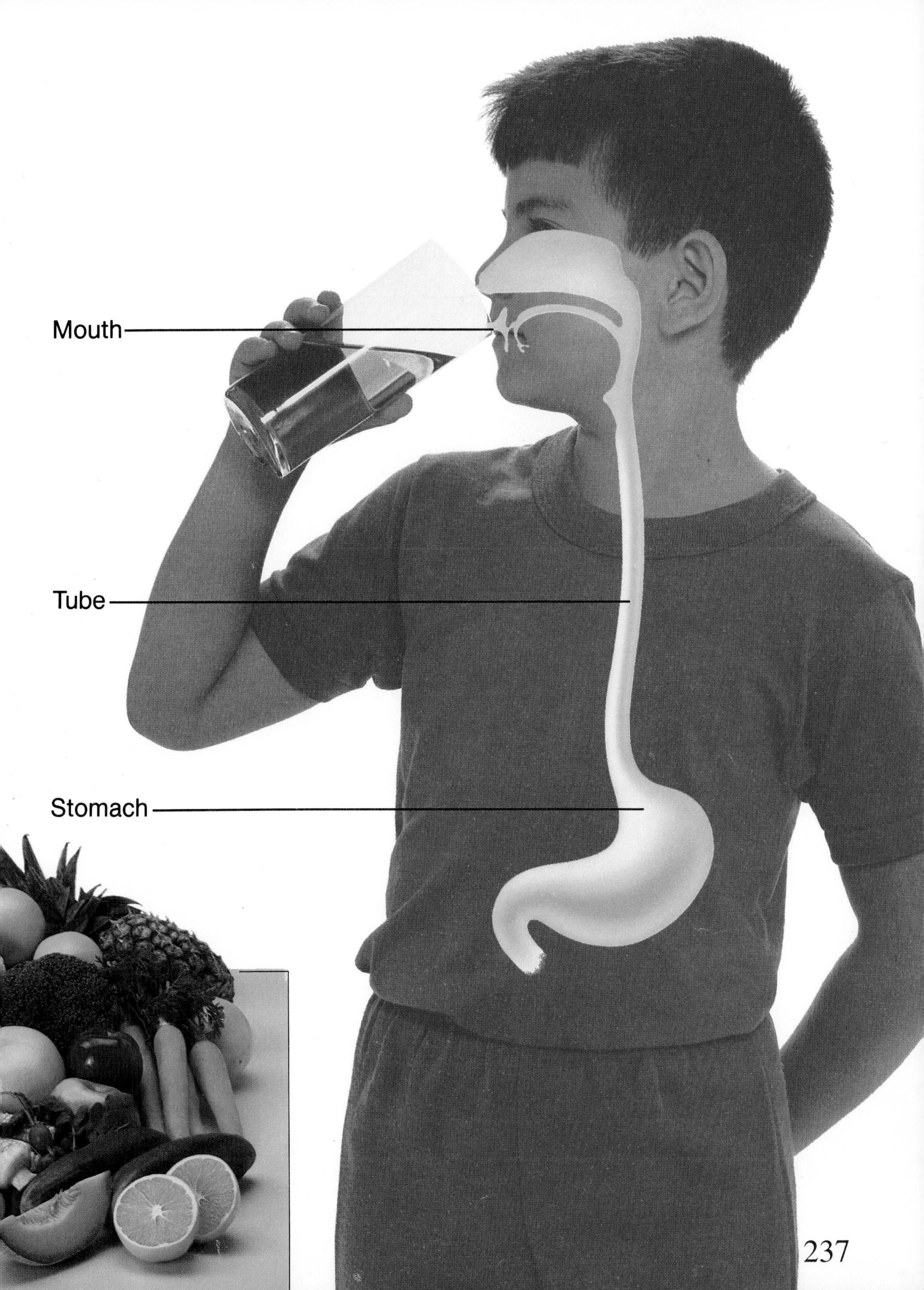
Mouth
Tube
Stomach

Blood carries the changed food to every part of your body. You need food to work and to have fun like the children in the picture.

Your body cannot use some parts of food. These parts move out of the body.

Lesson Review

1. What parts of your body change food?
2. How does food change in your mouth?

HUMAN BODY

Find Out

Would it help your stomach to chew your food into small or big pieces? Why?

Computers That Help People Walk

Some people cannot move their legs. A computer can help some of these people walk. Many of the wires that come from the legs of this man connect to a computer. The computer helps move his leg muscles.

Information goes from the leg muscles to the computer. Then the computer uses this information to move more muscles as the person takes a step.

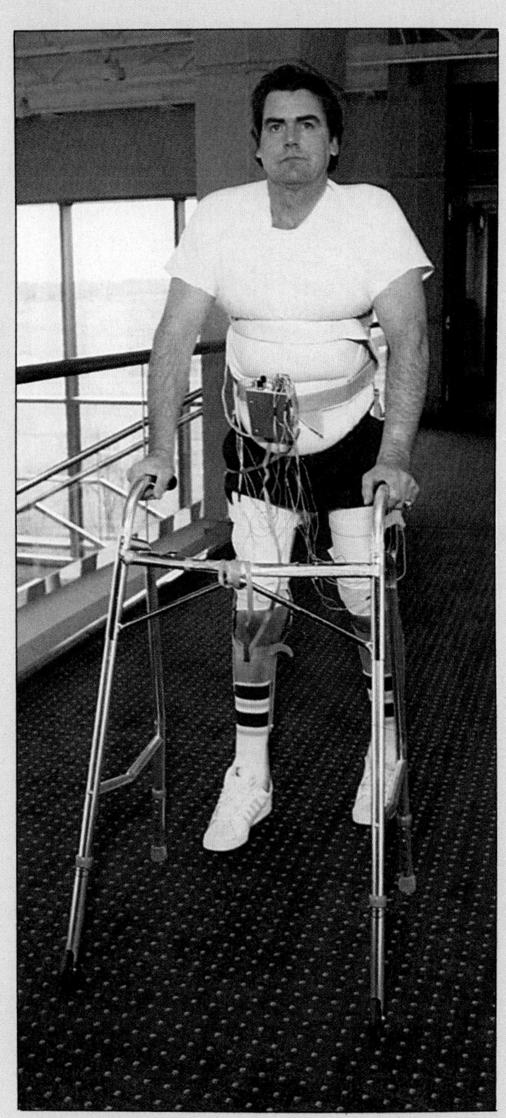

What Do You Think?

How does this computer work like some parts of the body?

Using a Ruler and Making a Graph

What can measuring fingers show?

1. Use your own paper and a metric ruler. Measure each finger as you see here. Write down the numbers on your paper.

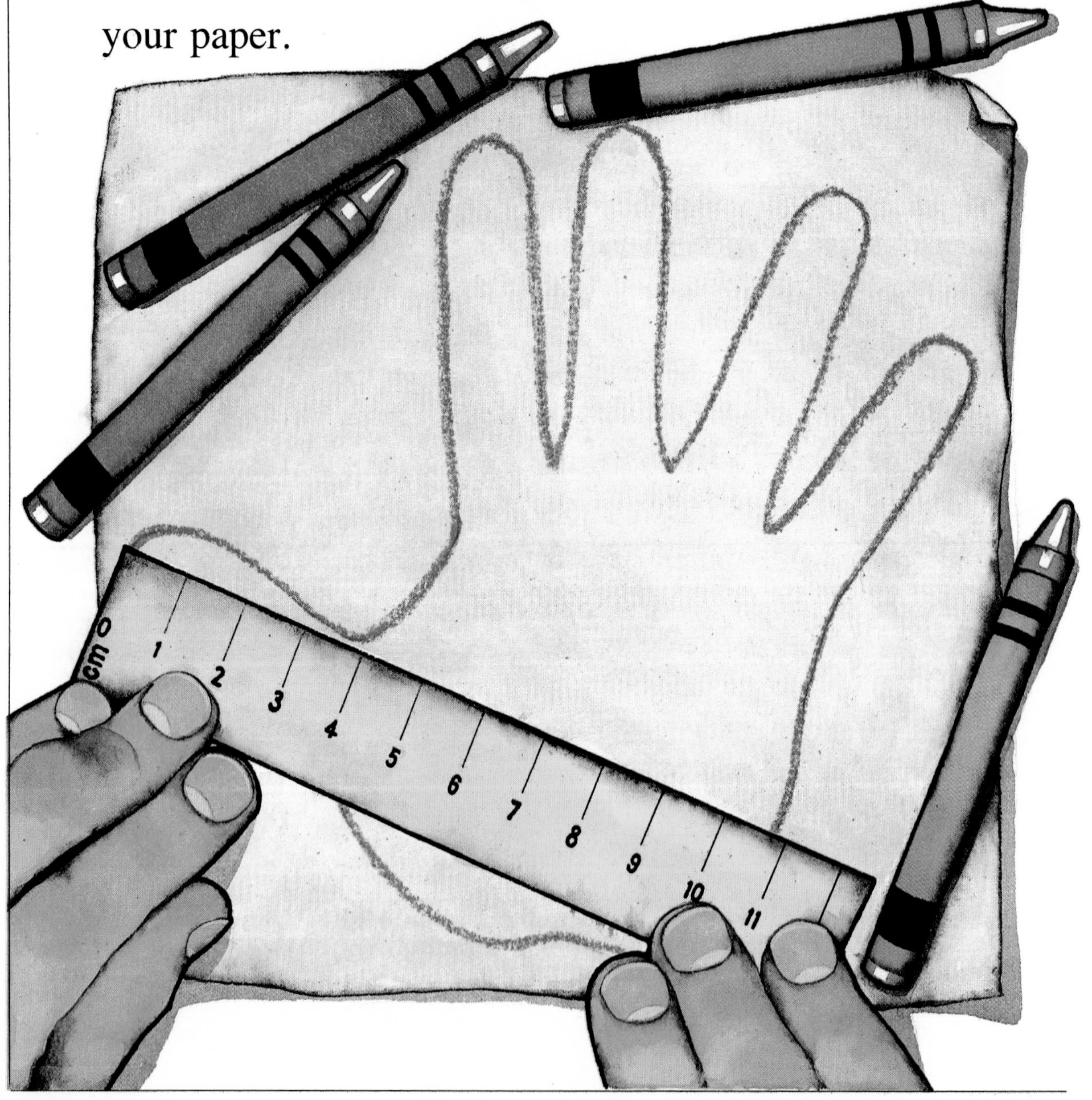

2. Draw a chart like this one. Use the numbers you wrote. Color in a row to show how long each finger is. Use a different color for each row.

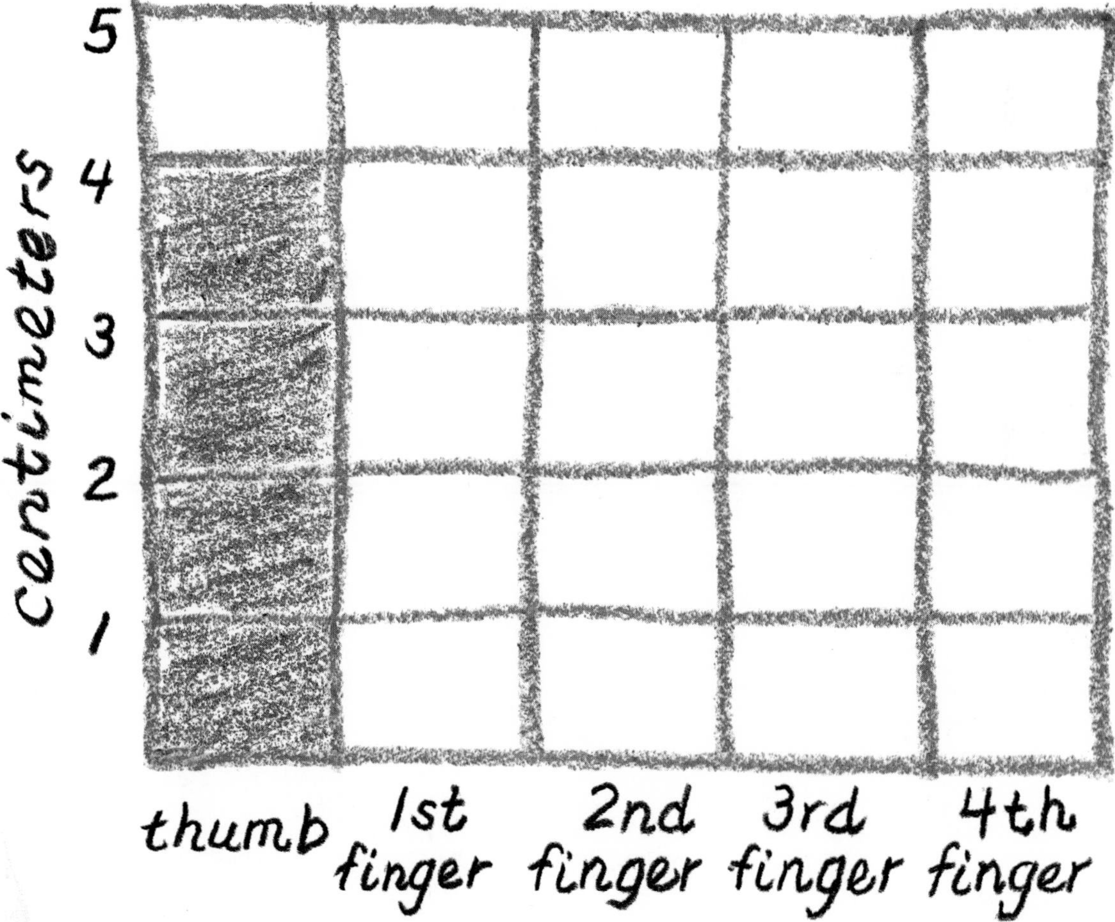

3. Look at your chart. Which finger is the same as the thumb?

Chapter 10 Review

Review Chapter Ideas

1. Tell what bones do in the body.
2. Tell what muscles do.
3. Tell where you see the brain in the picture. Tell what the brain does.
4. Find the heart and lungs in the picture. Tell what each does.
5. Name the part of the body in the picture that changes food.
6. Tell how the body changes food.

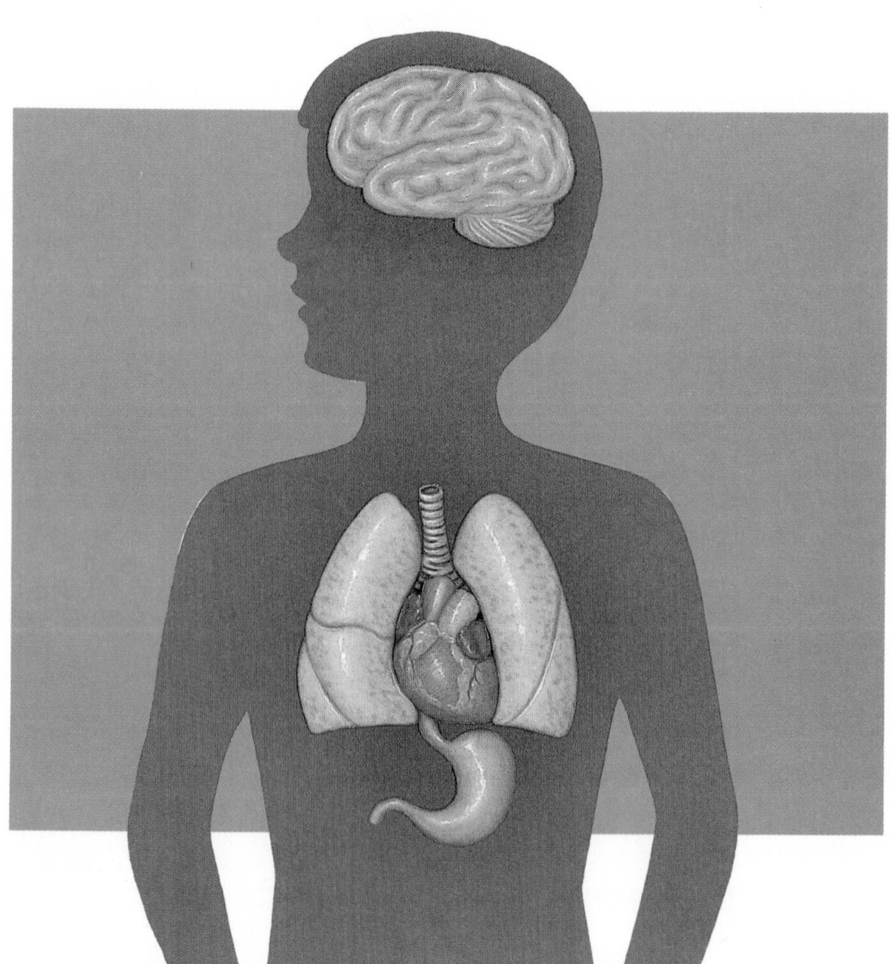

Review Science Words

Match the words and the pictures.

1. bones
2. brain
3. lungs
4. stomach

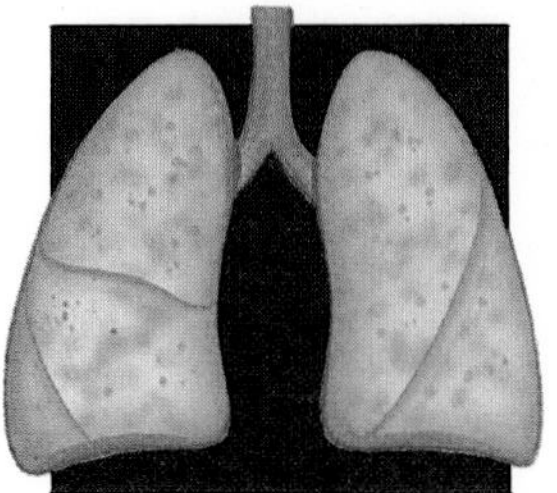
a.

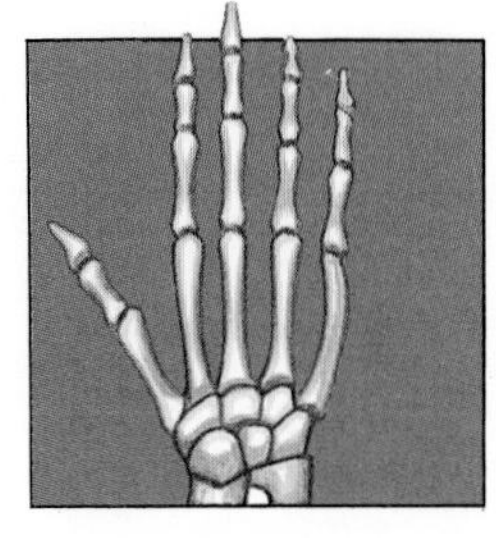
b.

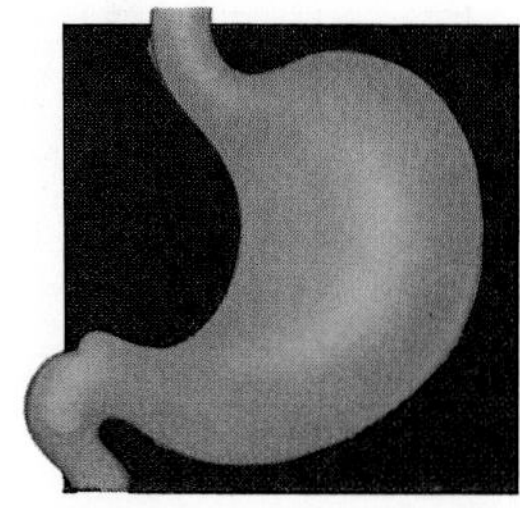
c.

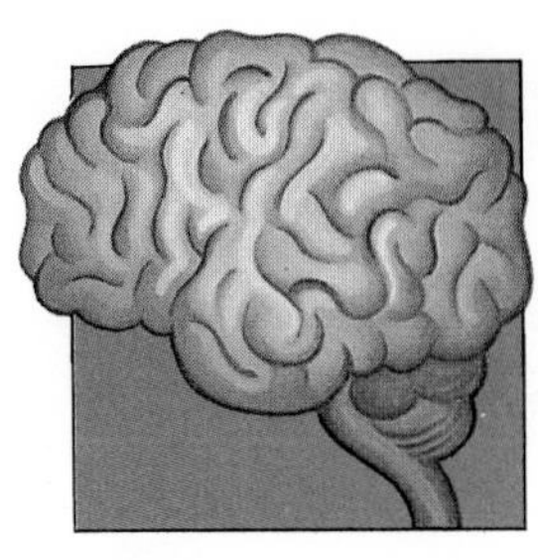
d.

Tell what each word means.

5. blood
6. nerves
7. oxygen
8. muscles
9. heart

Use Science Ideas

How will this girl use her brain, bones, muscles, and stomach?

Chapter 11

Keeping Healthy

When you stay healthy you can play, work, study, and exercise. How do you stay healthy?

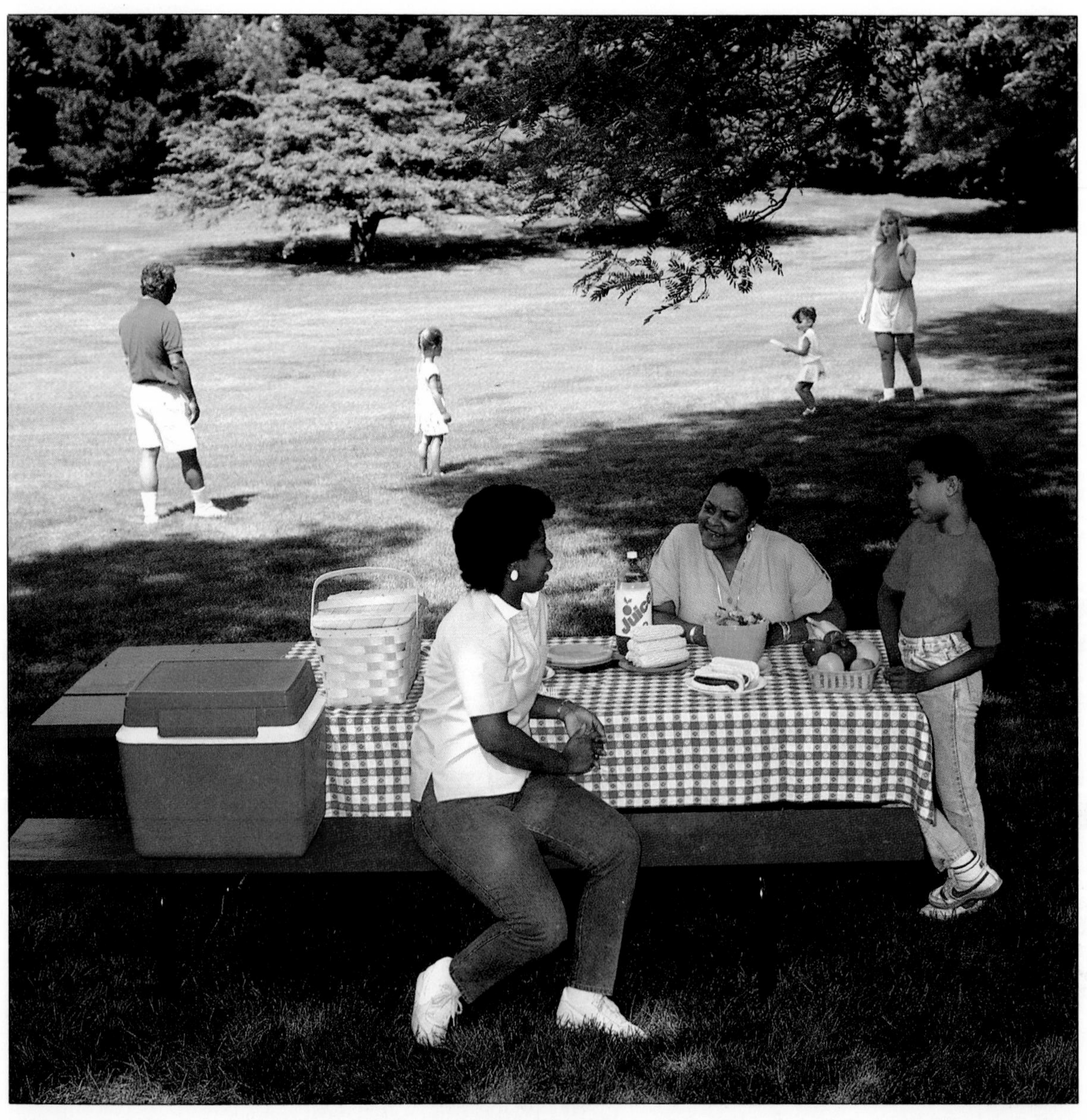

Starting the Chapter

You probably want to stay healthy. One way to stay healthy is to use your muscles to keep them strong. Try using your muscles while you sit. Then read more about staying healthy.

TRY THIS

Using Muscles

Put your hands on your desk. Push down as hard as you can. Count to ten. Put your hands together in front of you. Press as hard as you can. Count to ten. What muscles did you use each time?

Lesson 1 What Do You Need for Good Health?

You need food to stay healthy. Food helps you grow. It helps you work and play without getting tired.

You need different foods every day. The different foods you see here help your body work well. Which foods here do you enjoy eating?

You also need to drink plenty of water. Drinking water helps your body work well.

You need **exercise** to stay healthy. Exercise helps keep your heart and lungs healthy. Exercise helps you build strong muscles.

Many different kinds of exercise are good for your body. You help keep your body healthy when you run, ride a bicycle, and jump rope. What kinds of exercise do you like?

You need rest and sleep to stay healthy. Rest and sleep help your body work and feel better. Most children your age need about ten or eleven hours of sleep each day. How can you tell these children got enough sleep?

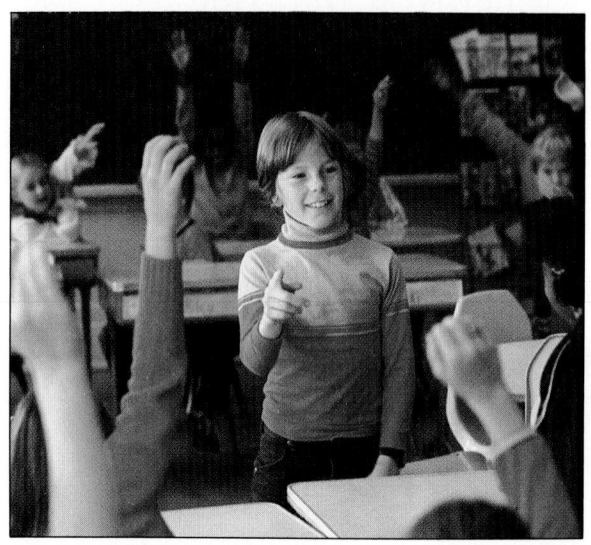

Lesson Review

1. What three things do you need for good health?
2. What kinds of exercise can help you stay healthy?

LIFE SCIENCE
Find Out
CONNECTION

Animals need rest and sleep to stay healthy. What animals sleep during the day? What animals sleep at night?

Science and People

George Washington Carver

George Washington Carver taught people about farming. He began to study peanuts. He found that peanuts were a good food for people. He found ways to make cheese, milk, and flour from peanuts. He also showed people how to make ink and soap from peanuts. George Washington Carver showed people how to find new ways to use foods.

What Do You Think?

Why was George Washington Carver's work important?

Lesson 2 What Helps Protect You from Sickness?

Germs are tiny living things. You cannot see them. They can get inside your body through your nose and mouth and through cuts in your skin. Some kinds of germs can make you sick.

Dirt can have germs in it. Keeping clean can protect you from some germs that could make you sick. Wash your hands like this to help get rid of germs. Use soap and warm water.

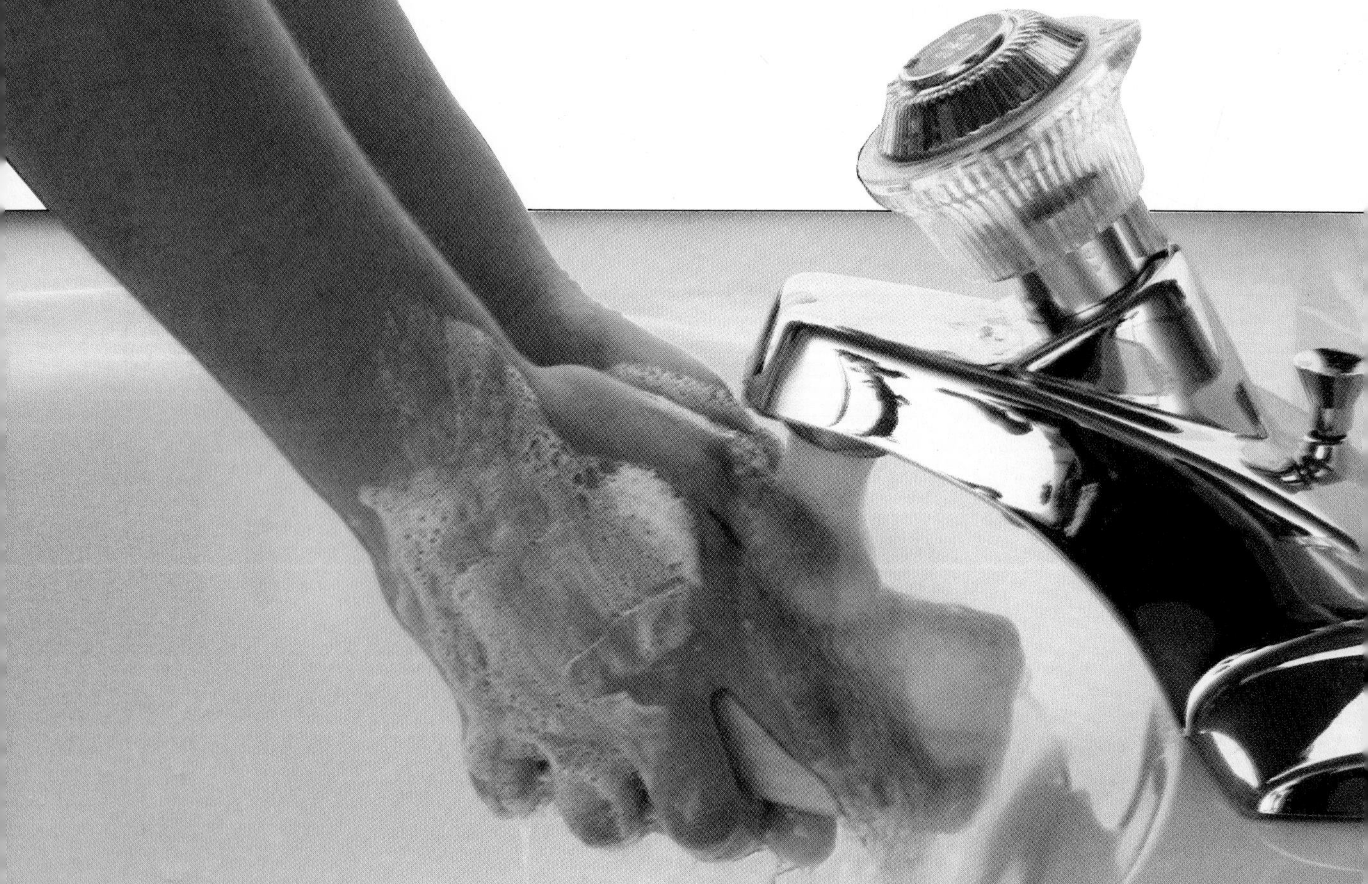

Objects can have germs on them. You can protect yourself from sickness by keeping objects like pencils out of your mouth.

Some **medicines** can protect you from sickness. Sometimes you get these medicines in shots. The medicine this child is taking will keep him from getting a sickness called polio.

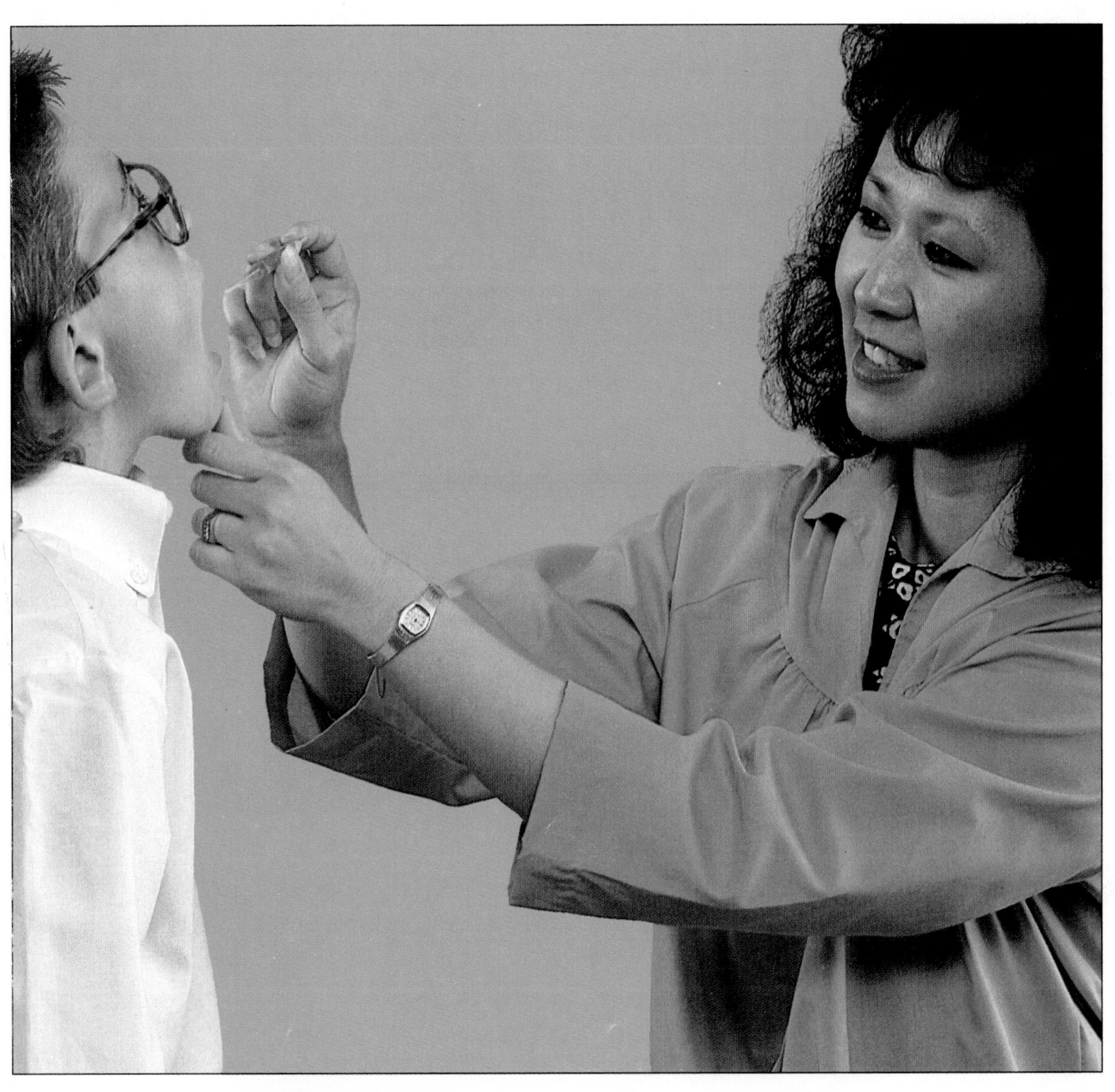

If you do get sick from germs, your body works hard to help you get well. Special parts of your body work to get rid of the germs that made you sick. You can help your body by getting extra rest as this child does. Also remember to eat healthy foods.

Lesson Review

1. What do some sicknesses come from?
2. What can you do to help keep yourself from getting sick?

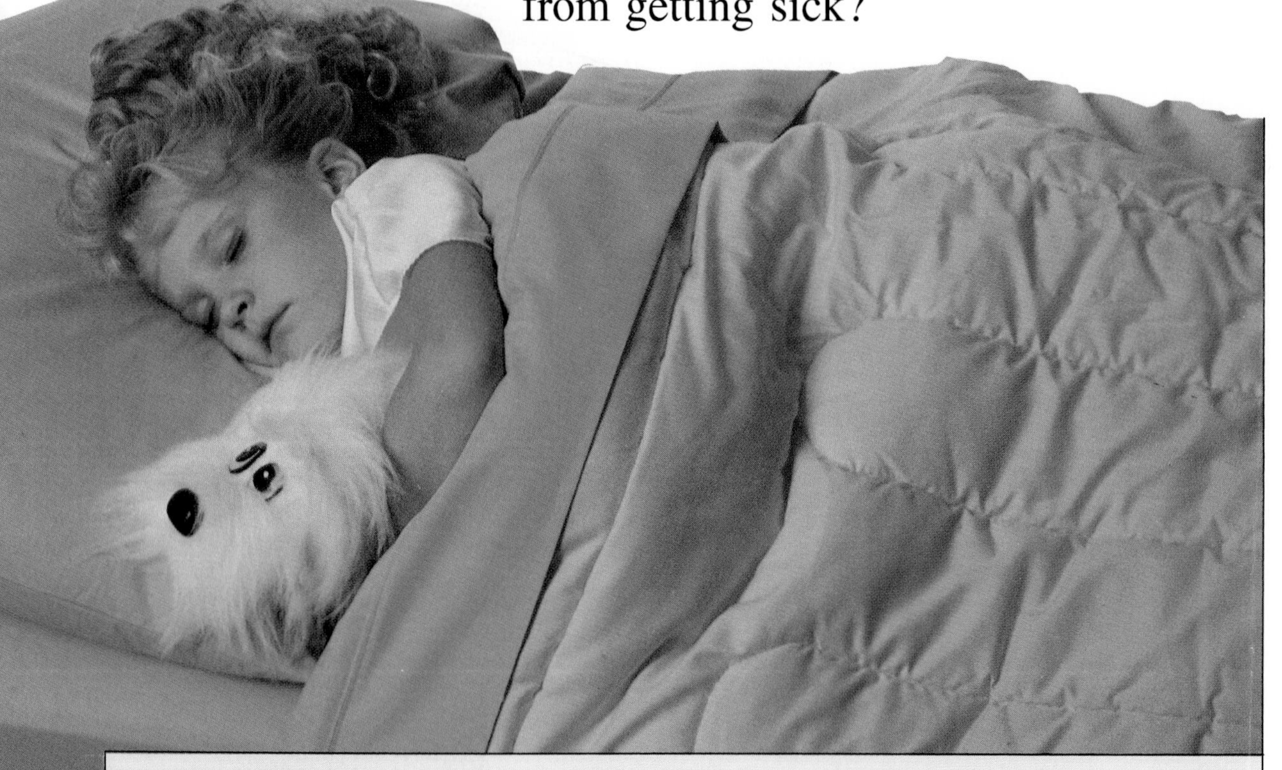

HUMAN BODY

Find Out

Shots can protect you from some sickness. Ask an adult which shots you have had.

ACTIVITY

Protecting Yourself from Germs

Follow the Directions

1. Wash your hands.
2. Pretend you have a cut on your hand. Cover it with tape like this to protect it from germs.
3. Play and work for a few hours.
4. Take off the tape.
5. Find out if the place under the tape looks clean or dirty.

Tell What You Learned

Tell how putting a bandage on a cut protects against germs. Tell another way to keep germs out of a small cut.

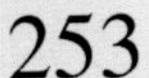

Lesson 3 What Can You Do to Stay Safe?

You can stay safe on the street. Cross streets carefully. Watch **traffic signals.** Look left, right, and then left again. Wait to cross until you see no cars each time.

Follow the bicycle rules where you live. Ride on the sidewalk if you can. Ride a bicycle that is the right size for you.

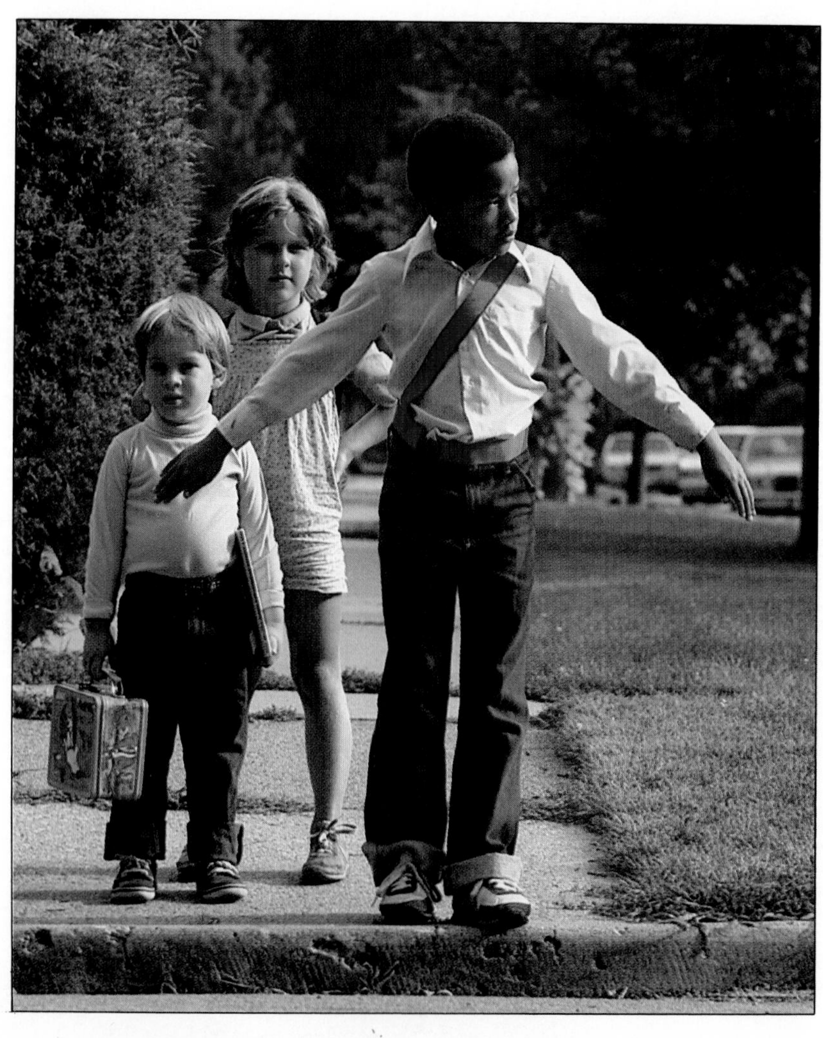

Be safe in your home. Never take any medicine by yourself. Only your parents or someone they ask should give you medicine. They can read the label and use the medicine safely.

Some things used in homes can be **poisons.** They can hurt your skin or eyes. Do not breathe them in or taste them. Use things like the picture shows only with help from an adult.

Stay safe at school. The teacher will help you work safely. Learn the school rules for a fire drill and follow them.

Play safely in the gym. Follow the teacher's directions. Help other students. How are these children playing safely?

Lesson Review

1. How can you stay safe on the street?
2. What can you do to be safe at home and school?

HUMAN BODY

Find Out

How does wearing a safety belt when riding in a car help keep you safe?

Observing Safety Signs

Follow the Directions

1. Make two safety signs like these.
2. Make one sign with yellow paper.
3. Make one sign with dark paper.
4. Observe the signs in a dark room.

Tell What You Learned

Which sign was easier to see? What other colors do you think would be good for safety signs?

Making and Using a Graph

What healthy snacks did the children eat most?

1. Look at the healthy snacks each child ate. Use your own paper. Write the name of each child and what snacks each child ate.

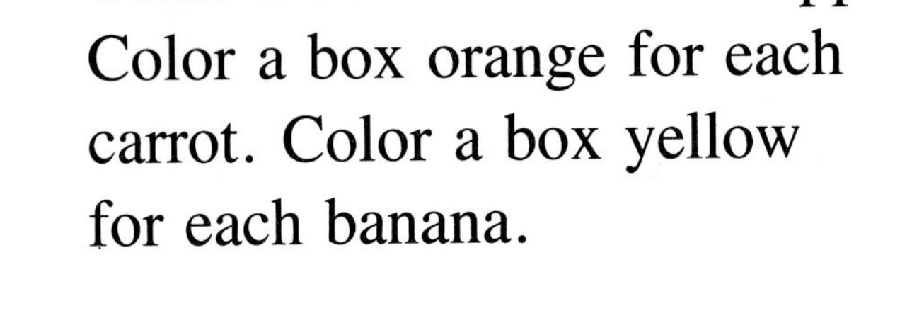

2. Draw a graph like this one. Color a box red for each apple. Color a box orange for each carrot. Color a box yellow for each banana.

3. What food did the children eat most for a healthy snack?

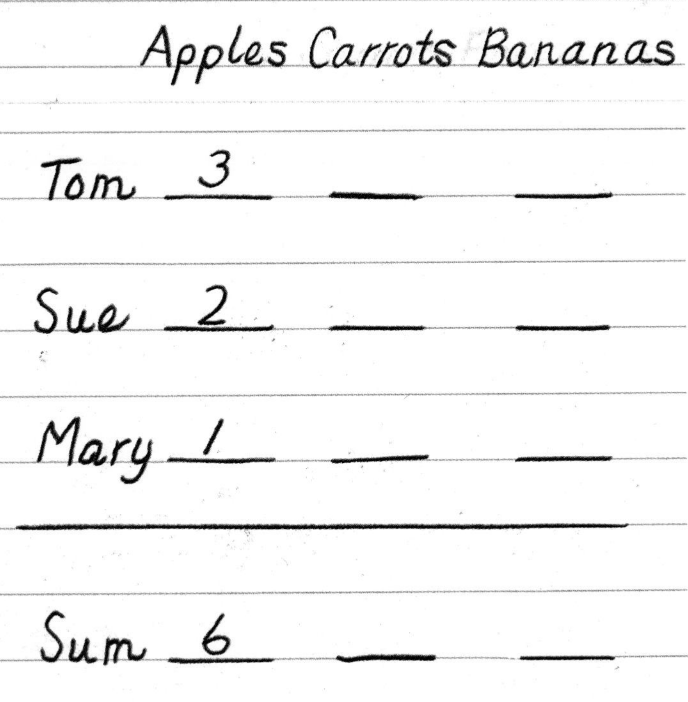

	Apples	Carrots	Bananas
Tom	3	___	___
Sue	2	___	___
Mary	1	___	___
Sum	6	___	___

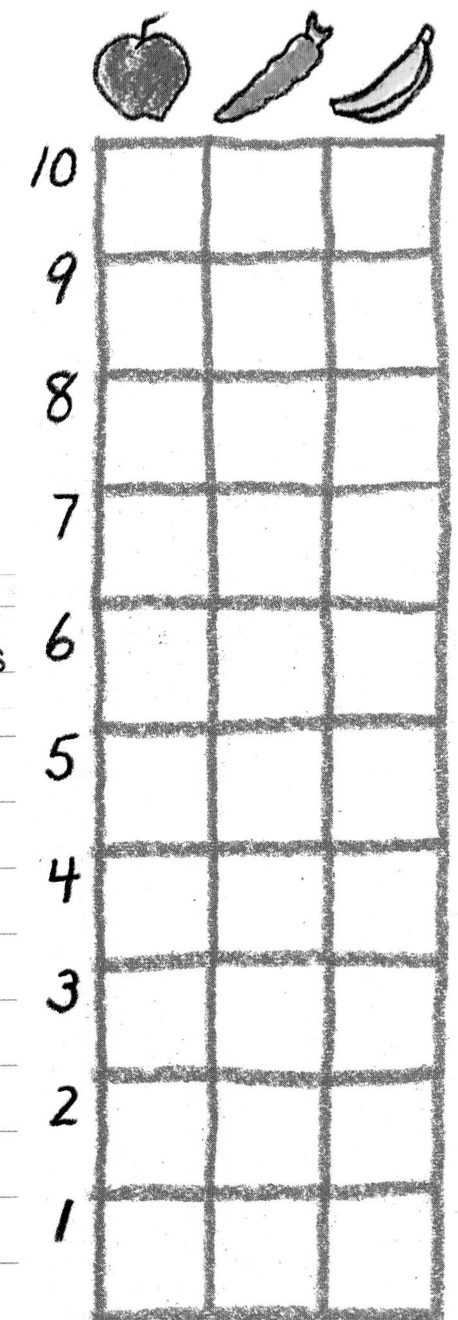

Chapter 11 Review

Review Chapter Ideas

1. Tell three ways to stay healthy.
2. Tell what healthy food does for your body.
3. Name what some kinds of sickness come from.
4. Tell two ways to help keep yourself from getting sick.
5. Tell how to cross a street safely.
6. Look at the picture. Tell how to be safe with medicines.

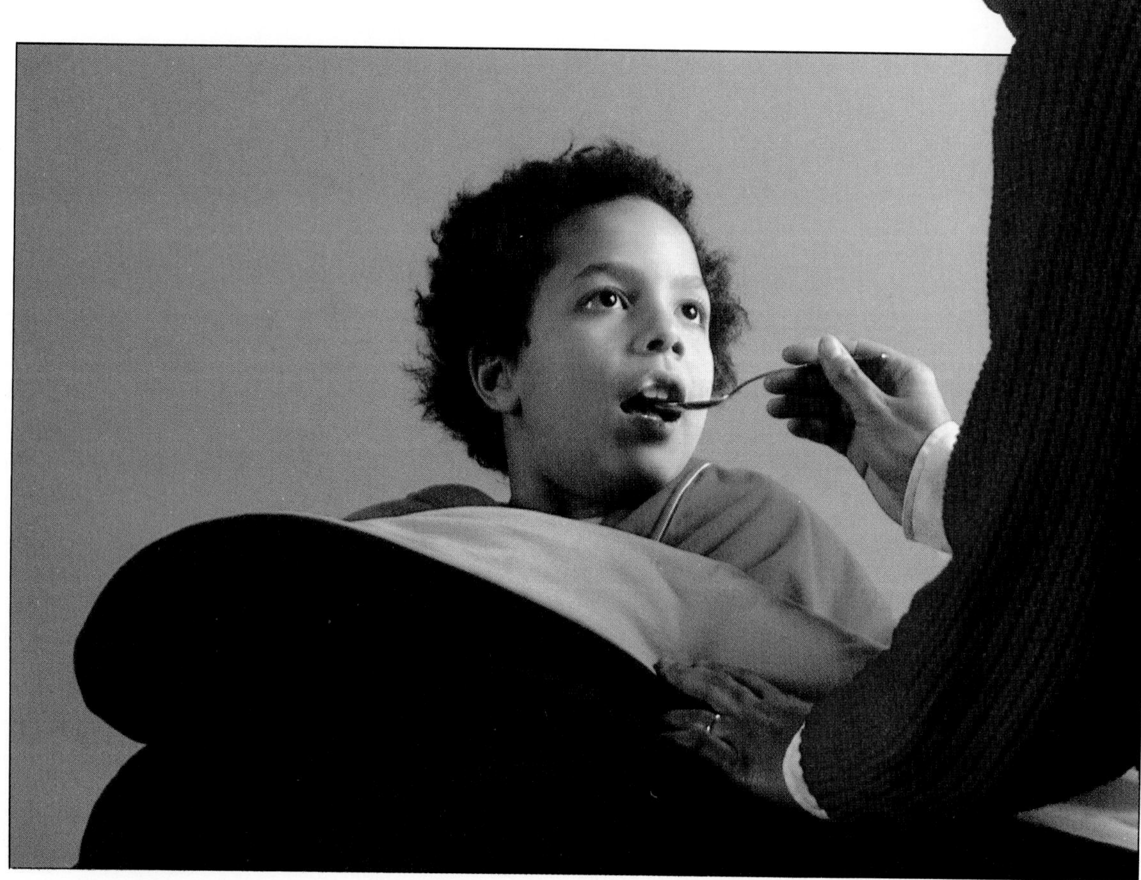

Review Science Words

Match the words and the pictures.

1. poison
2. traffic signal
3. medicines
4. exercise

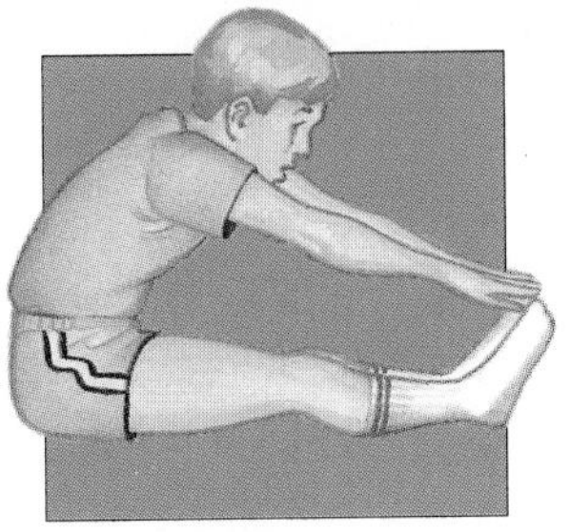

a.

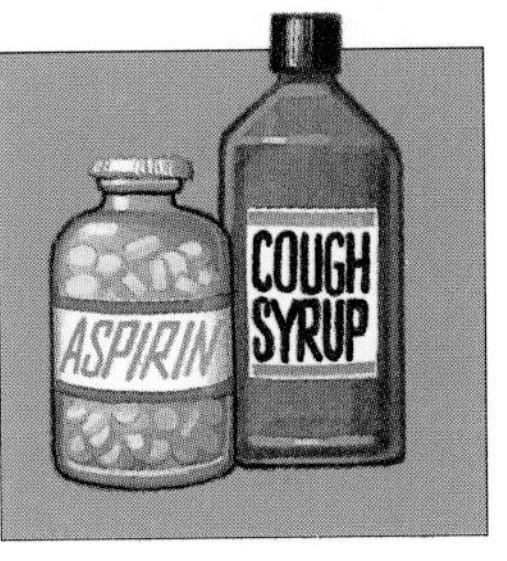

b.

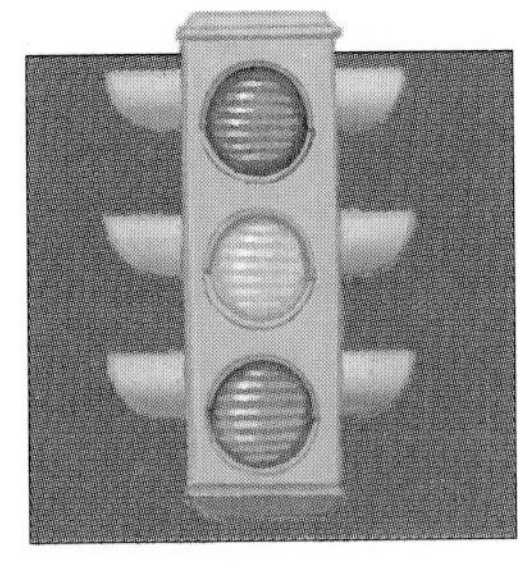

c.

d.

Tell what the word means.

5. germ

Use Science Ideas

Which child can be seen better by drivers?

Doctor

Doctors have many different kinds of jobs. Some doctors take care of children from the time they are born until they are teenagers.

These doctors check to see if children are growing well. They check different parts of the body, such as the eyes, ears, and nose. They ask children how they feel. They help sick children get better.

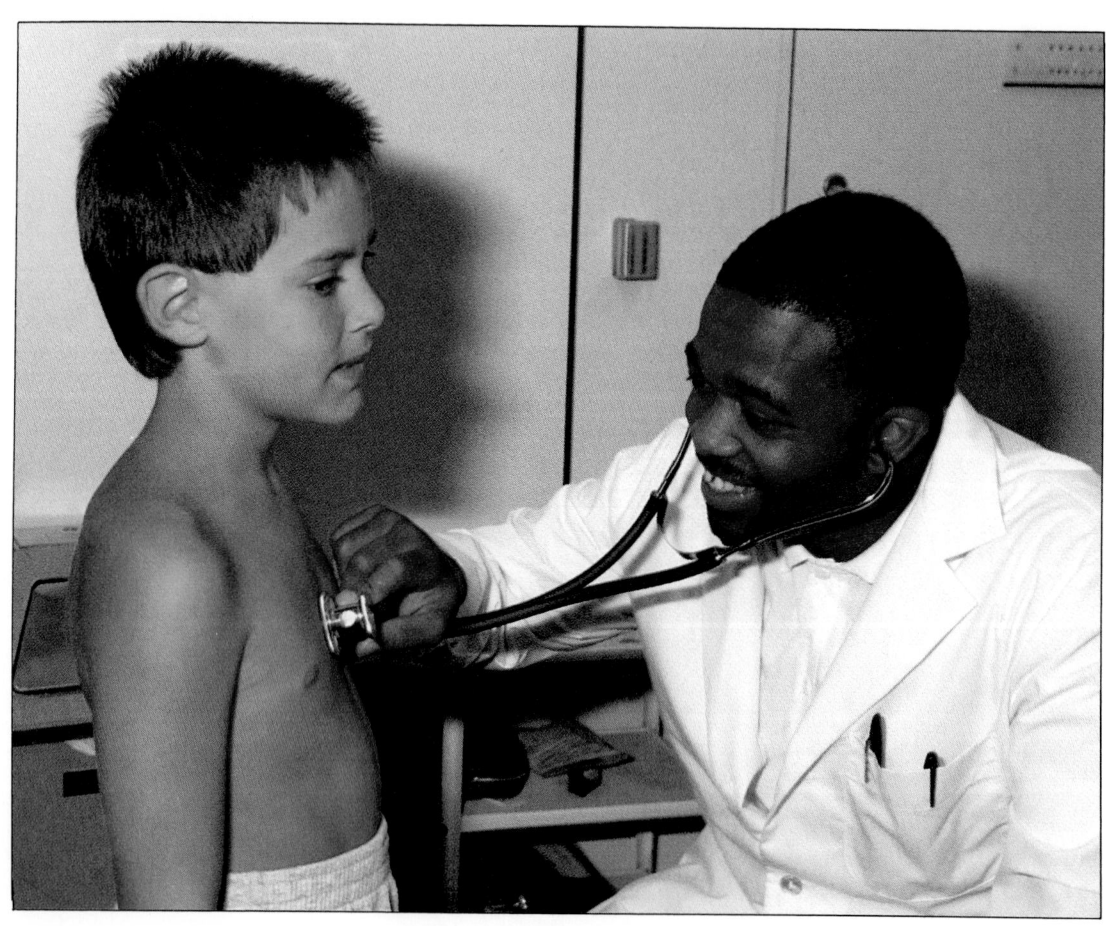

X Rays

How are X rays used to take pictures inside the body?

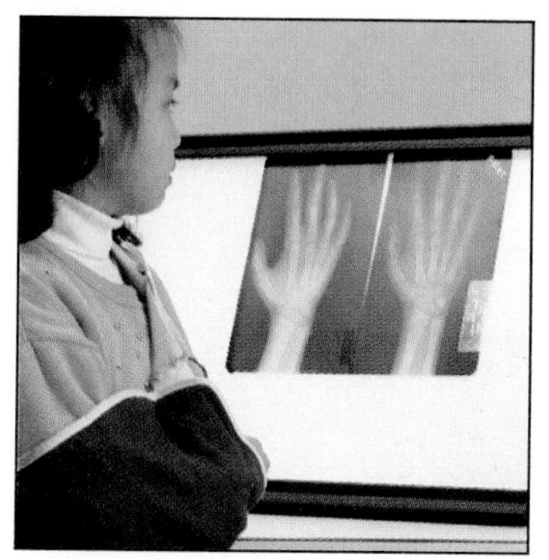

Special machines shoot X rays just as a flashlight shoots a beam of light. The X rays go through the body onto a piece of film. Notice how the machine is shooting X rays through the hand. Only hard or thick parts of the body stop the rays. The parts that stop the X rays cause shadows. The film will show shadows of bones, teeth, or thick parts of the body. What shadows does the girl see on the film?

Unit 4 Review

Answer the Questions

1. How do muscles and bones work together?
2. What body part controls everything a person does?
3. What is one job of the heart and of the lungs?
4. How do pieces of food change after you eat them?
5. What are three things you should do to help yourself stay healthy?
6. How can a person keep some kinds of sickness away?
7. How can you protect yourself from germs?

Study the Pictures

How can you be safe with these?

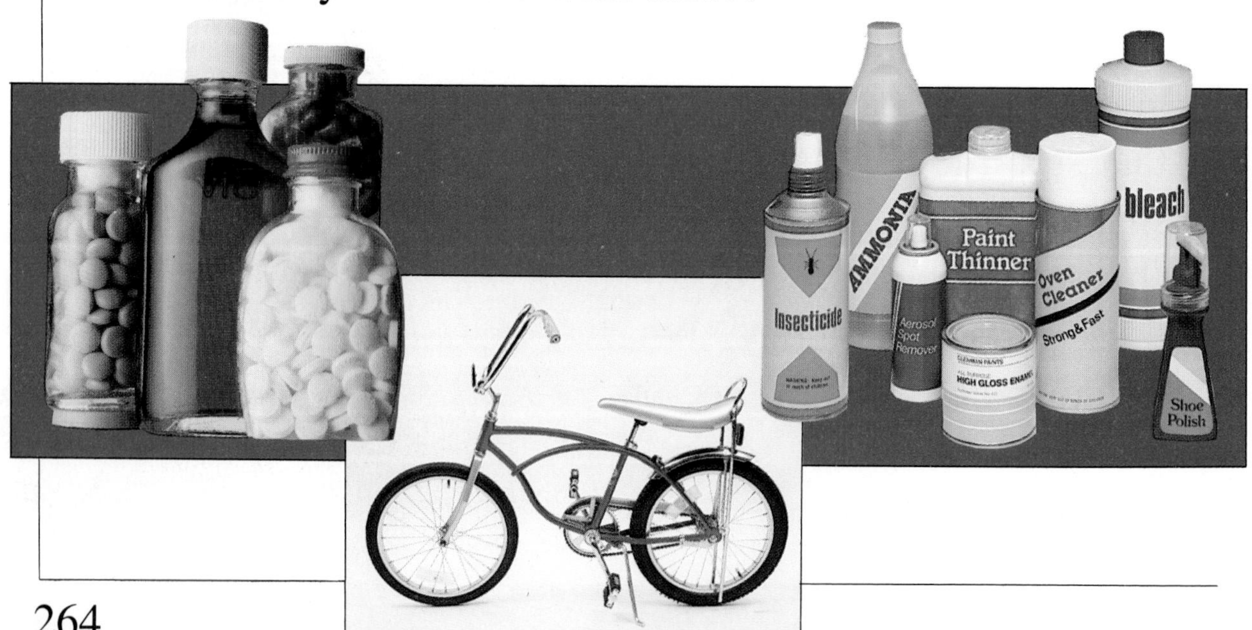

What to Do

1. Use your own paper. Finish this story.
   Today I used my bones and muscles to ___.
   Write as many ways as you can remember.
2. Look back at the foods on pages 246 and 247. Draw a picture of a meal you would like using some of these foods.
3. Make a poster that shows two ways to stay healthy. Write a title on the poster.

Independent Study Guide

Answer the questions for each chapter.
Use your own paper. Write the best word.

Chapter 1 Study Guide

Use your own paper. Write the best word.

LESSON 1
pages 16–19

1. Some flowers grow at the top of a ____.
   leaf stem root

LESSON 2
pages 20–21

2. The leaves and other green parts of plants make ____.
   water sunlight food

LESSON 3
pages 24–26

3. As a new plant grows, it uses food from the inside of the ____.
   seed roots flower

LESSON 4
pages 28–29

4. Plants grow in different kinds of ____.
   wind sunlight habitats
5. A pond is a ____ habitat.
   dry wet desert

Chapter 2 Study Guide

LESSON 1
pages 36–40

1. Animals with fur on their bodies are ____.
   birds mammals scales
2. Birds have wings and ____ on their bodies.
   feathers scales fur

3. Turtles, snakes, and lizards are ▒▒.
fish birds reptiles

LESSON 2
pages 42–43

4. The forest is a squirrel's ▒▒.
work habitat pond

LESSON 3
pages 44–46

5. Some animals live in caves for ▒▒.
protection food people

6. Many animals ▒▒ in the winter.
work hibernate shelter

LESSON 4
pages 48–50

7. Baby mammals are born ▒▒.
alive parents grown

8. Baby birds and ▒▒ hatch from eggs.
people elephants tadpoles

Chapter 3 Study Guide

LESSON 1
pages 58–60

1. A dinosaur footprint left in rock is a ▒▒.
picture fossil puzzle

2. The climate is the kind of ▒▒ the earth has over a very long time.
shape rocks weather

LESSON 2
pages 62–66

3. Dinosaurs with long, sharp teeth ate ▒▒.
leaves meat flowers

4. Dinosaurs with flat teeth ate ▒▒.
animals plants meat

LESSON 3
pages 68–69

5. The ▒▒ lived after dinosaurs disappeared.
snails flying reptiles mammals

LESSON 4

pages 70–72

6. ___ materials can change the plants and fish living in a lake, river, or ocean.
   Harmful   New   Old

LESSON 5

pages 74–75

7. People can save ___ by using electricity carefully.
   sand   fuel   soil

Chapter 4 Study Guide

Use your own paper. Write the best word.

LESSON 1

pages 88–89

1. Most matter takes up space and has ___.
   color   weight   fur
2. Floating and sinking are ___ of matter.
   weights   kinds   properties

LESSON 2

pages 92–96

3. The desk you are sitting at is a ___.
   solid   gas   liquid
4. Look at the pictures below. Tell which one does not have its own shape.

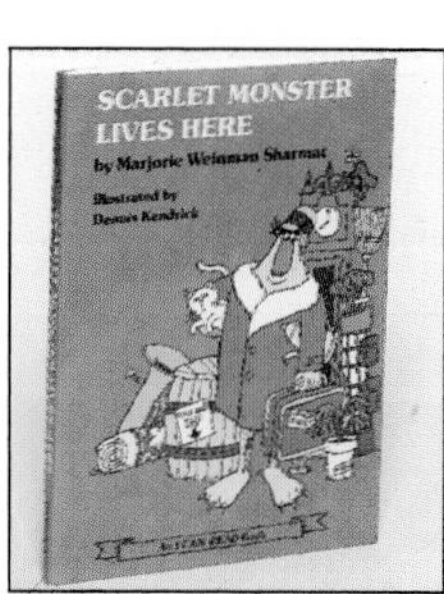

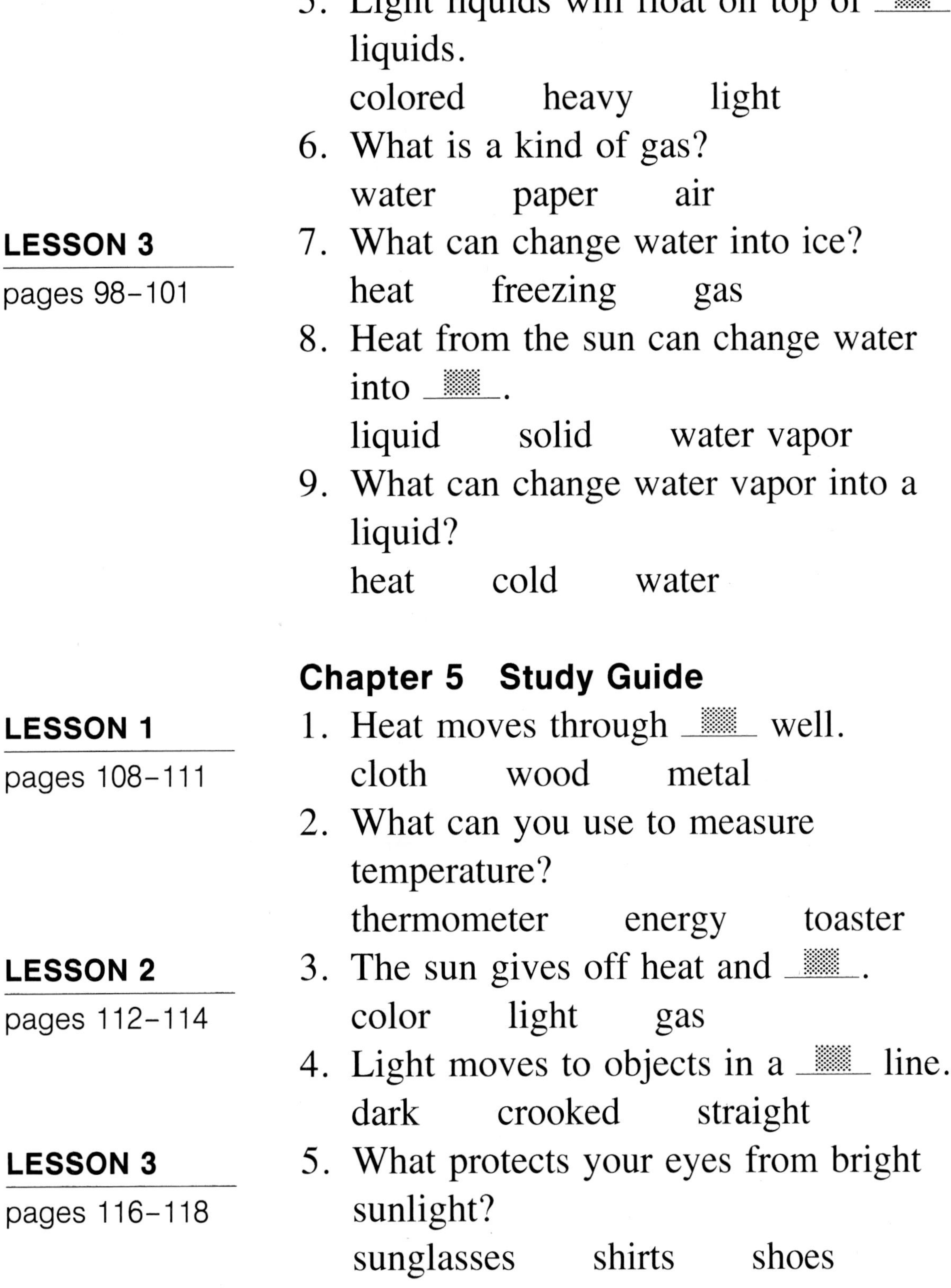

5. Light liquids will float on top of ____ liquids.
   colored heavy light
6. What is a kind of gas?
   water paper air

LESSON 3
pages 98–101

7. What can change water into ice?
   heat freezing gas
8. Heat from the sun can change water into ____.
   liquid solid water vapor
9. What can change water vapor into a liquid?
   heat cold water

Chapter 5 Study Guide

LESSON 1
pages 108–111

1. Heat moves through ____ well.
   cloth wood metal
2. What can you use to measure temperature?
   thermometer energy toaster

LESSON 2
pages 112–114

3. The sun gives off heat and ____.
   color light gas
4. Light moves to objects in a ____ line.
   dark crooked straight

LESSON 3
pages 116–118

5. What protects your eyes from bright sunlight?
   sunglasses shirts shoes

LESSON 4
pages 120–122

6. You hear sounds when objects ____.
   vibrate   move   bounce

LESSON 5
pages 124–125

7. Sound can warn you of ____.
   information   danger   radios

Chapter 6 Study Guide

Use your own paper. Write the best word.

LESSON 1
pages 132–133

1. You use ____ when you move your chair.
   machines   force   light

LESSON 2
pages 134–136

2. The ____ of magnets push or pull the hardest.
   middle   sides   poles
3. What pole pulls toward the north pole?
   north pole   south pole   east pole

LESSON 3
pages 138–139

4. What uses electricity to make light?
   fire   sun   lamp

LESSON 4
pages 142–143

5. Only use an electric appliance if your hands are ____.
   clean   empty   dry

Chapter 7 Study Guide

LESSON 1
pages 156–158

1. Fresh water has very little ____ in it.
   ice   soil   salt
2. Most groundwater goes into rivers and ____.
   oceans   ponds   rain

LESSON 2

pages 160–163

3. People cannot drink ocean water because it is ▒▒.
cold warm salty

LESSON 3

pages 166–169

4. Water with harmful wastes in it is ▒▒.
polluted clean salty

LESSON 4

pages 170–171

5. What is air made of?
liquids gases salt

LESSON 5

pages 172–173

6. What pollutes the air?
toys sailboats cars

Chapter 8 Study Guide

LESSON 1

pages 180–184

1. What is a way the weather can change?
shape temperature color
2. Look at the picture below. What season does this weather remind you of?

summer
winter
fall

LESSON 2

pages 186–189

3. What are clouds made of?
water soil salt

LESSON 3

pages 192–193

4. The warmest weather in the world is at the ▒▒.
North Pole South Pole Equator

Chapter 9 Study Guide

LESSON 1

pages 200–204

1. The sun is a ball of glowing ▒▒.
   oil coal gases

LESSON 2

pages 206–207

2. Earth is a ▒▒.
   sun star planet

LESSON 3

pages 210–211

3. Most stars look ▒▒ because they are very far from the earth.
   big bright small

Chapter 10 Study Guide

LESSON 1

pages 224–227

1. Your bones help you ▒▒.
   learn move see

LESSON 2

pages 228–230

2. You use your ▒▒ when you think.
   brain muscles bones

LESSON 3

pages 232–234

3. What pumps blood to your body?
   lungs heart bones

LESSON 4

pages 236–238

4. ▒▒ carries changed food to every part of the body.
   Blood Juice Muscles

Chapter 11 Study Guide

LESSON 1

pages 246–248

1. You need food and ▒▒ for good health.
   water candy bicycles

LESSON 2

pages 250–252

2. Keeping ▒▒ can protect you from some germs.
   friends clean food

LESSON 3

pages 254–256

3. Do not breathe in or taste ▒▒.
   oxygen water poisons

Using Scientific Methods

Almost every day scientists learn new things about the world. They try to find the answers to problems. Scientists use scientific methods to help them with problems. They use these steps in their methods. Sometimes scientists use the steps in different order. You can use these steps to find answers too.

Explain the Problem

Ask a question like this. Does wind make waves?

Make Observations

Tell about the size, color, or shape of things.

Give a Hypothesis

Try to answer the problem. Think of different ideas. Then do an experiment to test your ideas.

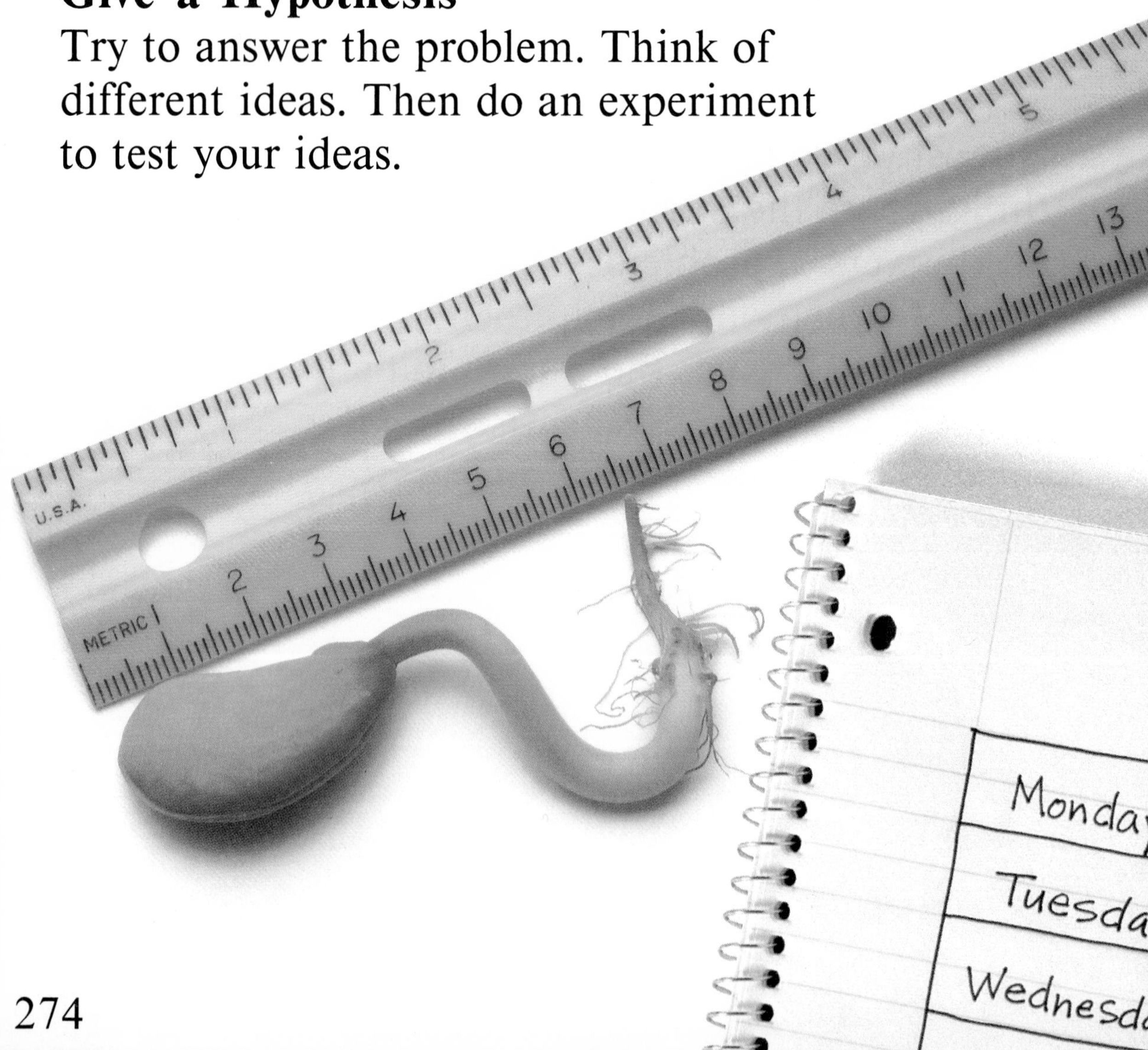

Make a Chart or Graph

Write what you learn in the experiment in your chart or graph.

Make Conclusions

Decide if your hypothesis is right or wrong.

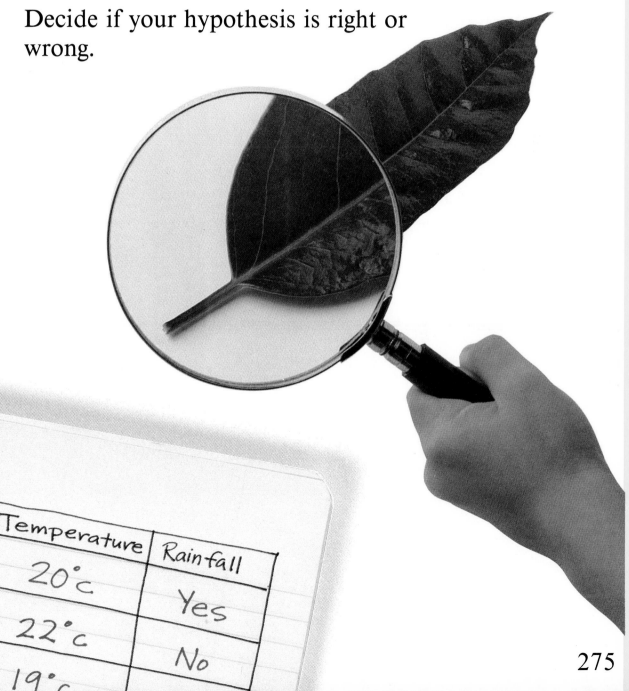

Safety in Science

Scientists are careful when they do experiments. You also need to be careful. Here are some safety rules to remember.

- Read each experiment carefully.
- Wear cover goggles when needed.
- Clean up spills right away.
- Wash your hands after each experiment.

- Never taste or smell unknown things.
- Do not shine lights in someone's eyes.
- Clean up when you finish an experiment.

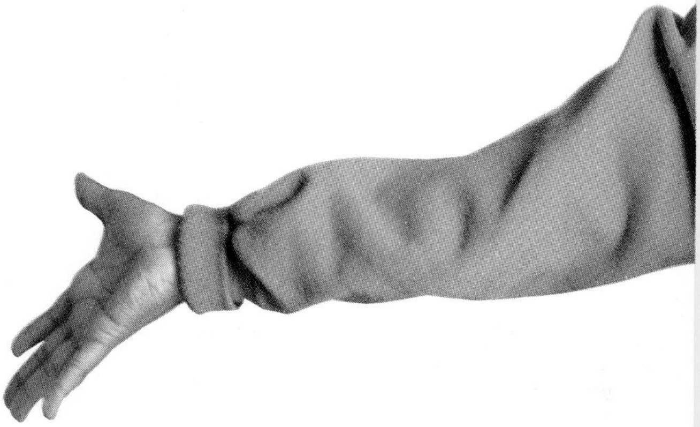

Chapter 1 Experiment Skills

Maria and Juan were pulling weeds in their yard. They wondered why such tall plants had such short roots. Juan decided that some parts of a plant grow more than other parts.

Problem

Do some parts of plants grow more than other parts?
Give your hypothesis.
Then find out if your hypothesis is right.
Read the experiment to find out.

Follow the Directions

1. Make a chart like the one below.
2. Gently lay the plant on a paper.
3. Mark how long the plant's roots and stems are.
4. Put the plant back into the pot. Wait one week.
5. Measure how many centimeters the roots and stems grew. Write the answers in your chart.
6. Circle in the chart the part that grew the most.

Write Your Conclusion

Do some parts of plants grow more than other parts?

Plant part	Grew
stems	__ cm
roots	__ cm

Chapter 2 Experiment Skills

Sam heard crickets chirping in his basement. He wondered what crickets use as food. His dad told him to catch a cricket. Then he could feed it to find out.

Sam decided to feed the cricket different foods. He thought maybe a cricket would like meat and fruit.

Problem

Do crickets eat meat and fruit?
Give your hypothesis.
Then find out if your hypothesis is right.
Read the experiment to find out.

Follow the Directions

1. Make a chart like the one below.
2. Make air holes in a box.
3. Place your cricket in the box.
4. Give the cricket a bit of meat and a bit of apple. Give it a little water too.
5. Check the cricket each day for two days.
6. Tell in the chart what food is left each day.
7. Circle in the chart the food that the cricket liked better.

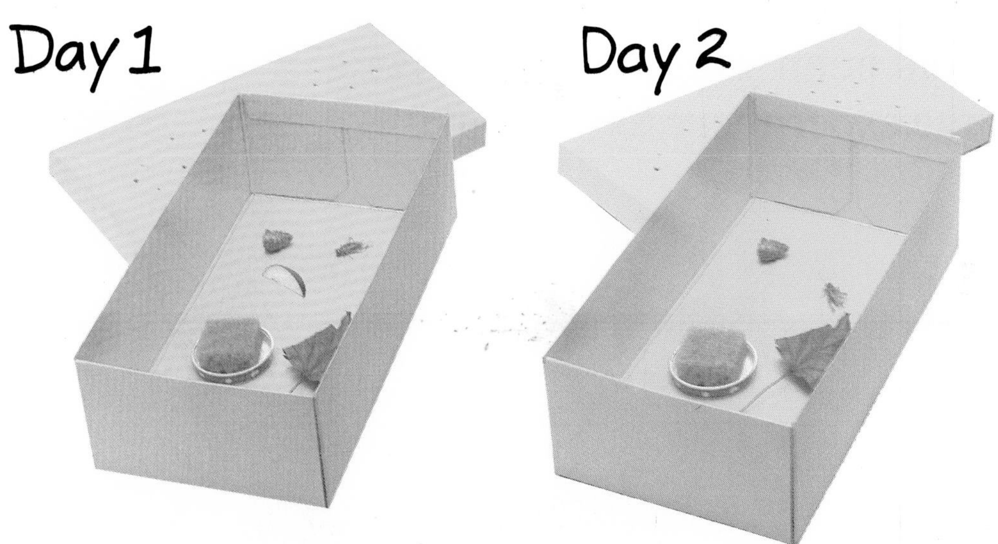

Write Your Conclusion

Do crickets eat fruit and meat?

Cricket	Food
day 1	
day 2	

Chapter 3 Experiment Skills

Cindy and Kathy walked into their classroom on a Monday morning. Kathy looked at the plants near the window. She asked Cindy what was wrong with them. On Friday the plants had looked fine. Now their leaves drooped. Cindy told Kathy that the plants needed water.

Problem

Does a plant need water to live?
Give your hypothesis.
Then find out if your hypothesis is right.
Read the experiment to find out.

Follow the Directions

1. Make a chart like the one below.
2. Place two healthy plants in a window. Mark them plant 1 and plant 2.
3. Add 50 milliliters of water to plant 2 every other day. Milliliters are marked mL on the cup.
4. Watch both plants for two weeks.
5. Tell in the chart if the plants look healthy or not healthy.

After 2 weeks

Write Your Conclusion

Does a plant need water to live?

Plant	After 2 weeks
1. without water	
2. with water	

Chapter 4 Experiment Skills

Beth wants to add a rock to her fish bowl. She drops a big rock into the bowl. Water runs out of the bowl. The fish seems frightened. Beth wishes she had put in a smaller rock.

Her mother says, "A rock takes up space in the water. A big rock takes up more space than a smaller rock. Let's find out what size rock you should use."

Problem

Does a big rock take up more space than a smaller rock?
Give your hypothesis.
Then find out if your hypothesis is right.
Read the experiment to find out.

Follow the Directions

1. Make a chart like the one below.
2. Fill a bowl to the middle with water. Tape how high the water is.
3. Place a big rock in the water. Tell in the chart if the water goes up.
4. Place a small rock in the water. Tell in the chart if the water goes up.
5. Circle in the chart the rock that makes the water go up more.

Write Your Conclusion

Does a big rock take up more space than a smaller rock?

Rock	Water in bowl
big	
small	

Chapter 5 Experiment Skills

Kathy and Eddie are reading a book together. They notice their shadows on the pages. Suddenly Kathy says, "I can make a shadow grow bigger. Then I can make it grow smaller."

"Can you really?" asks Eddie. "Our shadows on the book do not change size."

"Come on." says Kathy, "I'll show you how I can do it."

Problem

Can you make a shadow change size?
Give your hypothesis.
Then find out if your hypothesis is right.
Read the experiment to find out.

Follow the Directions

1. Make a chart like the one below.
2. Place a toy and a flashlight on a table.
3. Tape a sheet of paper behind the toy.
4. Turn the flashlight on.
5. Look at the shadow.
6. Move the light farther from the toy. Look at the shadow again.
7. See which shadow is larger. Write your answer in your chart.

Write Your Conclusion

Can you make a shadow change size?

Light	Shadow
close up	
far away	

Chapter 6 Experiment Skills

Marie wants to do magic tricks at a birthday party. She wants to use a magnet to make objects appear to move by themselves. Marie knows she must hide the magnet to do the trick. She wonders if she can hide the magnet under cardboard or plastic.

Problem

Does a magnet attract metal objects through cardboard and plastic?
Give your hypothesis.
Then find out if your hypothesis is right.
Read the experiment to find out.

Follow the Directions

1. Make a chart like the one below.
2. See if the magnet can attract paperclips through cardboard. Write yes or no in the chart.
3. See if the magnet attracts paperclips through plastic. Write yes or no in your chart.

Tell Your Conclusion

Does a magnet attract metal objects through cardboard and through plastic?

Attracts clips	Magnet
through cardboard	
through plastic	

Chapter 7 Experiment Skills

Bob passed a pond on his way to school. The water looked very clear. It rained later that morning. The water looked muddy and dirty at lunchtime. Bob wonders if the water will be clear later.

Problem

Can dirty water become clear?
Give your hypothesis.
Then find out if your hypothesis is right.
Read the experiment to find out.

Follow the Directions

1. Make a chart like the one below.
2. Find a jar with a lid. Put some dirt and stones in it. Add water.
3. Close the jar and shake it. Watch what happens. Is the water clear? Write yes or no in your chart.
4. Leave the jar for one hour. See where the dirt goes. Does the water get clear? Write your answer in your chart.

Tell Your Conclusion

Can dirty water become clear?

Time	Clear water
after shaking	
after one hour	

Chapter 8 Experiment Skills

Steve wondered why the towel still felt cold and wet. It had hung outside for hours. Yesterday a wet towel dried quickly outside. It was a warm, sunny day.

Steve knew that water evaporates. It moves from the towel to the air. He decided a towel dried faster in warm air than cold air. Steve thought of a way to see if he was right.

Problem

Does water evaporate faster in warm air than in cold air?

Give your hypothesis.

Then find out if your hypothesis is right.

Read the experiment to find out.

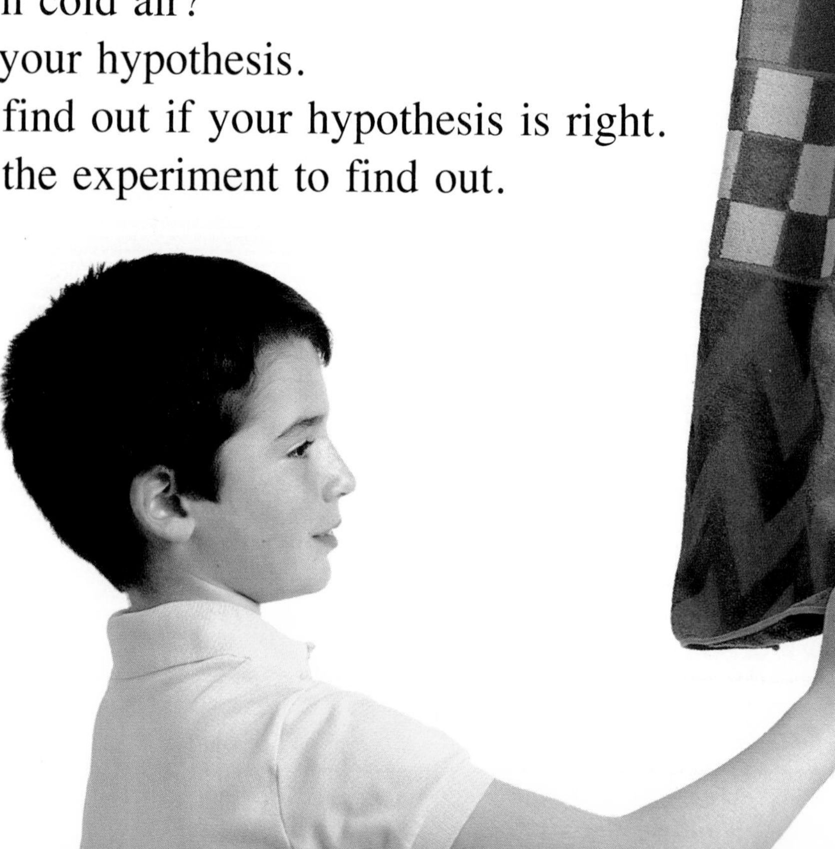

Follow the Directions

1. Make a chart like the one below.
2. Fill two cups with the same amount of water. Tape how high the water is in each cup.
3. Put one cup in a cold place. Put the other cup in a warm place.
4. Wait three days. Tell in the chart if each cup has lost water.
5. Circle in the chart where the most water evaporated.

Tell Your Conclusion

Does water evaporate faster in warm air than in cold air?

Place	Water evaporated
cold	
warm	

Chapter 9 Experiment Skills

Kay is playing on the playground after school. It is a bright and sunny afternoon. Suddenly she notices the shadow of the flag pole. The shadow is very long. She remembers that sometimes shadows are short. She wonders if shadows change size during the day. Kay decides to find out.

Problem

Is a shadow shorter at noon than it is in the afternoon?
Give your hypothesis.
Then find out if your hypothesis is right.
Read the experiment to find out.

Follow the Directions

1. Make a chart like the one below.
2. Set up a short stick. Put a sheet of paper on the ground. The shadow of the stick should fall on it.
3. Measure the shadow at noon. Write your answer in your chart.
4. Measure the shadow later in the afternoon. Write your answer in your chart.
5. Circle the time when the shadow is longer.

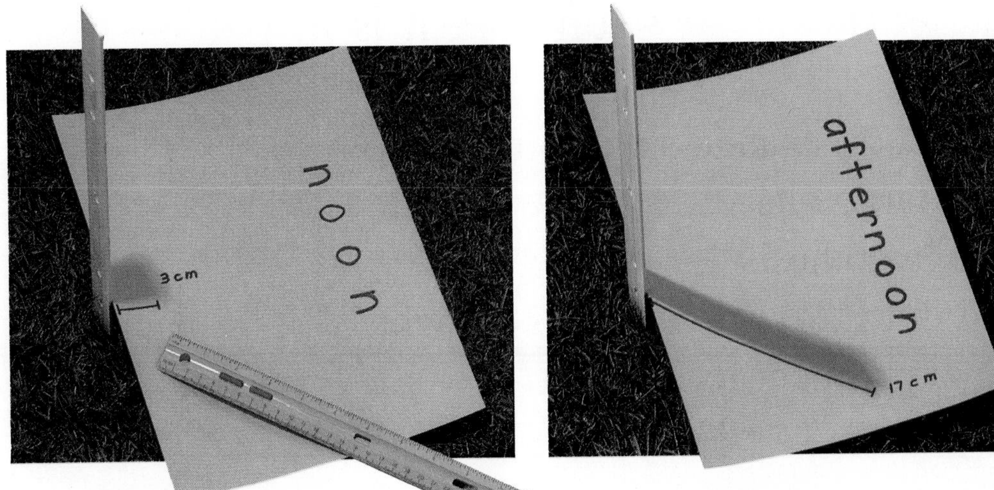

Tell Your Conclusion

Is a shadow shorter at noon than it is in the afternoon?

Time	Shadow
noon	__ cm
afternoon	__ cm

Chapter 10 Experiment Skills

James has a baby sister. Sometimes his mother lets him feed her. The baby food is soft and is made up of little pieces of food. Large pieces of food might make the baby sick.

James knows his body changes the food he eats. His body breaks food into smaller and smaller pieces. He wonders if small bits change faster and easier than large bits.

Problem

Does your body change small bits of food faster than large bits?
Give your hypothesis.
Then find out if your hypothesis is right.
Read the experiment to find out.

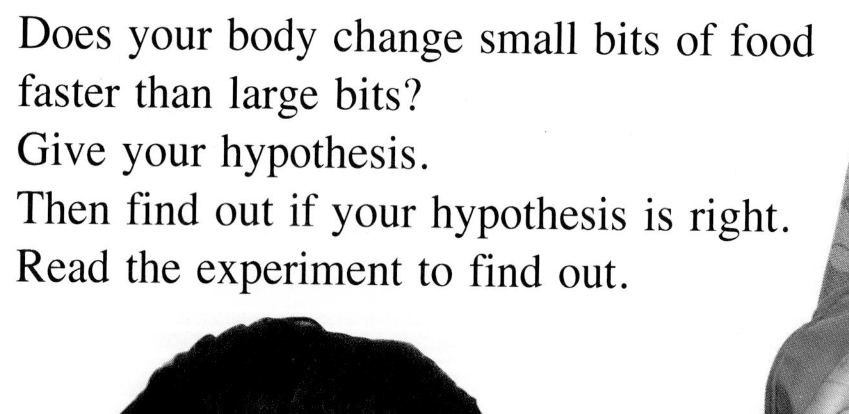

Follow the Directions

1. Make a chart like the one below.
2. Put warm water in two bags.
3. Put two whole crackers in bag 1. Put pieces of two crackers in bag 2.
4. Shake each bag ten times. Tell in your chart if the food in each bag changes.
5. Circle in your chart which food changed faster.

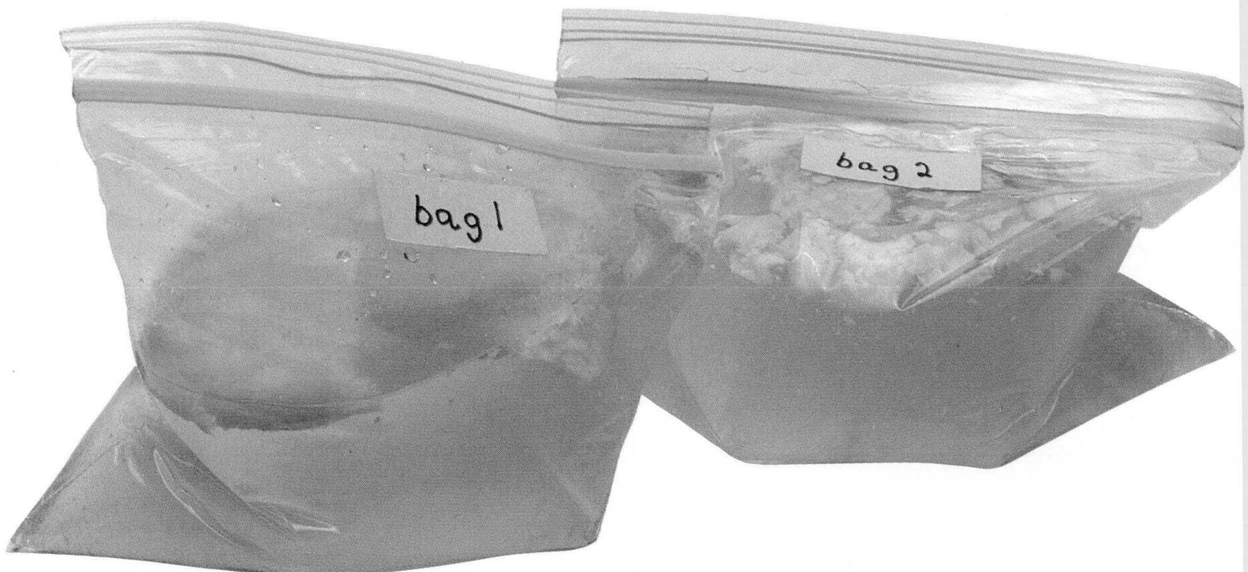

Tell Your Conclusion

Does your body change small bits of food faster than large bits?

Crackers	Change
Whole	
pieces	

Chapter 11 Experiment Skills

Jenny fell and cut her knee. Her father washed the cut with soap and water. He put a bandage on it. He told Jenny that the skin was broken. He said that skin protects the body. It helps keep germs from getting inside.

Jenny thought about skin on other things. She wondered if skin protects plants too.

Problem

Does skin protect fruits?
Give your hypothesis.
Then find out if your hypothesis is right.
Read the experiment to find out.

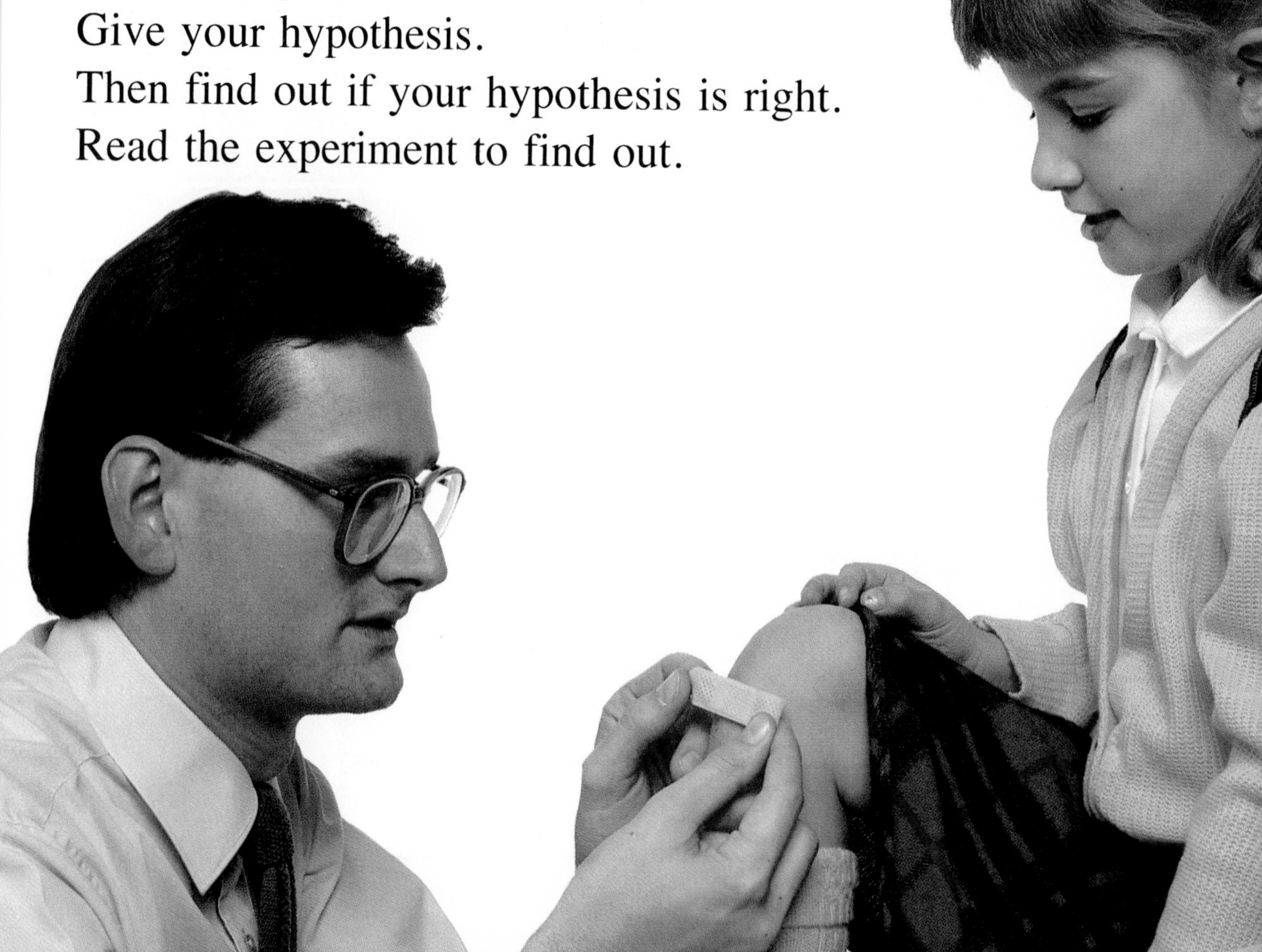

Directions

1. Make a chart like the one below.
2. Get two hard apples. Use a plastic knife to cut the skin of apple 1. Let the apple stand for one hour.
3. Look at the inside of apple 1. Tell in your chart how it looks.
4. Cut apple 2. Look at the inside right away. Tell in your chart how the inside looks.

Write Your Conclusion

Does skin protect fruits?

Skin	Inside of apple
apple 1	
apple 2	

Glossary

A

amphibian *Amphibians* live in water and on land.

B

blood The liquid that goes to all parts of your body.

bones Your *bones* give your body shape.

brain You use your *brain* when you think, feel, and move.

bud The new part of a plant that may become a leaf, a stem, or a flower.

C

Celsius thermometer The thermometer that uses the metric system.

climate The *climate* is the kind of weather a place has.

coal *Coal* is used as fuel.

coverings Feathers, fur, and fish scales are some animal *coverings*.

D

dam A *dam* holds back water.

desert A warm, dry habitat is called a *desert*.

dinosaur *Dinosaurs* lived long ago.

E

eardrum A small part inside your ear.

earth The *earth* is a planet.

electric appliance A toaster is an *electric appliance*.

electricity *Electricity* is a kind of energy.

energy Heat is *energy* in motion.

Equator The weather at the *Equator* is very warm.

evaporate When water changes to a gas, it *evaporates*.

exercise *Exercise* helps you stay healthy.

F

factory Smoke from a *factory* can pollute the air.

flower A *flower* is a part of a plant.

flying reptile *Flying reptiles* lived long ago.

force A *force* is a push or a pull.

fossil *Fossils* can be parts or marks of plants and animals.

fuel *Fuel* is anything that can be burned to make a fire.

G

gas *Gases* have no shape of their own.

germ *Germs* can get into your body through your mouth.

globe A *globe* is a model of the earth.

groundwater The water that soaks into the ground.

H

habitat The place where a plant or animal lives.

heart Your *heart* pumps blood to every part of your body.

heat The *heat* from a fire can warm us.

hibernate Some animals *hibernate* in winter.

hypothesis A *hypothesis* is an answer to a problem.

I

insect *Insects* have three body parts and six legs.

L

leaf Roots, stems, and *leaves* are all parts of plants.

light *Light* is a kind of energy.

liquid Water is a *liquid.*

lungs The *lungs* take in air.

M

magnet A *magnet* attracts other metal objects.

mammal People, horses, and cats are all *mammals*.

matter *Matter* can be a solid, a liquid, or a gas.

medicine Some *medicines* can protect you from sickness.

moon The *moon* orbits the earth.

muscles Your body has many different *muscles*.

N

nerves *Nerves* go to all parts of your body.

North Pole The *North Pole* has very cold weather.

O

orbit The earth *orbits* the sun.

oxygen *Oxygen* is a gas.

P

planet Mars is a *planet*.

poison Do not taste *poisons*.

poles A magnet has two *poles*.

polluted Air or water that is dirty is *polluted*.

pond A small body of water is a *pond*.

properties Color and size are *properties* of matter.

R

reptile Snakes are *reptiles*.

root A *root* is a part of a plant.

S

salt water Ocean water is *salt water*.

scales Many fish have *scales* covering their bodies.

season Winter is a *season*.

seed If you plant a *seed* in the ground it might grow.

solid A book is a *solid*.

sound *Sounds* are a kind of energy.

South Pole The *South Pole* has very cold weather.

star You might see a *star* in the sky at night.

stem A *stem* is a part of a plant.

stomach Your *stomach* breaks down food.

sun The *sun* warms the earth.

T

tadpole A young frog is called a *tadpole*.

temperature *Temperature* is the measure of how hot something is.

thermometer Use a *thermometer* to measure temperature.

traffic signal Watch the *traffic signal* carefully.

V

vibrate When an object *vibrates*, it moves back and forth very quickly.

W

water vapor Water that is in the form of a gas.

wind vane A *wind vane* points in the direction of the wind.

Index

A **bold-faced** number indicates a page with a picture about the topic.

Acknowledgments

Unless otherwise acknowledged, all photos are the property of Scott, Foresman & Company. Page positions are as follows: (T)top, (B)bottom, (C)center, (L)left, (R)right, (INS)inset.

V-T: C.C.Lockwood/Cactus Clyde Productions **V-B:** Dr. David Schwimmer/Bruce Coleman Inc. **VIII:** NASA **XII:** David R. Frazier Photolibrary **2:** NASA **5:** NASA **6L:** John Bova/Photo Researchers **6R:** John Bova/Photo Researchers **7L:** John Bova/Photo Researchers **7R:** John Bova/Photo Researchers **12:** c Mickey Pfleger 1987 **14:** Walter Chandoha **16R:** Lynn M. Stone **16-17:** David Muench **17TL:** Lawrence Migdale **17TR:** Robert E. Lyons/Color Advantage/Robert E. Lyons **17BL:** Lynn M. Stone **17BR:** Lynn M. Stone **20-21:** Frank Siteman/Photographic Resources, Inc. **23:** Terrence Moore/Woodfin Camp & Associates **24:** H.Chaumeton/Nature Photographique **25:** Dwight R. Kuhn **28:** Lynn M. Stone **29:** Don and Pat Valenti **33L:** Don and Pat Valenti **33R:** Don and Pat Valenti **34:** Walter Chandoha **36TL:** Jim Brandenburg/Brandenburg Pictures **36TR:** Y.Arthus-Bertrand/Peter Arnold, Inc. **36BL:** Dwight R. Kuhn **36BR:** Wolfgang Bayer Productions **37R:** Gwen Fidler **37BL:** Lynn M. Stone **37TL:** Don and Pat Valenti **37CL:** J.R.Woodward/VIREO **38BL:** Dwight R. Kuhn **38TR:** Bill Ivy **38TL:** D. Wilder **38BR:** D. Wilder **39:** Fred Bavendam/Peter Arnold, Inc. **40L:** Don and Pat Valenti **40C:** Dwight R. Kuhn **40R:** Dwight R. Kuhn **42:** C.C.Lockwood/Cactus Clyde Productions **43R:** Lynn M. Stone **43C:** Bill Ivy **43L:** Don and Pat Valenti **44:** Gerald Cubitt **45TL:** Lynn M. Stone **45TR:** Bill Ivy **45B:** Wolfgang Kaehler **46:** Wolfgang Bayer Productions **48:** Galen Rowell/Peter Arnold, Inc. **51:** Craig Buchanan **54TL:** Marty Snyderman **54TR:** J. Serrao **54BL:** Dwight R. Kuhn **54BR:** Jim Brandenburg **56:** Ron Testa/Field Museum of Natural History, Chicago **58L:** Field Museum of Natural History, Chicago **58C:** (c)Grant Heilman Photography, Specimen from North Museum, Franklin and Marshall College **58R:** Breck P. Kent/Earth Scenes **59L:** Dr. David Schwimmer/Bruce Coleman Inc. **60:** David R. Frazier Photolibrary **66:** Courtesy of the Trustees of the British Museum **71:** Michael Collier/Stock Boston **72:** Cactus Clyde Productions/C.C.Lockwood/Cactus Clyde Productions **73:** Mark A. Philbrick/Brigham Young University **80:** Larry Lefever/Grant Heilman Photography **82L:** Lynn M. Stone **82C:** Jim Brandenburg **82R:** Carl Roessler **84:** Roger Ressmeyer—Starlight **86:** (c) Mickey Pfleger 1987 **95:** Martha Cooper/Peter Arnold, Inc. **96:** Ellis Herwig/Taurus Photos, Inc. **98:** P.M.DeRenzis/The Image Bank **99:** Milt & Joan Mann/Cameramann International, Ltd. **100:** Joseph A. DiChello **106:** John Kelly/The Image Bank **109:** Camerique/H. Armstrong Roberts **112:** John Apolinski **114:** Alan Schein/Manhattan Views **120L:** Johnny Johnson/DRK Photo **120R:** Lynn M. Stone **122:** Bob Hahn/Taurus Photos, Inc. **130:** Baron Wolman **131:** David R. Frazier Photolibrary **141T:** The Bettmann Archive **141B:** Courtesy Ford Motor Company **152:** Craig Aurness/West Light **154:** Tom Algire **156:** Lawrence Hudetz **158:** James F. Pribble/Taurus Photos, Inc. **162-163:** Fred Bavendam/Peter Arnold, Inc. **162L:** Lawrence Hudetz **162C:** Lawrence Hudetz **162:** Lawrence Hudetz **165:** The Cousteau Society, Inc. **166:** Robert Alan Soltis/Sportschrome, Inc. **167:** Steve Proehl/The Image Bank **168:** Milt & Joan Mann/Cameramann International, Ltd. **170-171:** Sharon Green/Sportschrome, Inc. **172-173:** Milt & Joan Mann/Cameramann International, Ltd. **176:** Tom Algire **177:** Jefrey L. Rotman **178:** Tom Ives **180:** Lynn M. Stone **181L:** Jeff Patrick **182:** Lynn M. Stone **183:** Tom Algire **184:** R.J.Erwin/DRK Photo **188:** Jim Brandenburg/Brandenburg Pictures **191:** NDAA **196:** Don and Pat Valenti **197:** Harald Sund **198:** R. Hamilton Smith **200:** NASA **202:** NASA **204:** Gregory G. Dimijian/Photo Researchers **209:** Albert Moldvay/PSI **210-211** Jerry Schad/Science Source/Photo Researchers **216:** Bob Daemmrich **220:** Jeffry Myers/West Stock **222:** Alvis Upitis/The Image Bank **226:** Roger Ressmeyer—Starlight **238:** Don and Pat Valenti **239:** Courtesy Wright State Universtiy, Dayton, Ohio **249T:** P.H.Polk, Tuskegee Institute, Ala.

TAAS Practice Tests

Practice reading skills.
Practice writing skills.
Learn about science.
Answer the questions on your own paper.

Unit 1 TAAS Practice Test

Reading ■ Read the story. Answer the questions.

Different Animals

Think about ways animals are alike. All animals need food. They also need air, water, and shelter to stay alive.

Think about ways animals are different. Some animals walk or run. Some animals fly. Some animals swim.

Different kinds of animals have different kinds of coverings. Most mammals have hair or fur. Feathers cover most birds. Scales cover the bodies of fish. Amphibians live on land and in water. They have wet, smooth skin. Turtles, alligators, and lizards are *reptiles.* These animals have rough, dry skin.

Some animals live in water. Whales are mammals that live in water. Some animals live in forests. You might have seen deer in a forest. Some animals live in deserts. Many reptiles live in deserts. Some animals, such as earthworms, even live under the ground.

1. What is the story mostly about?
   A. Animals have different coverings.
   B. Animals are alike and different.
   C. Most amphibians live on land.
   D. Different kinds of animals live in different places.

2. What kind of animal has a covering of fur?
   A. a mammal
   B. a bird
   C. an amphibian
   D. a reptile

3. What does the story ask you to do?
   A. Look at pictures of animals.
   B. Think about ways animals are alike and different.
   C. Describe reptiles.
   D. Name animals that eat plants.

4. The word *reptile* means
   A. fish.
   B. insect.
   C. rough, dry animal.
   D. wet, smooth animal.

5. Sara wants a puppy Her mother says she can have a puppy. How does Sara probably feel?
   A. angry
   B. happy
   C. sad
   D. scared

Writing ■ Follow the instructions below.

6. Pretend that you own a pet store. You want to find a good home for the puppy in the picture. Write a story for a newspaper. Describe the puppy. Tell why it would make a good pet.

Reading ■ Read the story. Answer the questions.

Dinosaurs

When dinosaurs lived on the earth, there were no people or buildings. The land was covered with big trees. The climate on earth was probably very warm.

Some dinosaurs were smaller than cats. Other dinosaurs were taller than five-story buildings.

Dinosaurs that had sharp teeth and claws ate meat. Dinosaurs that had flat teeth ate plants.

The *Apatosaurus* was a large dinosaur that moved slowly. It ate leaves from trees and plants.

The *Tyrannosaurus* dinosaur ran on its strong back legs. Its speed helped it catch animals to eat.

Ankylosaurus means *stiff lizard.* This dinosaur had spikes on its tail to protect it.

Dinosaurs lived on earth for many years. Then they disappeared from the earth.

7. What could be real in this story?
 A. Dinosaurs lived close to people.
 B. All dinosaurs ate other animals.
 C. All dinosaurs were larger than people.
 D. Dinosaurs disappeared from the earth.

8. Where did dinosaurs probably live?
 A. near cavemen
 B. in zoos
 C. in cold climates
 D. in warm climates

9. If *Stego-* means *plated,* what does *Stegosaurus* mean?
A. plated fish
B. plated lizard
C. plated bird
D. plated giant

10. Which dinosaur had spikes on its tail?
A. Ankylosaurus
B. Apatosaurus
C. Tyrannosaurus
D. Stegosaurus

Writing ■ Read the story and choose the word or group of words that belongs in each space.

Long ago, mammals (11) different from those living today. After dinosaurs disappeared, mammals (12) everywhere on earth. Some of them (13) like animals we see now.

11. A. are
B. was
C. were
D. will be

12. A. lived
B. live
C. living
D. alive

13. A. is looking
B. was looking
C. looks
D. looked

Reading ▪ Read the story. Answer the questions.

Learning About Plants

Plants are made up of different parts. Flowers, leaves, stems, and roots are some plant parts.

Most plants need air, water, and sunlight to live and grow. They use air, water, and sunlight to make food. They also use materials from the soil.

Different plants grow in different places. Some plants are used to make clothing or food. Farmers grow and sell these plants. Farmers in Texas grow cotton and *sorghum*. Cotton is used to make clothing. Sorghum is used to feed cattle. Texas farmers also grow corn and wheat. Corn and wheat are used for food.

14. The word *sorghum* in this story means
A. a plant.
B. a farm.
C. a cow.
D. a city.

15. If a plant does not get enough sunlight, it will
A. live much longer.
B. make flowers.
C. grow taller.
D. die.

16. What could be real in this story?
A. Corn is used to make clothing.
B. Wheat is grown in Texas.
C. Plants have only two parts.
D. Plants need darkness to grow.

17. What do people make from wheat?
    A. rope baskets
    B. food
    C. clothing
    D. rugs

18. What must a corn farmer do first?
    A. sell corn
    B. grow corn
    C. pick corn
    D. make food out of corn

Writing ■ Follow the instructions below.

19. Write a description of this picture for your teacher. Use describing words to tell how the leopard looks. Tell as much about the leopard as you can.

20. Write a story about a leopard that lives in a forest. Write about what happens first. Then write what happens next, and so on. Be sure to tell how the leopard's covering helps it stay safe.

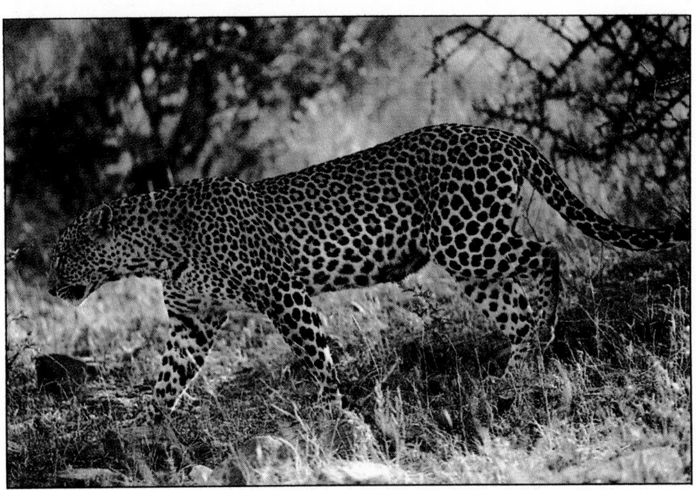

Writing ■ Read the story. Decide which choice below is the best way to rewrite each underlined part of the story. If the underlined part is correct as it is written, mark "D. No Mistake."

John read about seeds. <u>He put seeds in a line. From smallest to largest.</u> **21** He put them in groups by color and shape. <u>John thought about the different kinds of plants the seeds came from.</u> **22** He put the seeds into bean, fruit tree, and flower groups.

21. A. He put seeds. From smallest to largest.
B. He put seeds in a line from smallest to largest.
C. He put seeds in a line; from smallest to largest in size.
D. No Mistake

22. A. John thought about the different plants. Seeds came from.
B. John thought. About different plants seeds came from.
C. John thought about kinds of plants the seeds. Came from.
D. No Mistake

Writing ■ Read the story and decide which type of mistake is in each underlined part. If the underlined part is correctly written, mark "D. No Mistake."

Pumpkins grow on vines. <u>The vine's</u> (23) grow from pumpkin seeds. <u>In october, many pumpkins</u> (24) are picked. They have <u>seeds inside that kan be planted.</u> (25)

23. A. Spelling
    B. Capitalization
    C. Punctuation
    D. No Mistake

24. A. Spelling
    B. Capitalization
    C. Punctuation
    D. No Mistake

25. A. Spelling
    B. Capitalization
    C. Punctuation
    D. No Mistake

Writing ■ Follow the instructions below.

26. Write a story about the tadpole in the picture. Tell how the tadpole will change as it grows.

Unit 2 TAAS Practice Test

Reading ■ Read the story. Answer the questions.

What Is Matter?

Anything that takes up space and has weight is called matter. A book takes up space on a shelf. The air in a balloon takes up space. The milk in a glass takes up space. The book, air, and milk are made of matter.

How can you describe matter? You can tell what *properties* matter has. Shape, color, and size are properties of matter. Taste and smell are properties of matter.

Matter can be a solid, a liquid, or a gas. A solid has a certain size and shape. It takes up space. Look at a book in your classroom. A book is a solid.

A liquid takes up space. It has weight. It does not have its own shape. Milk is a liquid. When you pour milk from a pitcher to a cup, the milk changes shape.

A gas takes up space. It does not have its own shape. You cannot see most gases. Air is one kind of gas. Air in a balloon takes the shape of the balloon. If you let air out of a balloon, the air spreads out and fills a larger space.

1. What is real?

A. Milk is a gas.

B. Solids take up space.

C. A gas does not take up space.

D. Liquids cannot change shape.

2. What is a gas?
   A. air
   B. milk
   C. a book
   D. water

3. What is the story mostly about?
   A. Gases and liquids can change shape.
   B. Matter is grouped in different ways.
   C. Anything that takes up space and has weight is made of matter. Matter can be gas, liquid, or solid.
   D. A book is a solid. Milk is a liquid. Air is a gas.

4. In this story, *properties* means
   A. a piece of land.
   B. a thing that belongs to someone.
   C. a way to group matter.
   D. something that tells what matter is like.

5. If you let air out of a bicycle tire
   A. the air would fill a larger space.
   B. the air would not change shape.
   C. the air would not fill space.
   D. nothing would happen.

Writing ■ Follow the instructions below.

6. Write a story for your class about this picture. Tell what would happen first, second, and so on.

Reading ▪ Read the story. Answer the questions.

What Is Heat?

Heat is one kind of energy. Many objects in homes, such as toasters, give off heat. People use heat for cooking and washing dishes.

Heat can move from one place to another. Think about cooking food on a stove. First, the heat energy moves from the stove to the pan. Then the energy moves to the food in the pan. Then the heat energy moves into the air around the pan.

Heat moves through metal well. Heat does not move well through cloth and wood.

A metal spoon in a pan of hot food would get hot. A wooden one would stay cool.

Cloth can protect your hands from heat. Use cloth potholders if you touch a hot pan or *remove* it from the stove.

7. In this story, the word *remove* means
   A. move from a place.
   B. move to a place.
   C. move quickly.
   D. move sideways.

8. When cooking, what happens first?
   A. Heat moves from food to the air.
   B. Heat energy moves from the stove to the pan.
   C. Heat energy moves from the pan to the air.
   D. Heat energy moves from the pan to the food.

9. What could be real in this story?
   A. Wooden spoons get hot.
   B. Cloth potholders cause burns.
   C. Heat moves through metal.
   D. Fires cannot warm the air.

10. Wood stays cooler than metal because
   A. wood carries heat easily.
   B. metal cannot get hot.
   C. metal gives off heat.
   D. heat does not move well through wood.

Writing ■ Read the story and choose the word or group of words that belongs in each space.

Last week, I (11) about sunlight. The teacher (12) us to protect our eyes and skin from bright sunlight. Yesterday I (13) to school. I (14) a hat to protect my skin.

11. A. learn
   B. learned
   C. am learning
   D. will learn

12. A. tell
   B. telled
   C. were telling
   D. told

13. A. walked
   B. am walking
   C. will walk
   D. were walking

14. A. weared
   B. did wore
   C. wore
   D. is wearing

Reading ■ Read the story. Answer the questions.

What Can Electricity Do?

Electricity is a kind of energy. Most of the electricity people use is made in special places. It travels through wires from these places to your home.

Suppose a person plugs in a lamp and turns it on. The lamp wire carries electricity. It makes the light go on.

Some machines are *wireless.* They can use electric energy from batteries. The electricity moves to toys, radios, and other machines.

Be sure to use electricity safely. Ask an adult for help whenever you use an electric appliance. Do not use an appliance that has a broken cord.

Electricity moves through water. Only use electric appliances if your hands are dry and you are in a dry place.

15. How should you use an electric appliance?
A. carelessly
B. with wet hands
C. with adult help
D. in a wet place

16. In this story, the word *wireless* means
A. electric appliance.
B. without an electric cord.
C. with a wire.
D. easily carried.

17. How can wireless machines get energy?
A. from wires
B. from lamps
C. from batteries
D. from water

18. What is the fourth paragraph mostly about?

A. using electricity safely

B. talking with adults about electricity

C. broken electric cords

D. people of all ages using electric appliances

19. Using electricity near water is dangerous because

A. water stops electric energy.

B. electric energy cannot travel through water.

C. water can break electric cords.

D. electricity moves through water.

Writing ■ Follow the instructions below.

20. Write a story about the police car. Tell what happens first. Tell other things that happen. Describe sounds the car might make. Tell whether the sounds are high or low. Tell whether they are loud or soft.

Writing ■ Read the story. Decide which choice below is the best way to rewrite each underlined part of the story. If the underlined part of the story is correct as written, mark "D. No Mistake."

<u>Light is a kind of energy.</u> You need light to
21
see. <u>Suppose you. Were reading a book.</u>
22
Light would help you see the book. <u>The</u>
23
<u>sun. Fires. Light bulbs give off light.</u>

21. A. Light is a kind. Energy.
    B. Light, kind of energy.
    C. Kind of light, kind of energy.
    D. No Mistake

22. A. Suppose. Reading a book.
    B. Suppose you were reading a book.
    C. Suppose you. Reading a book.
    D. No Mistake

23. A. The sun and fires. Light bulbs give off light.
    B. The sun, fires, and light bulbs. Give off light.
    C. The sun gives off light. Fires and light bulbs give off light.
    D. No Mistake

Writing ■ Read the story and decide which type of mistake is in each underlined part. If the underlined part is correctly written, mark "D. No Mistake."

Most magnets are metal? Magnets kan
24 25
push or pull some metal objects. poles are
26
the parts of magnets that push or pull
27
hardest.

24. A. Spelling
    B. Capitalization
    C. Punctuation
    D. No Mistake

25. A. Spelling
    B. Capitalization
    C. Punctuation
    D. No Mistake

26. A. Spelling
    B. Capitalization
    C. Punctuation
    D. No Mistake

27. A. Spelling
    B. Capitalization
    C. Punctuation
    D. No Mistake

Writing ■ Follow the instructions below.

28. Look at the blocks in the picture. Write a story telling about different ways you could group them.

Unit 3 TASS Practice Test

Reading ■ Read the story. Answer the questions.

What Makes Clouds, Rain, and Snow?

Rosa wants to play outside. Rain begins to fall. Rosa feels sad.

Some clouds are dark. Others are white and fluffy. All clouds are made in the same way.

Clouds are made of tiny drops of water. The sun heats the water from oceans, rivers, lakes, and ponds. Then the water *evaporates.*

Water becomes water vapor when it evaporates. You cannot see water vapor. Water vapor gets cold as it moves high into the sky. Cold water vapor changes into tiny drops of water that make clouds.

The drops of water in clouds float in the air. The drops can move and bump into each other. They join together to make bigger drops that get too heavy to stay in the clouds. They fall from the clouds as rain.

Some clouds are high where the air is cold. These clouds make snow. Bits of ice and water drops in the clouds bump together and freeze.

The bits of ice get bigger. When they get too heavy, they fall from the cloud as snow. If air below the cloud is cold, the falling snow does not melt. The snow falls and covers the ground.

1. The word *evaporates* means
   A. to turn into water.
   B. becomes water vapor.
   C. to rain.
   D. to turn into ice.

2. What happens first?
   A. Snow falls.
   B. Bits of ice in clouds get bigger.
   C. Clouds get heavy.
   D. Ice and water in clouds freeze.

3. Why is Rosa sad?
   A. It is sunny.
   B. She wants rain.
   C. She cannot play outside.
   D. It is snowing.

4. Ice falls from clouds as snow because
   A. water vapor gets cold.
   B. ice is lighter than a cloud.
   C. air below the clouds is warm.
   D. the bits of ice get too heavy to stay in the clouds.

Writing ■ Follow the instructions below.

6. Look at the picture of a snowstorm. Imagine that this snow is falling near your home. Write a story telling what happens during such a storm.

Reading ■ Read the story. Answer the questions.

The Sun

The sun is the closest star to the earth. It is a ball of glowing gases.

The sun is much bigger than the earth. It looks small because it is far away from the earth.

The sun gives light and warmth to the earth. Living things on earth need light and warmth.

The light from the sun makes day on the earth. The part of the earth the sun shines on has day. The part of the earth away from the sun has night.

Day and night happen because the earth is always turning. As it turns, different parts have day and night.

While the earth turns, it also moves around the sun. This trip around the sun takes one year. This path around the sun is called an orbit.

The Equator gets direct sunlight all year. It stays warm. The North Pole and the South Pole do not get direct sunlight. They stay cold all of the time.

6. What could *not* be real?

A. The sun is a star.

B. Earth moves in an orbit around the sun.

C. Day and night happen because the earth is always turning.

D. Snow falls often at the Equator.

7. How long is the earth's trip around the sun?
   A. one month
   B. one year
   C. one day
   D. one week

8. If the sun stopped shining, the earth might
   A. get hotter.
   B. move faster.
   C. not have living things.
   D. always have day.

9. What is this story mostly about?
   A. the sun
   B. the earth
   C. heat and light
   D. the earth's orbit

10. Day and night happen because
   A. the sun is large.
   B. the earth is close to the sun.
   C. the earth is always turning.
   D. the sun moves around the earth.

Writing ■ Read the story and choose the word or group of words that belongs in each space.

Last evening, Jarrod (11) outside. He saw stars. They (12) tiny. Many stars are large. They look small because they are far away.

11. A. goed
   B. went
   C. goes
   D. will go

12. A. am looking
   B. looks
   C. will look
   D. looked

Reading ■ Read the story. Answer the questions.

Clean Water Is Important

Living things need clean water to stay healthy. Fish and plants that live in water can die if the water is *polluted.*

People need clean water. People use water for cooking and cleaning. They use water for taking baths and washing clothes. People even use water for fun.

Some people have jobs using boats on water. They use the boats for fishing. They use the boats to take people and things from place to place.

Some food people eat comes from oceans, lakes, and rivers. Fish, shellfish, and seaweed are some of these foods.

Polluted water has germs that make people and animals sick. It might have harmful wastes from a factory. Oil spilled from a ship might pollute the water.

People should not use polluted water. They should not swim or fish in it. People should not eat fish from polluted water.

Not all clear water is clean. Some water that looks clear might be *unsafe* to drink or use.

People can help keep rivers and lakes clean. They should throw trash and garbage into proper containers. They should not throw trash and garbage into water. People also can try not to use more clean water than they need.

13. In this story, the word *polluted* means
A. clean.
B. dirty.
C. cold.
D. useful.

14. What can you do to help keep water clean?
A. Leave water running.
B. Throw trash into water.
C. Throw trash into proper containers.
D. Use water for cooking.

15. In this story, the word *unsafe* means
A. clear.
B. good-tasting.
C. clean.
D. dangerous.

16. What is the story mostly about?
A. Clean water is important. People can help keep it clean.
B. Food comes from water.
C. Trash should be put into containers.
D. Not all clear water is clean.

Writing ■ Follow the instructions below.

17. The picture shows birds in the springtime. Write sentences describing what you see in the picture.

Writing ■ Read the story. Decide which choice below is the best way to rewrite each underlined part of the story. If the underlined part is correct as it is written, mark "D. No Mistake."

<u>In many places the weather does not</u>
18
<u>change very much. In different seasons.</u>

Many places stay cool most of the year.

<u>Many places stay warm. Most of the year.</u>
19

18. A. In many places, the weather does not change very much. In different seasons.
B. In many places. The weather does not change, in different seasons.
C. In many places, the weather does not change very much in different seasons.
D. No Mistake

19. A. Many places stay warm most of the year.
B. Many places. Stay warm most of the year.
C. Many places. Stay warm. Most of the year.
D. No Mistake

Writing ■ Read the story and decide which type of mistake is in each underlined part. If the underlined part is correctly written in the story, mark "D. No Mistake."

Jacques cousteau studies oceans and living
20
things in oceans, He writes books aynd
21 22
movies about oceans. He also helps protect
23
the ocean and ocean animals.

20. A. Spelling
B. Capitalization
C. Punctuation
D. No Mistakes

21. A. Spelling
B. Capitalization
C. Punctuation
D. No Mistakes

22. A. Spelling
B. Capitalization
C. Punctuation
D. No Mistake

23. A. Spelling
B. Capitalization
C. Punctuation
D. No Mistake

Writing ■ Follow the instructions below

24. In many places, the four seasons have different weather. Write a story telling how the seasons might change in one of these places.

Unit 4 TASS Practice Test

Reading ■ Read the story. Answer the questions.

Staying Healthy?

One thing you need to stay healthy is food. Food helps you grow. It helps you work and play without getting tired.

You need many kinds of foods. Different foods work together in your body to keep you healthy. Drinking water also helps your body work well.

Another thing your body needs to stay healthy is *exercise.* Exercise helps keep your heart and lungs healthy. It helps you build strong muscles. Different kinds of exercise are good for you. You help keep your body healthy when you run and ride a bicycle.

You need rest and sleep to stay healthy. Rest and sleep help your body work better.

Suppose you do not get enough sleep. You might feel tired and cross. You might make mistakes in school.

You can work well in school when you get enough sleep. Most children your age need about ten or eleven hours of sleep each day.

1. What does the word *exercise* mean in this story?
   A. active use of the body
   B. getting enough sleep
   C. eating enough food
   D. staying healthy

2. What is this story mostly about?
   A. You need to run every day.
   B. You need enough sleep everyday.
   C. Food helps you grow.
   D. You need food, water, exercise, and enough sleep each day.

3. If you do not sleep, you probably feel
   A. surprised.
   B. sad.
   C. tired and cross.
   D. happy.

4. How many hours of sleep do most children your age need each night?
   A. 5 or 6
   B. 7 or 8
   C. 10 or 11
   D. 12 or 13

5. What could be real in this story?
   A. You need only one kind of food.
   B. Children need five hours sleep daily.
   C. Running is not good exercise.
   D. You need to drink plenty of water.

Writing ■ Follow the instructions below.

6. Write a story describing the items in the picture. Tell how a person who plays sports can stay safe.

Reading ■ Read the story. Answer the questions.

How You Stay Safe

Wherever you are, there are things you can do to stay safe.

You can stay safe on the street. Wherever you cross the street, stop at the *curb* first. Watch traffic signals. Look left, right, and then left again. Wait to cross until you see no cars each time.

Follow the bicycle rules where you live. Ride on the sidewalk if you can. Ride a bicycle that is the right size.

You can be safe in your home. Never take any medicine by yourself. Only your parents or someone they ask should give you medicine.

Some things used in homes can be poisons. They can hurt your skin or eyes. Do not breathe them in or taste them.

You can stay safe at school. Follow your school rules when a fire alarm sounds. Know what to do if you are not with your class.

7. The word *curb* in the story means
A. the street.
B. the grass.
C. the playground.
D. the end of the sidewalk.

8. Before crossing the street, look
A. left then right.
B. only to the left.
C. left, right, and left again.
D. straight ahead.

9. Some household cleaners have poisons in them. You need help from an adult to use these cleaners because
A. poisons are for adults.
B. poisons can hurt you.
C. poisons are safe.
D. poisons are weak.

10. What might happen if you ride a bicycle that is too big for you?
A. You will look older.
B. You might have an accident.
C. Your parents will like it.
D. You will ride safely.

Writing ■ Read the story and choose the word or group of words that belongs in each space.

Last week, I (11) to the doctor. She (12) at my eyes and ears. She listened to my heart. The doctor (13) me I (14) well.

11. A. go
B. went
C. gone
D. will go

12. A. looks
B. is looking
C. were looking
D. looked

13. A. told
B. tells
C. tell
D. will tell

14. A. is growing
B. were growing
C. was growing
D. grows

Writing ■ Read the story. Decide which choice below is the best way to rewrite each underlined part of the story. If the underlined part is correct as it is written, mark "D. No Mistake."

<u>Muscles have some of the same jobs that bones do.</u> (15) <u>Muscles help protect the inside. Parts of your body.</u> (16)

15.
A. Muscles have some of the same jobs. Bones do.
B. Muscles have some, of the same jobs that bones do.
C. Muscles have. Some of the same jobs that bones do.
D. No Mistake

16.
A. Muscles help protect. The inside parts of your body.
B. Muscles help protect the inside parts of your body.
C. The inside parts of your body, muscles protect.
D. No Mistake

Writing ■ Follow the instructions below.

17. Think of an exercise you know. Write a letter to a classmate telling how to do the exercise.

Writing ▪ Read the story and decide which type of mistake is in each underlined part. If the underlined part is correctly written, mark "D. No Mistake."

<u>In september,</u> I played soccer. The coach
18
<u>talked too us about</u> keeping <u>fit We do</u>
19 **20**
exercises to <u>keep our muscles strong,</u>
21

18. A. Spelling
B. Capitalization
C. Punctuation
D. No Mistake

19. A. Spelling
B. Capitalization
C. Punctuation
D. No Mistake

20. A. Spelling
B. Capitalization
C. Punctuation
D. No Mistake

21. A. Spelling
B. Capitalization
C. Punctuation
D. No Mistake

Writing ▪ Follow the instructions below.

22. Look at the pictures and write what each of the traffic signs and signals mean. Tell what you should do when you see them.